TAMAKO NIWA

First Course in Japanese

PART 1

UNIVERSITY OF WASHINGTON PRESS   **Seattle and London**

FIRST COURSE IN JAPANESE is published in three parts:

1. Units I and II
2. Units III and IV
3. Character Workbook

Acknowledgments

The writer is indebted to a grant from the Ford Foundation administered by the Washington Foreign Language Program at the University of Washington for the development of materials for use in high schools in the State of Washington. She would also like to express her gratitude to the various schools and teachers who experimented with the original draft, Mr. William C. Callaghan (Franklin High School, Seattle), Mr. Yoneichi Matsuda (Ingraham High School, Seattle) and Mrs. Ikuko Matsumoto (Lewis and Clark High School, Spokane). The writer is most indebted to Mrs. Kazue Akinaga, the Japanese teachers at the University of Washington and Mrs. Kikuko Makihara for their many helpful suggestions which contributed greatly to the writing of this text. The writer wishes to express her gratitude to Mrs. Susan Dubin for her helpful comments and the meticulous care she took in the typing of this text. However, it is the writer who is solely responsible for all inconsistencies and deficiencies of the text, for which she asks the readers' indulgence.

                                        T. N.

Contents

Introduction

This is a beginning text in Japanese designed for those who wish to commence slowly and gradually progress to a faster pace of study. The constructions studied progress from the simple to the more complex. The text has been primarily designed for young adults such as high-school students, with the idea that a freshman may progress at a slower pace than a senior. The scope of the grammar covered in this text is much the same as that of the text, Basic Japanese for College Students; high-school students who have completed this text should be able to continue at the next level in any university using the above college text.

The romanized part of the text is in four units, with each unit (except the fourth) consisting of eight lessons and a review. The fourth unit consists of six lessons. Each lesson is composed of a pattern passage, grammar explanation, drills, cultural notes (when desirable), and exercises. Each unit concentrates on a particular aspect of grammar. Unit I introduces the semi-formal level verbs and the copula, Unit II emphasizes the verbal adjective, Unit III concentrates on more complex verb forms and conjunctions, and Unit IV treats polite or honorific language. Grammatical analysis is based on modern linguistic concepts rather than on traditional Japanese grammar.

The aim of this text is to teach the student about Japan and the Japanese at the same time that he is learning the language. The pattern passages focus on the activities of Yukio Yamada and his family. By the time the student has reached the end of the text he will be acquainted with the life of a Tokyo family of the economic and social level of the Yamadas. This is one of the fortunate families whose home was spared in the destructive fires during the Second World War. It is a big house and probably some modern changes were made in recent times. Not all of this information appears in the text, but a discerning teacher will be able to conduct, in Japanese, many enlightening and enjoyable discussions with the students on various aspects of Japanese life based on the hints in the text.

Material for the study of Japanese writing has been designed to be used along with the romanized text, beginning with Unit II of the latter. The Japanese text not only teaches the writing but also serves as a review of material already learned.

Methods of Teaching

The text is adaptable to various methods of aural-oral teaching. Depending on the classroom situation it may even be advisable to let the students do some of the basic learning from the tapes of the drills, which are available. The following, however, is the method recommended.

1. With the exception of the exercises, the student should NEVER be permitted to look at his book during class.

2. The teacher should speak almost exclusively in Japanese and at his REGULAR PACE OF SPEECH, using ONLY vocabulary and forms already familiar to the student. He should particularly avoid stressing any particles.

3. MEMORIZATION should be a major part of the homework. The pattern passage should be committed to memory. The <u>first</u> example of each drill introducing a new grammar point should be committed to memory.

4. In introducing drills, the teacher should make every use of visual aids and PERFORM AS AN ACTOR, in order to convey the meanings of the sentences.

5. Within each lesson, the drills are grouped according to the grammar point being introduced to enable the teacher to plan each hour and thus vary the method and pace of teaching.

6. Part of the hour each day SHOULD BE SPENT CONVERSING freely, emphasizing the form being introduced.

7. Part of the hour should be spent in chorused and individual drilling to enable the student to gain some fluency in the new construction. This also gives the teacher the opportunity to correct pronunciation before bad habits become ingrained.

8. The importance of learning by review should be emphasized. Thus, homework and memorization should be on material already covered under the direction of the teacher.

Grammar

In this text, the parts of speech are six. They are: 1) the verb, 2) the verbal adjective, 3) the copula, 4) particles, 5) <u>sono</u>-type noun modifiers, and 6) nouns. The first three of the series are conjugated, while the last three never change in form. A noun is defined as something which does not change in form and which is not a particle or a <u>sono</u>-type word. Thus, one must be aware that the noun category is quite broad.

The politeness levels have been divided into two categories--the semi-formal and the honorific or formal language. The informal level or familiar speech is also introduced in some of the later lessons in the pattern-passage conversations among members of the Yamada family. Hawever, as the semi-formal and formal language is more commonly used with friends and acquaintances, these levels are the ones primarily taught. Within the levels of semi-formal and formal language, the endings of the conjugated forms (the verb, the verbal adjective, and the copula) may be informal or semi-formal. For example, the verb "eat" at the semi-formal level has an informal form <u>taberu</u> and a semi-formal form <u>tabemasu</u>; at the formal level, "I eat" has an informal form <u>itadaku</u> and a semi-formal form <u>itadakimasu</u> while "you eat" has the informal form <u>meshiagaru</u> and the semi-formal form <u>meshiagarimasu</u>.

Pronunciation

The five basic vowels in Japanese today are <u>a</u>, <u>i</u>, <u>u</u>, <u>e</u> and <u>o</u>. (For the pronunciation of these vowels it is recommended that one mimic the teacher or follow the tape.) Each of these vowels may be held, <u>a</u> becoming <u>aa</u>, <u>i</u> becoming <u>ii</u>, etc. In the case of the held vowels, <u>aa</u>, <u>ii</u>, etc., the single unit is simply held longer but never changes in quality.

The basic Japanese syllables are one of the above vowels, combinations of a consonant (or consonants) and one of the vowels, or the nasal "n." The following are the basic syllables. The forms in parentheses indicate the spelling used in this text.

a	ka	sa	ta	na	ha	ma	ya	ra	wa	n (nasal)
										(or m)
i	ki	si	ti	ni	hi	mi		ri		
		(shi)	(chi)							
u	ku	su	tu	nu	hu	mu	yu	ru		
		(tsu)			(fu)					
e	ke	se	te	ne	he	me		re		
o	ko	so	to	no	ho	mo	yo	ro		

ga	za	da	ba	pa
gi	zi		bi	pi
	(ji)			
gu	zu	du	bu	pu
		(zu)		
ge	ze	de	be	pe
go	zo	do	bo	po

kya	(sha)	(cha)	nya	hya	mya	rya
kyu	(shu)	(chu)	nyu	hyu	myu	ryu
kyo	(sho)	(cho)	nyo	hyo	myo	ryo
gya	(ja)		bya	pya		
gyu	(ju)		byu	pyu		
gyo	(jo)		byo	pyo		

(The syllables in parentheses in the last group are all palatalized.)

Mention must also be made of the so-called "whispered" vowels i and u. These are not indicated in the text, because it is hoped that students will not be looking at their texts and also that they will learn from mimicking the teacher. These vowels become whispered only when they occur between the consonants k, s, t and h, or as a final after one of these consonants. Examples are shi̱ta, hi̱to, -masu̱ ka, and fu̱tatsu̱.

The student is also advised to use the nasal g in non-initial positions. This is the preferred pronunciation in the Tōkyō dialect.

Accent

The pitch accent in Japanese is one to which English speakers are not accustomed and one to which they must pay special attention. Pitch may affect the meaning, as in the examples ȳonda and yonda, the former meaning "read" and the latter meaning "called." Within an utterance, that is, between two pauses, there may be several pitch accents but they are not all the same height in pitch. It is recommended that one listen closely to the teacher's pronunciation of pitch.

There are four patterns of pitch. An illustration with nouns and proper names as examples would be the following four types: 1) head-high, Shimizu, 2) intermedially-high, Yoshimura, 3) tail-high, yama desu, and 4) flat (in which the first syllable of the series is somewhat lower than the remainder), Tanaka. Accent marks are indicated in the text in the above manner. Pitch marks have been omitted from the sections which the students might be seeing in class, such as the exercise section. Thus, in class recitation, there is a check on the student to see if he has memorized the proper pitch for each phrase. The pitch patterns followed in this text are those of the Tokyo dialect which is the basis for standard Japanese today. However, accents change from generation to generation and there are some which are now in a state of flux. In such cases, an attempt has been made to use the one which is most prevalent. Pitch accents of individual words have been based on the reference work, Nihongo Akusento Jiten by Haruhiko Kindaichi.

First Course in Japanese

Part 1

LESSON 1

Yukio:	Ohayoo gozaimasu.[1]		Yukio:	Good morning.
Okaasan:	Ohayoo gozaimasu.		Mother:	Good morning.
Yukio:	Nanji desu ka?		Yukio:	What time is it?
Okaasan:	Shichiji desu.		Mother:	It's seven o'clock.
	(sitting down to eat)			
Yukio:	Itadakimasu.[2]		Yukio:	Itadakimasu.

GRAMMAR

I-1.1 The copula desu

Desu has the meanings "am," "is" and "are" and the choice of meaning is determined by context. In this lesson, desu appears only after nouns.

EXAMPLES:

Yukio desu.	I am Yukio (literally, "am Yukio").
	It's Yukio (literally, "is Yukio").
Tokee desu.	It's a clock (literally, "is a clock").
	They are clocks (literally, "are clocks").
Ichiji desu.	It's one o'clock (literally, "is one o'clock").

I-1.2 Nouns

In the case of most Japanese nouns, there is no distinction in form between singular and plural. For example, tokee may mean "clock" or "clocks"; context determines which meaning is intended.

I-1.3 -san

San is a suffix which is added to names of people as an expression of politeness. It also occurs after names of jobs or professions when referring to individuals in those professions. It is comparable to the use of "Mr.," "Mrs." and "Miss" in English. SAN IS NEVER ADDED WHEN GIVING ONE'S OWN NAME.

EXAMPLES:

Yukio-san desu.	It's Yukio.
Hon'ya san desu.	It's the bookseller.

I-1.4 Interrogative particle ka

The particle ka occurring at the end of a sentence makes the sentence an interrogative one.

EXAMPLES:

Yukio-san desu.	It's Yukio.
Yukio-san desu ka?	Is it Yukio?
Ichiji desu ka?	Is it one o'clock?

3

Tokee desu ka?   Is it a clock? Do you mean a clock?
Nan desu ka?   What is it?

(Nani is an interrogative word meaning "what." The form nan occurs rather
than nani before a word beginning with "d," such as desu and also before counters
(to be discussed later) such as ji meaning "o'clock" as in nanji, "what hour" or
"what o'clock." Both the forms nan and nani occur interchangeably before a word
beginning with "t" or "n." (Before other consonants or vowels, nani occurs.)

I-1.5 ...ka, ...ka
     Two interrogative sentences of similar pattern uttered in sequence indicates
choice; "is it _____ or is it _____" is the meaning.

EXAMPLES:
     Ichiji desu ka, niji desu ka?   Is it one o'clock or is it two o'clock?
     Tanaka-san desu ka, Yamada-san   Is it Mr. Tanaka or is it Mr. Yamada?
        desu ka?

                                    DRILLS

1. Repetition (using a clock)

ichiji   one o'clock
niji   two o'clock
sanji   three o'clock
yoji   four o'clock
goji   five o'clock
rokuji   six o'clock
shichiji   seven o'clock
hachiji   eight o'clock
kuji   nine o'clock
juuji   ten o'clock
juu-ichiji   eleven o'clock
juu-niji   twelve o'clock

2. Substitution

Ichiji desu.   It's one o'clock.

(niji)   Niji desu.   It's two o'clock.
(sanji)   Sanji desu.   It's three o'clock.
(yoji)   Yoji desu.   It's four o'clock.
(goji)   Goji desu.   It's five o'clock.
(rokuji)   Rokuji desu.   It's six o'clock.
(shichiji)   Shichiji desu.   It's seven o'clock.
(hachiji)   Hachiji desu.   It's eight o'clock.
(kuji)   Kuji desu.   It's nine o'clock.
(juuji)   Juuji desu.   It's ten o'clock.

(juu-ichiji)   Juu-ichiji desu.   It's eleven o'clock.
(juu-niji)   Juu-niji desu.   It's twelve o'clock.

3. Response (using a clock)

Q. Nanji desu ka?   What time is it?
A. Ichiji desu.   It's one o'clock.

(Use list in Drill 2 above.)

4. Substitution

Ichiji desu ka, niji desu ka?   Is it one o'clock or two o'clock?

(niji, sanji)   Niji desu ka, sanji   Is it two o'clock or three o'clock?
                   desu ka?
(sahji, yoji)   Sanji desu ka, yoji   Is it three o'clock or four o'clock?
                   desu ka?
(yoji, goji)   Yoji desu ka, goji   Is it four o'clock or five o'clock?
                   desu ka?
(goji, roku-   Goji desu ka, rokuji   Is it five o'clock or six o'clock?
   ji)   desu ka?
(rokuji, shi-   Rokuji desu ka, shi-   Is it six o'clock or seven o'clock?
   chiji)   chiji desu ka?
(shichiji,   Shichiji desu ka, ha-   Is it seven o'clock or eight o'clock?
   hachiji)   chiji desu ka?
(hachiji, ku-   Hachiji desu ka, kuji   Is it eight o'clock or nine o'clock?
   ji)   desu ka?
(kuji, juuji)   Kuji desu ka, juuji   Is it nine o'clock or ten o'clock?
                   desu ka?
(juuji, juu-   Juuji desu ka, juu-   Is it ten o'clock or eleven o'clock?
   ichiji)   ichiji desu ka?
(juu-ichiji,   Juu-ichiji desu ka,   Is it eleven o'clock or twelve o'clock?
   juu-niji)   juu-niji desu ka?

5. Affirmative Response (using a clock)

Q. Ichiji desu ka?   Is it one o'clock?
A. Ee. Ichiji desu.   Yes, it's one o'clock.

(Use list in Drill 2 above.)

6. Negative Response (using a clock)

Q. Ichiji desu ka?   Is it one o'clock?
A. Iie. Niji desu.   No, it's two o'clock.

7. Repetition

Yukio-san desu.   It's Yukio.
Yamada-san desu.   It's Mr. Yamada.

(Substitute members of the class.)

8. Affirmative Response (indicating members of the class)

Q. _____-san desu ka?   Is it _____?
A. Ee. _____-san desu.   Yes, it's _____.

9. Negative Response (indicating members of the class)

Q. Yukio-san desu ka?   Is it Yukio?
A. Iie. _____-san desu.   No, it's _____.

10. Self-introduction (beginning with the teacher)

(Tanaka) desu.   I'm (Tanaka).

11. Response

Q. Tanaka-san desu ka, _____-san   Is it Mr. Tanaka or _____?
   desu ka?
A. _____ desu.   I'm _____.

(Use names of members of the class.)

12. Repetition (using objects)

Tokee desu.   It's a clock.
Empitsu desu.   It's a pencil.
Tekisuto desu.   It's a textbook.
Hon desu.   It's a book.
Booru pen desu.   It's a ballpoint pen.

13. Affirmative Response (using objects)

Q. Tokee desu ka?   Is it a clock?
A. Ee. Tokee desu.   Yes, it's a clock.

(Use list in Drill 12 above.)

14. Negative Response

Q. Empitsu desu ka?   Is it a pencil?
A. Iie. Booru pen desu.   No, it's a ballpoint pen.

(Use list in Drill 12 above.)

15. Response (using objects)

Q. Empitsu desu ka, booru pen desu   Is it a pencil or a ballpoint pen?
      ka?
A. Empitsu desu.   It's a pencil.

(Use list in Drill 12 above.)

CULTURAL NOTES

1. Greetings are always accompanied by a bow. The depth to which one bows when standing varies according to the degree of formality, ranging from a ninety-degree bow on formal occasions to a slight nod of the head.

2. Said by all individuals before beginning a meal and also said by guests invited to tea, etc., before taking the first bite of something or first sip of tea. It is said in the spirit of saying grace when uttered before a meal.

EXERCISES

A. Tell your friend that it is:

1. three o'clock
2. six o'clock
3. four o'clock
4. eight o'clock
5. two o'clock
6. ten o'clock
7. one o'clock
8. nine o'clock
9. seven o'clock
10. twelve o'clock
11. five o'clock
12. eleven o'clock

B. You are Yukio-san and it is now eight o'clock in the morning. Respond to the following greetings or questions accordingly.

1. Ohayoo gozaimasu.
2. Nanji desu ka?

3. Shichiji desu ka?
4. Hachiji desu ka?
5. Tanaka-san desu ka?
6. Yukio-san desu ka?
7. Michio-san desu ka, Yukio-san desu ka?
8. Hachiji desu ka, kuji desu ka?

C. Give the questions which prompted the following answers.

1. Ee. Kuji desu.
2. Ee. Yukio-san desu.
3. Ee. Yukio desu.
4. Sanji desu.
5. Iie. Yukio desu. (a sample question)
6. Iie. Rokuji desu. (a sample question)

Yukio:	(finishing his breakfast) Gochisoo-sama.[1]	Yukio:	Gochisoo-sama.
Okaasan:	Kyoo wa nanji ni kaerimasu ka?	Mother:	What time will you be returning today?
Yukio:	Goji-han goro ni kaerimasu. (putting on his shoes and preparing to leave)[2] Itte mairimasu.[3]	Yukio:	I'll return around five-thirty. Goodbye.
Okaasan:	Itte irasshai.[4]	Mother:	Goodbye.

GRAMMAR

I-2.1 Verbs (-masu ending)

The -masu ending has a future meaning, i.e. I "will (shall)" do something, or it signifies habitual occurrence, i.e., I "usually (often)" do that. The one ending -masu is used for all persons, first, second or third in both the singular and plural; one ending suffices for all these instances. (The form itself will be discussed later.)

EXAMPLES:

Kaerimasu.

I will return. I [usually] return.
You will return. You [usually] return.
He will return. He [usually] returns.
  She will return. She [usually] returns.
We will return. We [usually] return.
They will return. They [usually] return.

(This verb "return" is used only when returning home or to a place where one usually belongs.)

I-2.2 Particle wa

The particle wa follows a noun or a noun phrase and sets it off as the topic of the sentence. The part following the wa gives or asks some information pertaining to that topic.

EXAMPLES:

Yukio-san wa nanji ni kaerimasu ka?

At what time will Yukio-san return [home]? (As for Yukio, what time will he return?)

Kyoo wa goji ni kaerimasu.

Today, I will return at five. (Today-- as opposed to other days--I will return at five.)

I-2.3 Particle ni

When occurring in relation to time, ni follows a given moment of time when

9

some action or incident occurs. It may be compared with the prepositions "in,"
"on" and "at" in English in such phrases as "in May," "on Tuesday" or "at three
o'clock."

EXAMPLES:

Shichiji ni okimasu.	I get up at seven o'clock.
Hachiji ni tabemasu.	I eat at eight o'clock.
Nanji ni kaerimasu ka?	At what time do you return?

I-2.4 goro

Goro, meaning "about" or "around," occurs only after a given moment of time
when some action or incident occurs.

EXAMPLES:

Rokuji goro ni tabemasu.	I eat around six o'clock.
Kuji-han goro ni yasumimasu.	I go to bed around nine-thirty.
Rokuji-han goro ni okimasu.	I get up around six-thirty.

DRILLS

1. Repetition (using a clock)

ichiji-han	one-thirty
niji-han	two-thirty
sanji-han	three-thirty
yoji-han	four-thirty
goji-han	five-thirty
rokuji-han	six-thirty
shichiji-han	seven-thirty
hachiji-han	eight-thirty
kuji-han	nine-thirty
juuji-han	ten-thirty
juu-ichiji-han	eleven-thirty
juu-niji-han	twelve-thirty

2. Repetition (using a clock)

ichiji	one o'clock
ichiji-han	one-thirty
niji	two o'clock
niji-han	two-thirty
sanji	three o'clock
sanji-han	three-thirty
yoji	four o'clock
yoji-han	four-thirty
goji	five o'clock
goji-han	five-thirty
rokuji	six o'clock
rokuji-han	six-thirty

shichiji	seven o'clock
shichiji-han	seven-thirty
hachiji	eight o'clock
hachiji-han	eight-thirty
kuji	nine o'clock
kuji-han	nine-thirty
juuji	ten o'clock
juuji-han	ten-thirty
juu-ichiji	eleven o'clock
juu-ichiji-han	eleven-thirty
juu-niji	twelve o'clock
juu-niji-han	twelve-thirty

3. Substitution

Ichiji-han desu.   It's one-thirty.

(niji-han)	Niji-han desu.	It's two-thirty.
(sanji-han)	Sanji-han desu.	It's three-thirty.
(yoji-han)	Yoji-han desu.	It's four-thirty.
(goji-han)	Goji-han desu.	It's five-thirty.
(rokuji-han)	Rokuji-han desu.	It's six-thirty.
(shichiji-han)	Shichiji-han desu.	It's seven-thirty.
(hachiji-han)	Hachiji-han desu.	It's eight-thirty.
(kuji-han)	Kuji-han desu.	It's nine-thirty.
(juuji-han)	Juuji-han desu.	It's ten-thirty.
(juu-ichiji-han)	Juu-ichiji-han desu.	It's eleven-thirty.
(juu-niji-han)	Juu-niji-han desu.	It's twelve-thirty.

4. Substitution

Ichiji-han ni kaerimasu.   I will return at one-thirty.

(niji-han)	Niji-han ni kaerimasu.	I will return at two-thirty.
(sanji-han)	Sanji-han ni kaerimasu.	I will return at three-thirty.
(yoji-han)	Yoji-han ni kaerimasu.	I will return at four-thirty.
(goji-han)	Goji-han ni kaerimasu.	I will return at five-thirty.
(rokuji-han)	Rokuji-han ni kaerimasu.	I will return at six-thirty.
(shichiji-han)	Shichiji-han ni kaerimasu.	I will return at seven-thirty.
(hachiji-han)	Hachiji-han ni kaerimasu.	I will return at eight-thirty.
(kuji-han)	Kuji-han ni kaerimasu.	I will return at nine-thirty.
(juuji-han)	Juuji-han ni kaerimasu.	I will return at ten-thirty.
(juu-ichiji-han)	Juu-ichiji-han ni kaerimasu.	I will return at eleven-thirty.
(juu-niji-han)	Juu-niji-han ni kaerimasu.	I will return at twelve-thirty.

5. Repetition

Kuji-han ni kaerimasu.   I will return at nine-thirty.
Kuji-han ni okimasu.   I will get up at nine-thirty.

Kuji-han ni dekakemasu.   I will start out at nine-thirty.
Kuji-han ni tabemasu.   I will eat at nine-thirty.
Kuji-han ni yasumimasu.   I will go to bed at nine-thirty.

6. Repetition

Ichiji-han goro ni dekakemasu.   I will start out around one-thirty.
Niji-han goro ni dekakemasu.   I will start out around two-thirty.
Sanji-han goro ni dekakemasu.   I will start out around three-thirty.
Yoji-han goro ni dekakemasu.   I will start out around four-thirty.
Goji-han goro ni dekakemasu.   I will start out around five-thirty.
Rokuji-han goro ni dekakemasu.   I will start out around six-thirty.
Shichiji-han goro ni dekakemasu.   I will start out around seven-thirty.
Hachiji-han goro ni dekakemasu.   I will start out around eight-thirty.
Kuji-han goro ni dekakemasu.   I will start out around nine-thirty.
Juuji-han goro ni dekakemasu.   I will start out around ten-thirty.
Juu-ichiji-han goro ni dekakemasu.   I will start out around eleven-thirty.
Juu-niji-han goro ni dekakemasu.   I will start out around twelve-thirty.

7. Substitution

Ichiji ni tabemasu.   I eat at one o'clock.

(ichiji goro)	Ichiji goro ni tabemasu.	I eat around one o'clock.
(ichiji-han goro)	Ichiji-han goro ni tabemasu.	I eat around one-thirty.
(niji)	Niji ni tabemasu.	I eat at two o'clock.
(niji goro)	Niji goro ni tabemasu.	I eat around two o'clock.
(niji-han goro)	Niji-han goro ni tabemasu.	I eat around two-thirty.
(sanji)	Sanji ni tabemasu.	I eat at three o'clock.
(sanji goro)	Sanji goro ni tabemasu.	I eat around three o'clock.
(sanji-han goro)	Sanji-han goro ni tabemasu.	I eat around three-thirty.
(yoji)	Yoji ni tabemasu.	I eat at four o'clock.
(yoji goro)	Yoji goro ni tabemasu.	I eat around four o'clock.
(yoji-han goro)	Yoji-han goro ni tabemasu.	I eat around four-thirty.
(goji)	Goji ni tabemasu.	I eat at five o'clock.
(goji goro)	Goji goro ni tabemasu.	I eat around five o'clock.
(goji-han goro)	Goji-han goro ni tabemasu.	I eat around five-thirty.
(rokuji)	Rokuji ni tabemasu.	I eat at six o'clock.
(rokuji goro)	Rokuji goro ni tabemasu.	I eat around six o'clock.
(rokuji-han goro)	Rokuji-han goro ni tabemasu.	I eat around six-thirty.
(shichiji)	Shichiji ni tabemasu.	I eat at seven o'clock.
(shichiji goro)	Shichiji goro ni tabemasu.	I eat around seven o'clock.
(shichiji-han goro)	Shichiji-han goro ni tabemasu.	I eat around seven-thirty.
(hachiji)	Hachiji ni tabemasu.	I eat at eight o'clock.
(hachiji goro)	Hachiji goro ni tabemasu.	I eat around eight o'clock.
(hachiji-han goro)	Hachiji-han goro ni tabemasu.	I eat around eight-thirty.
(kuji)	Kuji ni tabemasu.	I eat at nine o'clock.
(kuji goro)	Kuji goro ni tabemasu.	I eat around nine o'clock.
(kuji-han goro)	Kuji-han goro ni tabemasu.	I eat around nine-thirty.

(juuji)	Juuji ni tabemasu.	I eat at ten o'clock.
(juuji goro)	Juuji goro ni tabemasu.	I eat around ten o'clock.
(juuji-han goro)	Juuji-han goro ni tabemasu.	I eat around ten-thirty.
(juu-ichiji)	Juu-ichiji ni tabemasu.	I eat at eleven o'clock.
(juu-ichiji goro)	Juu-ichiji goro ni tabemasu.	I eat around eleven o'clock.
(juu-ichiji-han goro)	Juu-ichiji-han goro ni tabemasu.	I eat around eleven-thirty.
(juu-niji)	Juu-niji ni tabemasu.	I eat at twelve o'clock.
(juu-niji goro)	Juu-niji goro ni tabemasu.	I eat around twelve o'clock.
(juu-niji-han goro)	Juu-niji-han goro ni tabemasu.	I eat around twelve-thirty.

8. Substitution

Yukio-san wa asa nanji ni okimasu ka?   What time does Yukio get up in the morn-
                                                        ing?

(Substitute names of members of the class.)

9. Response

Q. _____-san wa asa nanji ni oki-   What time do you get up in the morning,
      masu ka?   _____?
A. Rokuji-han ni okimasu.   I get up at six-thirty.

10. Repetition

Yukio-san wa yoru nanji ni yasumimasu   What time does Yukio go to bed at night?
  ka?

(Substitute names of members of the class.)

11. Response

Q. _____-san wa yoru nanji ni ya-   What time do you go to bed at night,
      sumimasu ka?   _____?
A. Kuji-han goro ni yasumimasu.   I go to bed around nine-thirty.

12. Response

Q. _____-san wa ban nanji ni tabe-   What time do you eat in the evening,
      masu ka?   _____?
A. Rokuji goro ni tabemasu.   I eat around six o'clock.

13. Response

Q. _____-san wa ohiru nanji ni ta-   What time do you eat at noon, _____?
   bemasu ka?
A. Juu-ichiji-han ni tabemasu.   I eat at eleven-thirty.

14. Repetition

Asa wa nanji ni tabemasu ka?   In the morning, what time do you eat?
Ohiru wa nanji ni tabemasu ka?   At lunchtime, what time do you eat?
Ban wa nanji ni tabemasu ka?   In the evening, what time do you eat?
Kyoo wa nanji ni tabemasu ka?   Today, what time will you be eating?
Ashita wa nanji ni tabemasu ka?   Tomorrow, what time will you be eating?

15. Progressive Substitution

Asa wa goji-han goro ni okimasu.   In the morning, I get up around
                                          five-thirty.

(rokuji)   Asa wa rokuji goro ni okimasu.   In the morning, I get up around
                                                    six o'clock.

(dekakemasu)   Asa wa rokuji goro ni dekake-   In the morning, I start out
               masu.   around six o'clock.

(ashita)   Ashita wa rokuji goro ni deka-   Tomorrow, I'll start out around
               kemasu.   six o'clock.

(juu-niji)   Ashita wa juu-niji goro ni de-   Tomorrow, I'll start out around
               kakemasu.   twelve o'clock.

(tabemasu)   Ashita wa juu-niji goro ni ta-   Tomorrow, I'll eat around twelve
               bemasu.   o'clock.

(ohiru)   Ohiru wa juuniji goro ni tabe-   At lunchtime, I eat around
               masu.   twelve o'clock.

(ichiji)   Ohiru wa ichiji goro ni tabe-   At lunchtime, I eat around one
               masu.   o'clock.

(kaerimasu)   Ohiru wa ichiji goro ni kaeri-   At lunchtime, I return home
               masu.   around one o'clock.

(kyoo)   Kyoo wa ichiji goro ni kaeri-   Today, I'll return home around
               masu.   one o'clock.

(shichiji)   Kyoo wa shichiji goro ni kaeri-   Today, I'll return home around
               masu.   seven o'clock.

(tabemasu)   Kyoo wa shichiji goro ni tabe-   Today, I'll eat around seven
               masu.   o'clock.

(ban)   Ban wa shichiji goro ni tabe-   In the evening, I eat around
               masu.   seven o'clock.

(hachiji)   Ban wa hachiji goro ni tabe-   In the evening, I eat around
               masu.   eight o'clock.

(kaerimasu)   Ban wa hachiji goro ni kaeri-   In the evening, I return home
               masu.   around eight o'clock.

(kyoo)   Kyoo wa hachiji goro ni kaeri-   Today, I'll return home around
               masu.   eight o'clock.

(juuji-han)   Kyoo wa juuji-han goro ni ka-   Today, I'll return home around
               erimasu.   ten-thirty.

(yasumimasu)	Kyoo wa juuji-han goro ni ya-sumimasu.	Today, I'll go to bed around ten-thirty.
(yoru)	Yoru wa juuji-han goro ni ya-sumimasu.	At night, I go to bed around ten-thirty.
(kuji)	Yoru wa kuji goro ni yasumi-masu.	At night, I go to bed around nine o'clock.
(tabemasu)	Yoru wa kuji goro ni tabemasu.	At night, I eat around nine o'clock.
(ashita)	Ashita wa kuji goro ni tabe-masu.	Tomorrow, I'll eat around nine o'clock.
(goji-han)	Ashita wa goji-han goro ni ta-bemasu.	Tomorrow, I'll eat around five-thirty.
(okimasu)	Ashita wa goji-han goro ni okimasu.	Tomorrow, I'll get up around five-thirty.
(asa)	Asa wa goji-han goro ni okimasu.	In the morning, I get up around five-thirty.

CULTURAL NOTES

1. Said at the end of a meal. A guest says a politer version, "Gochisoo-sama de gozaimashita," meaning, "It was a feast." This politer version is also said frequently by a dinner guest when leaving the home of the host. It is sometimes said by customers when leaving a restaurant noted for its cuisine.

2. Shoes are never worn inside a Japanese home. They are removed at the en-tranceway and slippers are worn indoors in the Western-style rooms but removed when entering a tatami room (a room with straw-mat flooring).

3. Said by a person when leaving his home or office or someplace where he is usually to be found. Literally, it means, "I'll go and return."

4. Said by the person remaining behind at home or in the office. It means, "Go and come back."

EXERCISES

A. Supply the missing particles.

1. Asa nanji _____ tabemasu ka?
2. Asa _____ shichiji _____ tabemasu.
3. Ban nanji _____ kaerimasu ka?
4. Ban goji-han goro _____ kaerimasu.
5. Ohiru _____ juu-niji _____ tabemasu ka?
6. Iie. Juu-ichiji-han _____ tabemasu.
7. Nanji _____ dekakemasu ka?
8. Yoru nanji _____ yasumimasu ka?
9. Yukio-san _____ kuji _____ yasumimasu ka?
10. Yukio-san _____ shichiji goro _____ okimasu ka?

B. Supply an appropriate verb.

1. Shichiji goro ni _____.
2. Asa hachiji-han ni _____ ka?
3. Ohiru wa nanji ni _____ ka?
4. Ban goji goro ni _____ ka?
5. Ban rokuji-han goro ni _____.
6. Yoru juuji goro ni _____.

C. Ask your neighbor:

1. what time he will get up tomorrow.
2. what time he eats in the morning.
3. what time he starts out in the morning.
4. whether he returns home at noon.
5. what time he eats in the evening.
6. what time he goes to bed at night.
7. what time he returns home in the evening.

LESSON 3

Yukio-san wa gakkoo e basu de ikimasu.   Yukio goes to school by bus. He doesn't
    Aruite ikimasen.   go on foot. (Literally, " he doesn't
                                               go walking.")

GRAMMAR

I-3.1 Verbs (-masen ending)
    The -masen ending is the negative of the -masu ending. It means that I (he,
etc.) "will not" do something or that I (he, etc.) "usually (often) do not" do
something. (The form itself will be discussed later.)

EXAMPLES:
    Kyoo wa ikimasen.   I'm not going today.
    Yoji-han ni okimasen.   I don't get up at four-thirty.
    Yukio-san wa kimasen.   Yukio doesn't come.

    This negative form is commonly used in inviting someone to do something; it
occurs then in the interrogative.

EXAMPLES:
    Kyoo ikimasen ka?   Won't you go today?
    Ashita kimasen ka?   Won't you come [over] tomorrow?

    The verbs "go" and "come," ikimasu and kimasu, are always used with reference
to the location of the speaker. For example, if A and B are talking on the telephone and A says he'll go to B's house, he will say, "Ikimasu." A will be going
away from where he presently is, over to B's home.

I-3.2 Verbs (-mashoo ending)
    The -mashoo ending has the meaning "let's"; when it is followed immediately
by the interrogative particle ka, it has the meaning "shall we" in the way of a
suggestion.

EXAMPLES:
    Ikimashoo.   Let's go.
    Ikimashoo ka?   Shall we go?
    Tabemashoo ka?   Shall we eat?
    Nanji ni tabemashoo ka?   At what time shall we eat?

I-3.3 Particle e
    The particle e means "to" or "towards" and indicates spatial motion.

EXAMPLES:
    Gakkoo e ikimasu.   He goes to school.
    Uchi e kimasu.   He comes to our house.
    Nihon e kaerimasu.   He will return to Japan.

17

I-3.4 Particle de
     The particle de indicates "with" or "by" what means an action takes place. It indicates the agent.

EXAMPLES:
     Kisha de ikimasu.   He goes by train.
     Takushii de kaerimasu.   I'm going home by taxi.

I-3.5 Response to a negatively phrased question
     The "yes" or "no" response to a negatively phrased question is different from the usual "yes" or "no" response to an affirmatively phrased question. One either agrees or disagrees with the statement, not the content of the statement.

EXAMPLES:
     Affirmatively phrased question:
     Goji ni kaerimasu ka?   Do you return home at five o'clock?
     Ee. Goji ni kaerimasu.   Yes, I return home at five o'clock.
     Iie. Goji ni kaerimasen.   No, I don't return home at five o'clock.

     Negatively phrased question:
     Goji ni kaerimasen ka?   Don't you return home at five o'clock?
     Ee. Goji ni kaerimasen.   No, I don't return home at five o'clock.
                                            (Yes, I agree with your statement. I
                                            don't return home at five o'clock.)

     Iie. Goji ni kaerimasu.   Yes, I return home at five o'clock. (No,
                                            I disagree with your statement. I re-
                                            turn home at five o'clock.)

                              DRILLS

1. Repetition (using objects)

Jettoki desu.   It's a jet plane.
Hikooki desu.   It's an airplane.
Basu desu.   It's a bus.
Tororii basu desu.   It's a trolley bus.
Densha desu.   It's a streetcar.
Chikatetsu desu.   It's a subway.
Takushii desu.   It's a taxi.
Jidoosha desu.   It's an automobile.
Kuruma desu.   It's a car.
Kisha desu.   It's a train.
Fuhe desu.   It's a boat.

2. Response (using objects)

Q. Nan desu ka?   What is it?
A. Jettoki desu.   It's a jet plane.

(Use list in Drill 1 above.)

3. Substitution

Basu de ikimasu.   I will go by bus.

(jettoki)   Jettoki de ikimasu.   I will go by jet plane.
(hikooki)   Hikooki de ikimasu.   I will go by plane.
(tororii basu)   Tororii basu de ikimasu.   I will go by trolley bus.
(densha)   Densha de ikimasu.   I will go by streetcar.
(chikatetsu)   Chikatetsu de ikimasu.   I will go by subway.
(takushii)   Takushii de ikimasu.   I will go by taxi.
(jidoosha)   Jidoosha de ikimasu.   I will go by automobile.
(kuruma)   Kuruma de ikimasu.   I will go by car.
(kisha)   Kisha de ikimasu.   I will go by train.
(fune)   Fune de ikimasu.   I will go by ship.

4. Response

Q. Nan de ikimasu ka?   How will you go? (By what means will you
                                                 go?)

A. Densha de ikimasu.   I'll go by streetcar.

(Use list in Drill 3 above.)

5. Substitution

Densha de ikimasen.   I'm not going by streetcar.

(jettoki)   Jettoki de ikimasen.   I'm not going by jet plane.
(hikooki)   Hikooki de ikimasen.   I'm not going by plane.
(basu)   Basu de ikimasen.   I'm not going by bus.
(tororii basu)   Tororii basu de ikimasen.   I'm not going by trolley bus.
(chikatetsu)   Chikatetsu de ikimasen.   I'm not going by subway.
(takushii)   Takushii de ikimasen.   I'm not going by taxi.
(jidoosha)   Jidoosha de ikimasen.   I'm not going by automobile.
(kuruma)   Kuruma de ikimasen.   I'm not going by car.
(kisha)   Kisha de ikimasen.   I'm not going by train.
(fune)   Fune de ikimasen.   I'm not going by ship.

6. Negative Response

Q. Yukio-san wa takushii de kimasu   Does Yukio come by taxi?
      ka?
A. Iie. Yukio-san wa takushii de   No, Yukio doesn't come by taxi.
      kimasen.

(Use list in Drill 5 above.)

7. Repetition

Kimasu.	I come.
Kimasen.	I don't come.
Ikimasu.	I go.
Ikimasen.	I don't go.
Tabemasu.	I eat.
Tabemasen.	I don't eat.
Dekakemasu.	I start out.
Dekakemasen.	I don't start out.
Kaerimasu.	I return.
Kaerimasen.	I don't return.
Yasumimasu.	I rest.
Yasumimasen.	I don't rest.
Okimasu.	I get up.
Okimasen.	I don't get up.

8. Negative Response

Q. Goji goro ni okimasu ka?   Do you get up around five o'clock?
A. Iie. Goji goro ni okimasen.   No, I don't get up around five o'clock.

(Shichiji-han goro ni dekakemasu ka?)   (Do you start out around seven-thirty?)
  Iie. Shichiji-han goro ni dekakema-   No, I don't start out around seven-
  sen.   thirty.
(Juuji goro ni dekakemasu ka?)   (Do you start out around ten o'clock?)
  Iie. Juuji goro ni dekakemasen.   No, I don't start out around ten
                                             o'clock.

(Rokuji goro ni okimasu ka?)   (Do you get up around six o'clock?)
  Iie. Rokuji goro ni okimasen.   No, I don't get up around six o'clock.
(Goji-han goro ni kaerimasu ka?)   (Do you return around five-thirty?)
  Iie. Goji-han goro ni kaerimasen.   No, I don't return around five-thirty.
(Yoji-han goro ni tabemasu ka?)   (Do you eat around four-thirty?)
  Iie. Yoji-han goro ni tabemasen.   No, I don't eat around four-thirty.
(Hachiji goro ni yasumimasu ka?)   (Do you go to bed around eight o'clock?)
  Iie. Hachiji goro ni yasumimasen.   No, I don't go to bed around eight
                                             o'clock.

9. Repetition

Gakkoo e ikimasu.	He goes to school.
Nihon e ikimasu.	He goes to Japan.
Amerika e ikimasu.	He goes to America.
Kaisha e ikimasu.	He goes to the office.
Machi e ikimasu.	He goes to town (downtown).

10. Response

	Q. Doko e ikimasu ka?	Where does he go?
(gakkoo)	A. Gakkoo e ikimasu.	He goes to school.

(kaisha)	A.	Kaisha e ikimasu.	He goes to the office.
(machi)	A.	Machi e ikimasu.	He goes downtown.
(Nihon)	A.	Nihon e ikimasu.	He goes to Japan.
(Amerika)	A.	Amerika e ikimasu.	He goes to America.

11. Repetition

Ikimashoo.	Let's go.
Kimashoo.	Let's come.
Tabemashoo.	Let's eat.
Okimashoo.	Let's get up.
Yasumimashoo.	Let's get to bed.
Kaerimashoo.	Let's return.
Dekakemashoo.	Let's start out.

12. Repetition

Ikimashoo ka?	Shall we go?
Kimashoo ka?	Shall we come?
Tabemashoo ka?	Shall we eat?
Okimashoo ka?	Shall we get up?
Yasumimashoo ka?	Shall we retire?
Kaerimashoo ka?	Shall we return?
Dekakemashoo ka?	Shall we start out?

13. Affirmative Response

| Q. | Ikimashoo ka? | Shall we go? |
| A. | Ee. Ikimashoo. | Yes, let's go. |

(kimashoo)	Kimashoo ka?	Shall we come?
	Ee. Kimashoo.	Yes, let's come.
(dekakemashoo)	Dekakemashoo ka?	Shall we start out?
	Ee. Dekakemashoo.	Yes, let's start out.
(kaerimashoo)	Kaerimashoo ka?	Shall we return?
	Ee. Kaerimashoo.	Yes, let's return.
(tabemashoo)	Tabemashoo ka?	Shall we eat?
	Ee. Tabemashoo.	Yes, let's eat.
(okimashoo)	Okimashoo ka?	Shall we get up?
	Ee. Okimashoo.	Yes, let's get up.
(yasumimashoo)	Yasumimashoo ka?	Shall we get to bed?
	Ee. Yasumimashoo.	Yes, let's get to bed.

14. Substitution

Gakkoo e aruite ikimasu ka?   Do you walk to school? (Do you go to
                                                  school walking?)

(kaisha)   Kaisha e aruite ikimasu ka?   Do you walk to the office?
(machi)   Machi e aruite ikimasu ka?   Do you walk to town?

15.   Substitution and Negative Response

Q. Aruite kimasu ka?   Do you come on foot?
A. Iie. Aruite kimasen. Basu de kimasu.   No, I don't come on foot. I
                                                     come by bus.

(densha)   Aruite kimasu ka?   Do you come on foot?
                Iie. Aruite kimasen. Densha   No, I don't come on foot. I
                  de kimasu.   come by streetcar.
(takushii)   Aruite kimasu ka?   Do you come on foot?
                Iie. Aruite kimasen. Takushii   No, I don't come on foot. I
                  de kimasu.   come by taxi.
(chikatetsu)   Aruite kimasu ka?   Do you come on foot?
                Iie. Aruite kimasen. Chika-   No, I don't come on foot. I
                  tetsu de kimasu.   come by subway.
(kuruma)   Aruite kimasu ka?   Do you come on foot?
                Iie. Aruite kimasen. Kuruma   No, I don't come on foot. I
                  de kimasu.   come by car.

16.   Affirmative Response to Negative Question

Q. Takushii de gakkoo e kimasen ka?   Don't you come to school by taxi?
A. Ee. Takushii de gakkoo e kimasen.   No, I don't come to school by taxi.

(Chikatetsu de machi e ikimasen ka?)   (Don't you go to town by subway?)
 Ee. Chikatetsu de machi e ikimasen.   No, I don't go to town by subway.
(Kuruma de kaisha e dekakemasen ka?)   (Don't you go to the office by car?)
 Ee. Kuruma de kaisha e dekakemasen.   No, I don't go to the office by car.
(Fune de Nihon e ikimasen ka?)   (Don't you go to Japan by boat?)
 Ee. Fune de Nihon e ikimasen.   No, I don't go to Japan by boat.
(Densha de uchi e kaerimasen ka?)   (Don't you return home by streetcar?)
 Ee. Densha de uchi e kaerimasen.   No, I don't return home by streetcar.

17.   Negative Response to Negative Question

Q. Takushii de gakkoo e kimasen ka?   Don't you come to school by taxi?
A. Iie. Takushii de gakkoo e kimasu.   Yes, I come to school by taxi.

(Chikatetsu de machi e ikimasen ka?)   (Don't you go to town by subway?)
 Iie. Chikatetsu de machi e ikimasu.   Yes, I go to town by subway.
(Kuruma de kaisha e dekakemasen ka?)   (Don't you go to the office by car?)
 Iie. Kuruma de kaisha e dekakemasu.   Yes, I go to the office by car.
(Fune de Nihon e ikimasen ka?)   (Don't you go to Japan by boat?)
 Iie. Fune de Nihon e ikimasu.   Yes, I go to Japan by boat.
(Densha de uchi e kaerimasen ka?)   (Don't you return home by streetcar?)
 Iie. Densha de uchi e kaerimasu.   Yes, I return home by streetcar.

EXERCISES

A. Reply negatively to the following questions.

1. Ashita ikimasu ka?
2. Ashita ikimasen ka?
3. Aruite kaerimasu ka?
4. Kyoo kaerimasen ka?
5. Hikooki de kaerimasu ka?
6. Kuruma de kimasen ka?
7. Yoji ni okimasu ka?
8. Rokuji ni okimasen ka?
9. Juu-ichiji ni tabemasu ka?
10. Shichiji goro ni yasumimasu ka?
11. Yukio-san wa kimasu ka?
12. Kyoo dekakemasu ka?

B. Supply the missing particles.

1. Yukio-san _____ rokuji _____ tabemasen.   Yukio doesn't eat at six
                                                      o'clock.
2. Basu _____ ikimasen.   Buses don't go there.
3. Basu _____ ikimasen.   I'm not going by bus.
4. Ashita dekakemasu. Kyoo _____ dekakemasen.   I'm starting out tomorrow. I'm
                                                      not going out today.
5. Nanji _____ okimasu ka?   What time do you get up?
6. Machi _____ ikimasu.   I go to town.
7. Yukio-san _____ gakkoo _____ kimasu ka?   Does Yukio come to school?
8. Goji goro _____ kaerimasu.   I'm returning around five
                                                      o'clock.

C. Suggest:

1. going to Japan.
2. going to America.
3. coming tomorrow.
4. returning around four o'clock.
5. getting up at seven o'clock.
6. going to the office.
7. going to the office at eight o'clock.
8. returning by streetcar.
9. returning by taxi.
10. going to America by ship.
11. returning to Japan by plane.
12. going by subway.

D. Ask (in the sense of invite) your friend: (using the negative interrogative)

1. to go tomorrow.
2. to go to town.
3. to walk back.
4. to eat some.
5. to return by train.
6. to go by car.

LESSON 4

Yukio-san no uchi no chikaku ni omise   Near Yukio's home, there is a store.
   ga arimasu. Yukio-san wa omise ni   Yukio dropped in at the store.
   yorimashita.

GRAMMAR

I-4.1   Verbs (-mashita ending)
     The -mashita ending indicates that an action has been completed or finished.
It often equals the past tense in meaning.

EXAMPLES:
     Kinoo ikimashita.   I went yesterday.
     Kinoo no ban tabemashita.   I ate it last night.
     Kinoo no asa kaerimashita.   He returned yesterday morning.

I-4.2   Verb arimasu
     The verb arimasu indicates existence, "is" or "are," and occurs in reference
to inanimate objects.   The phrase N (noun) ga (or wa) arimasu indicates the noun
which "exists" or the noun one "possesses." N (place noun) ni arimasu locates
where something is.   The latter combination, ni arimasu, is interchangeable with
desu.

EXAMPLES:
     Hon'ya ga arimasu.   There is a bookstore.
     Omise ga arimasu.   There is a store.
     Depaato wa arimasen.   There isn't a department store.
     Hon ga arimasu ka?   Is there a book? Do you have a book?
     Yukio-san wa empitsu ga arimasen.   Yukio doesn't have a pencil.

Compare with:

     Hon wa uchi ni arimasu.   The book is at home.
     Depaato wa doko ni arimasu ka?   Where is the department store?
     Omise ni wa arimasen.   There isn't one in the store.

Compare the following pairs:

     Hon'ya ni arimasu.   It's at a bookstore.
     Hon'ya desu.   It's at a bookstore.
                                           It is a bookstore.

     Uchi ni arimasu.   It's at home.
     Uchi desu.   It's at home.
                                           It's my home.

I-4.3   Comparison of wa and ga
     In form, the following two sentences differ only in the particle.

25

Yukio-san ga kimashita.   Yukio came.
Yukio-san wa kimashita.   Yukio came.

The difference in the particle results in a difference of emphasis in the meaning, as one can see from the English equivalents. Where the particle ga occurs, the information which is emphasized precedes the ga; where the particle wa occurs, the information which is emphasized follows the wa. In short, these two sentences are replies to very different questions.

Question 1.   Dare ga kimashita ka?   Who came?
               Yukio-san ga kimashita.   Yukio came.
Question 2.   Yukio-san wa kimashita   Did Yukio come or not?
                  ka, kimasen deshita ka?
               Yukio-san wa kimashita.   Yukio came.

(Note that the particle ga does not occur in combination with other particles but the particle wa may occur in combination with other particles, i.e., ni wa, de wa.)

I-4.4 Particle no
The particle no occurs between two nouns; the noun preceding the no is a modifier of the noun which follows it. The particle no is often equated with the English "of" or "'s."

EXAMPLES:
Yukio-san no empitsu desu.   It's Yukio's pencil.
Uchi no mae desu.   It's in front of our house.
Mae no uchi desu.   It's the house in front.

A noun may be modified by more than one phrase consisting of a noun plus no.

EXAMPLES:
Yukio-san no tsukue no soba ni   It's near Yukio's desk.
   arimasu.
Yamada-san no uchi no tonari desu.   It's next door to Mr. Yamada's home.

The final noun (i.e., the noun being modified) is often omitted when the object being discussed is clear.

EXAMPLES:
Yukio-san no desu.   It's Yukio's.
Uchi no mae no desu.   It's the one in front of our house.

I-4.5 Particle ni
The particle ni indicates motion "to" or "into." Ni and e are interchangeable when the action is directed towards a location. When the action is directed towards a person, the particle is usually ni.

EXAMPLES:
Omise ni yorimashita.   He dropped in at the store.
Omise e yorimashita.   He dropped in at the store.

(Note: When learning a new verb, it is recommended that the accompanying particle(s) also be memorized.)

I-4.6 Honorific prefix o
    Some nouns such as cha meaning "tea" are almost always preceded by the honor-
ific o, in informal as well as formal speech. Other nouns occur with or without
the honorific o, depending on the formality of the speech, with more usage of the
o in more honorific or formal speech. In these cases, the o before a noun may
have the meaning "your _____."

EXAMPLES:

    Mise no mae desu.   It's in front of the store.
    Omise no mae desu.   It's in front of the store.
    Yukio-san no okuruma desu ka?   Is it your car, Yukio?

DRILLS

1. Repetition (using drawings or slides)

Hon'ya desu.   It's a bookstore.
Depaato desu.   It's a department store.
Omise desu.   It's a store.
Yaoya desu.   It's a greengrocery. It's a fruit and
                                             vegetable store.

Pan'ya desu.   It's a bakery.
Eki desu.   It's a station.
Uchi desu.   It's a house.
Isu desu.   It's a chair.
Tsukue desu.   It's a desk.
Kokuban desu.   It's a blackboard.
Hako desu.   It's a box.

2. Substitution

Isu ga arimasu.   There's a chair.

(tsukue)   Tsukue ga arimasu.   There's a desk.
(kokuban)   Kokuban ga arimasu.   There's a blackboard.
(empitsu)   Empitsu ga arimasu.   There's a pencil.
(booru pen)   Booru pen ga arimasu.   There's a ballpoint pen.
(hon)   Hon ga arimasu.   There's a book.
(hon'ya)   Hon'ya ga arimasu.   There's a bookstore.
(pan'ya)   Pan'ya ga arimasu.   There's a bakery.
(yaoya)   Yaoya ga arimasu.   There's a greengrocery.
(omise)   Omise ga arimasu.   There's a store.
(depaato)   Depaato ga arimasu.   There's a department store.
(eki)   Eki ga arimasu.   There's a station.
(uchi)   Uchi ga arimasu.   There's a house.
(chikatetsu)   Chikatetsu ga arimasu.   There's a subway.
(gakkoo)   Gakkoo ga arimasu.   There's a school.
(kaisha)   Kaisha ga arimasu.   There's a business office.

3. Substitution

Pan ga arimasu ka?   Do you have bread?

(hon)   Hon ga arimasu ka?   Do you have a book?
(tekisuto)   Tekisuto ga arimasu ka?   Do you have a text?
(empitsu)   Empitsu ga arimasu ka?   Do you have a pencil?
(booru pen) Booru pen ga arimasu ka?   Do you have a ballpoint pen?
(isu)   Isu ga arimasu ka?   Do you have a chair?
(tsukue)   Tsukue ga arimasu ka?   Do you have a desk?
(kuruma)   Kuruma ga arimasu ka?   Do you have a car?
(jidoosha)   Jidoosha ga arimasu ka?   Do you have an automobile?
(uchi)   Uchi ga arimasu ka?   Do you have a house?
(tokee)   Tokee ga arimasu ka?   Do you have a watch?

4. Response

Q. Pan ga arimasu ka?   Do you have bread?
A. Ee. Arimasu.   Yes, I do.
A. Iie. Arimasen.   No, I don't.

(Use list in Drill 3 above.)

5. Response to a Negative Question

Q. Pan ga arimasen ka?   Isn't there any bread?
A. Ee. Arimasen.   No, there isn't any.
A. Iie. Arimasu.   Yes, there is some.

(Use list in Drill 3 above.)

6. Negative Response

Q. Tsukue ga arimasu ka?   Is there a desk?
A. Iie. Tsukue wa arimasen.   No, there isn't a desk.

(Isu ga arimasu ka?)   (Is there a chair?)
 Iie. Isu wa arimasen.   No, there isn't a chair.
(Hon'ya ga arimasu ka?)   (Is there a bookstore?)
 Iie. Hon'ya wa arimasen.   No, there isn't a bookstore.
(Pan'ya ga arimasu ka?)   (Is there a bakery?)
 Iie. Pan'ya wa arimasen.   No, there isn't a bakery.
(Hako ga arimasu ka?)   (Is there a box?)
 Iie. Hako wa arimasen.   No, there isn't a box.
(Tekisuto ga arimasu ka?)   (Is there a text?)
 Iie. Tekisuto wa arimasen.   No, there isn't a text.
(Booru pen ga arimasu ka?)   (Is there a ballpoint pen?)
 Iie. Booru pen wa arimasen.   No, there isn't a ballpoint pen.
(Kokuban ga arimasu ka?)   (Is there a blackboard?)
 Iie. Kokuban wa arimasen.   No, there isn't a blackboard.

7. Repetition (using a drawing)

Hon'ya no chikaku desu.   It's near the bookstore.
Hon'ya no tonari desu.   It's next door to the bookstore.
Hon'ya no mae desu.   It's in front of the bookstore.
Hon'ya no ushiro desu.   It's in back of the bookstore.
Hon'ya no soba desu.   It's near the bookstore.
Hon'ya no shita desu.   It's below the bookstore. It's under the
                                           bookstore.

Hon'ya no naka desu.   It's in the bookstore.
Hon'ya no yoko desu.   It's beside the bookstore.
Hon'ya no ue desu.   It's on top of the bookstore. It's above
                                           the bookstore.

8. Affirmative Response (using object)

Q. Tsukue no soba desu ka?   Is it near the desk?
A. Ee. Tsukue no soba desu.   Yes, it's near the desk.

(ue)   Tsukue no ue desu ka?   Is it on top of the desk?
(shita)   Tsukue no shita desu ka?   Is it under the desk?
(naka)   Tsukue no naka desu ka?   Is it in the desk?
(ushiro)   Tsukue no ushiro desu ka?   Is it in back of the desk?
(mae)   Tsukue no mae desu ka?   Is it in front of the desk?
(yoko)   Tsukue no yoko desu ka?   Is it beside the desk?

9. Substitution

Eki no tonari ni arimasu.   It's next door to the station.

(mae)   Eki no mae ni arimasu.   It's in front of the station.
(ushiro)   Eki no ushiro ni arimasu.   It's in back of the station.
(naka)   Eki no naka ni arimasu.   It's inside the station.
(chikaku)   Eki no chikaku ni arimasu.   It's near the station.
(yoko)   Eki no yoko ni arimasu.   It's beside the station.

10. Grammar

(Yaoya-san no tonari ni arimasu.)   (It's next door to the greengrocer's.)
 Yaoya-san no tonari desu.   It's next door to the greengrocer's.
(Yaoya-san no soba ni arimasu.)   (It's near the greengrocer's.)
 Yaoya-san no soba desu.   It's near the greengrocer's.
(Yaoya-san no mae ni arimasu.)   (It's in front of the greengrocer's.)
 Yaoya-san no mae desu.   It's in front of the greengrocer's.
(Yaoya-san no ushiro ni arimasu.)   (It's in back of the greengrocer's.)
 Yaoya-san no ushiro desu.   It's in back of the greengrocer's.
(Yaoya-san no yoko ni arimasu.)   (It's beside the greengrocer's.)
 Yaoya-san no yoko desu.   It's beside the greengrocer's.
(Yaoya-san no chikaku ni arimasu.)   (It's near the greengrocer's.)
 Yaoya-san no chikaku desu.   It's near the greengrocer's.

11. Do Drill 8 in reverse, using pan'ya for yaoya.

12. Progressive Substitution

Uchi no soba ni arimasu.   It's near our house.

(mae)	Uchi no mae ni arimasu.	It's in front of our house.
(desu)	Uchi no mae desu.	It's in front of our house.
(omise)	Omise no mae desu.	It's in front of the store.
(tonari)	Omise no tonari desu.	It's next door to the store.
(ni arimasu)	Omise no tonari ni arimasu.	It's next door to the store.
(eki)	Eki no tonari ni arimasu.	It's next door to the station.
(chikaku)	Eki no chikaku ni arimasu.	It's near the station.
(desu)	Eki no chikaku desu.	It's near the station.
(depaato)	Depaato no chikaku desu.	It's near the department store.
(naka)	Depaato no naka desu.	It's inside the department store.
(ni arimasu)	Depaato no naka ni arimasu.	It's inside the department store.
(hako)	Hako no naka ni arimasu.	It's inside the box.
(ue)	Hako no ue ni arimasu.	It's on top of the box.
(desu)	Hako no ue desu.	It's on top of the box.
(isu)	Isu no ue desu.	It's on top of the chair.
(shita)	Isu no shita desu.	It's underneath the chair.
(ni arimasu)	Isu no shita ni arimasu.	It's underneath the chair.
(tsukue)	Tsukue no shita ni arimasu.	It's underneath the desk.
(ushiro)	Tsukue no ushiro ni arimasu.	It's in back of the desk.
(desu)	Tsukue no ushiro desu.	It's in back of the desk.
(kokuban)	Kokuban no ushiro desu.	It's in back of the blackboard.
(yoko)	Kokuban no yoko desu.	It's beside the blackboard.
(ni arimasu)	Kokuban no yoko ni arimasu.	It's beside the blackboard.
(pan'ya)	Pan'ya no yoko ni arimasu.	It's beside the bakery.
(chikaku)	Pan'ya no chikaku ni arimasu.	It's near the bakery.
(desu)	Pan'ya no chikaku desu.	It's near the bakery.
(yaoya)	Yaoya no chikaku desu.	It's near the greengrocery.
(soba)	Yaoya no soba desu.	It's near the greengrocery.
(ni arimasu)	Yaoya no soba ni arimasu.	It's near the greengrocery.
(uchi)	Uchi no soba ni arimasu.	It's near our house.

13. Response (using objects)

Q. Empitsu wa doko ni arimasu ka?   Where is the pencil?
A. Hako no naka ni arimasu.   It's in the box.

(After various examples with the pencil, use other objects already taught.)

14. Negative Response

Q. Isu no ue ni arimasu ka?   Is it on top of the chair?
A. Iie. Isu no ue ni wa arimasen.   No, it isn't on top of the chair.

(Tsukue no ue ni arimasu ka?)   (Is it on top of the desk?)
 Iie. Tsukue no ue ni wa arimasen.   No, it isn't on top of the desk.
(Tsukue no soba ni arimasu ka?)   (Is it near the desk?)
 Iie. Tsukue no soba ni wa arimasen.   No, it isn't near the desk.
(Kokuban no soba ni arimasu ka?)   (Is it near the blackboard?)
 Iie. Kokuban no soba ni wa arimasen.   No, it isn't near the blackboard.
(Kokuban no yoko ni arimasu ka?)   (Is it beside the blackboard?)
 Iie. Kokuban no yoko ni wa arimasen.   No, it isn't beside the blackboard.
(Depaato no yoko ni arimasu ka?)   (Is it beside the department store?)
 Iie. Depaato no yoko ni wa arimasen.   No, it isn't beside the department
                                                     store.

(Depaato no chikaku ni arimasu ka?)   (Is it near the department store?)
 Iie. Depaato no chikaku ni wa arima-   No, it isn't near the department store.
   sen.
(Omise no chikaku ni arimasu ka?)   (Is it near the store?)
 Iie. Omise no chikaku ni wa arimasen.   No, it isn't near the store.
(Omise no mae ni arimasu ka?)   (Is it in front of the store?)
 Iie. Omise no mae ni wa arimasen.   No, it isn't in front of the store.

15. Substitution

Yukio-san no uchi desu.   It's Yukio's home.

(hon)   Yukio-san no hon desu.   It's Yukio's book.
(empitsu)   Yukio-san no empitsu desu.   It's Yukio's pencil.
(booru pen)   Yukio-san no booru pen desu.   It's Yukio's ballpoint pen.
(jidoosha)   Yukio-san no jidoosha desu.   It's Yukio's automobile.
(pan)   Yukio-san no pan desu.   It's Yukio's bread.
(tsukue)   Yukio-san no tsukue desu.   It's Yukio's desk.

16. Response

Q. _____-san no hon desu ka?   Is it _____'s book?
A. Ee. _____-san no desu.   Yes, it's _____'s.

(Substitute names of students and objects already taught.)

17. Repetition

_____-san no hon wa doko ni arimasu   Where is _____'s book?
  ka?

(Substitute names of students and objects already taught.)

18. Response

Q. _____-san no hon wa doko ni ari-   Where is _____'s book?
   masu ka?

A. Tsukue no ue ni arimasu.   It's on top of the desk.

(Substitute names of students and various objects which are in view.)

19. Substitution

Yukio-san no uchi e yorimashita.   They dropped by at Yukio's home.

(ikimashita)   Yukio-san no uchi e   They went to Yukio's home.
                    ikimashita.
(dekakemashita)   Yukio san no uchi e   They started out for Yukio's home.
                    dekakemashita.
(kaerimashita)   Yukio-san no uchi e   They returned to Yukio's home.
                    kaerimashita.

20. Negative Response to a Negative Question

(hon'ya)   Kinoo hon'ya ni yorimasen   Didn't you drop in at the book-
                    deshita ka?   store yesterday?
                    Iie. Kinoo hon'ya ni yo-   Yes, I dropped in at the book-
                    rimashita.   store yesterday.

(Yukio-san no   Kinoo Yukio-san no uchi ni   Didn't you drop in at Yukio's
  uchi)   yorimasen deshita ka?   home yesterday?
                    Iie. Kinoo Yukio-san no uchi Yes, I dropped in at Yukio's
                    ni yorimashita.   home yesterday.
(omise)   Kinoo omise ni yorimasen   Didn't you drop in at the store
                    deshita ka?   yesterday?
                    Iie. Kinoo omise ni yorima-   Yes, I dropped in at the store
                    shita.   yesterday.
(kaisha)   Kinoo kaisha ni yorimasen   Didn't you drop in at the of-
                    deshita ka?   fice yesterday?
                    Iie. Kinoo kaisha ni yori-   Yes, I dropped in at the office
                    mashita.   yesterday.
(yaoya)   Kinoo yaoya ni yorimasen   Didn't you drop in at the
                    deshita ka?   greengrocery yesterday?
                    Iie. Kinoo yaoya ni yorima-   Yes, I dropped in at the green-
                    shita.   grocery yesterday.

EXERCISES

A. Fill in the following blanks with one or more (as many as possible) of the
    following: kinoo, kyoo, ashita.

    1. _____ ikimashita.
    2. _____ yorimashita.
    3. _____ yorimashoo.
    4. _____ yorimasu.

5. _____ kaerimashita.
6. _____ yorimasen.
7. _____ kimasen.
8. _____ tabemasu.
9. _____ dekakemashoo.
10. _____ dekakemashita.

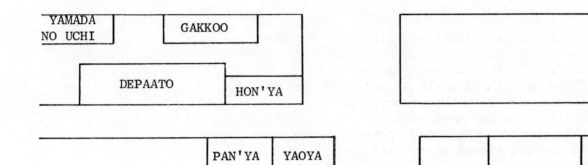

B. On the basis of the above plan, indicate whether the following statements are
   true (ee) or false (iie).

1. Depaato no tonari ni hon'ya ga arimasu.
2. Hon'ya wa eki no mae ni arimasu.
3. Hon'ya no shita ni pan'ya ga arimasu.
4. Pan'ya wa hon'ya no mae ni arimasu.
5. Yaoya wa pan'ya no tonari desu.
6. Eki no yoko ni jidoosha ga arimasu.
7. Gakkoo wa depaato no yoko desu.
8. Yamada-san no uchi wa gakkoo no chikaku desu.
9. Gakkoo wa depaato no ushiro desu.
10. Depaato no ushiro wa gakkoo desu.
11. Depaato no ushiro ni gakkoo ga arimasu.
12. Gakkoo wa depaato no naka ni arimasu.
13. Yamada-san no uchi wa gakkoo no soba ni arimasu.
14. Pan'ya wa yaoya no tonari ni arimasu.

C. Answer the following questions on the basis of the above plan.

1. Gakkoo ga arimasu ka?
2. Gakkoo wa doko ni arimasu ka?
3. Tanaka-san no uchi ga arimasu ka?
4. Yamada-san no uchi ga arimasu ka?
5. Yamada-san no uchi wa doko ni arimasu ka?
6. Hon'ya ga arimasu ka?

7. Hon'ya wa doko ni arimasu ka?
8. Hon'ya no mae ni nani ga arimasu ka?
9. Pan'ya wa doko ni arimasu ka?
10. Yaoya ga arimasu ka?
11. Yaoya wa doko ni arimasu ka?
12. Eki no yoko ni nani ga arimasu ka?
13. Depaato wa doko ni arimasu ka?
14. Eki no tonari ni hon'ya ga arimasu ka?

D. Tell (ask, suggest that) your friend:

1. that there is a department store.
2. that the department store is near the station.
3. that it isn't in the department store.
4. that it was in the bookstore.
5. what is next door to the department store.
6. go to the department store with you.
7. that you went to Mr. Yamada's home yesterday.
8. that you dropped in at the school.
9. if there is a store next door to the greengrocery.
10. that it's Yukio's.
11. where Mr. Yamada's car is.
12. where the station is.

(Omise no naka)	(In the store)

Ten'in: Irasshaimase![1]

Clerk: Welcome!

Yukio: Kono chokoreeto o kudasai.
Ikura desu ka?

Yukio: I'd like this chocolate, please.
(Please give me this choco-
late.) How much is it?

Ten'in: Gojuuen desu.[2]

Clerk: It's fifty yen.

Yukio: (paying the money) Hai.[3]
Gojuuen.

Yukio: (paying the money) Here you are.
Fifty yen.

Ten'in: Maido arigatoo gozaimasu.[4]

Clerk: Thank you. (Thank you for your
continued patronage.)

(Yukio wa chokoreeto o kaimashita.
Gojuuen deshita. Okane o gojuuen
dashimashita.)

(Yukio bought the chocolate. It was
fifty yen. He paid (presented) fifty
yen.)

GRAMMAR

I-5.1 The copula deshita

Deshita is the perfective of the copula desu (see 1.1) and means "was" or
"were."

EXAMPLES:

Kinoo deshita.	It was yesterday.
Yukio-san deshita.	It was Yukio.
Gojuuen deshita ka?	Was it fifty yen?
Nan deshita ka?	What was it?

I-5.2 Particle o

The particle o occurs after nouns and indicates the noun to be the direct
object of the verb.

EXAMPLES:

Chokoreeto o kaimashita.	I bought some chocolates.
Pan o kudasai.	Please give me some bread.
Shimbun o kaimashoo ka, zasshi o kaimashoo ka?	Shall we buy a newspaper or a magazine?

I-5.3 Kono, sono, ano, and dono

Kono, sono, ano, and dono occur only as noun modifiers and precede the noun.
Kono means "this" or "these"; sono means "that" or "those" and refers, in location, to something not far distant from the person being addressed, and in time,
to something which has just been mentioned; ano means "that" or "those" way over
there and refers, in location, to something away from both the speaker and the
addressee, and in time, to something mentioned some time back and understood by
both. Dono is the interrogative equivalent, "which."

EXAMPLES:

Kono jidoosha o kaimasu.	I'm going to buy this car.
Sono jidoosha wa Yamada-san no desu.	That car is Mr. Yamada's.
Ano jidoosha o onegai shimashita.	I ordered (requested) that car (we were talking about).
Dono jidoosha ga Yamada-san no desu ka?	Which car is Mr. Yamada's?

DRILLS

1. Repetition

Okashi o kudasai.	Please give me some cakes.
Chokoreeto o kudasai.	Please give me some chocolates.
Shimbun o kudasai.	Please give me some newspapers.
Zasshi o kudasai.	Please give me some magazines.
Okane o kudasai.	Please give me some money.

2. Substitution (pointing to objects)

Sono shimbun o kudasai.   Please give me that newspaper.

(okashi)	Sono okashi o kudasai.	Please give me that cake.
(chokoreeto)	Sono chokoreeto o kudasai.	Please give me that chocolate.
(zasshi)	Sono zasshi o kudasai.	Please give me that magazine.
(empitsu)	Sono empitsu o kudasai.	Please give me that pencil.
(booru pen)	Sono booru pen o kudasai.	Please give me that ballpoint pen.
(okane)	Sono okane o kudasai.	Please give me that money.
(tekisuto)	Sono tekisuto o kudasai.	Please give me that text.
(hon)	Sono hon o kudasai.	Please give me that book.
(pan)	Sono pan o kudasai.	Please give me that bread.
(tokee)	Sono tokee o kudasai.	Please give me that clock.
(hako)	Sono hako o kudasai.	Please give me that box.

3. Response (offering the object)

A. Sono shimbun o kudasai.   Please give me that newspaper.
B. Hai. Doozo.   Here you are. Please (take it).
                                              (offering the object)

(Use list in Drill 2 above.)

4. Substitution

Kono zasshi desu ka?   Do you mean this magazine? (Is it this
                                        magazine?)

(Use list in Drill 2 above.)

5. Conversation

A. Sono zasshi o kudasai.   Please give me that magazine.
B. Kono zasshi desu ka?   Do you mean this magazine?
A. Ee. Onegai shimasu.   Yes, please. (I request it.)
B. Hai. Doozo.   Here you are.

(Use list in Drill 2 above.)

6. Substitution

Sono hon o onegai shimasu.   I'd like that book, please.

(empitsu)   Sono empitsu o onegai shimasu.   I'd like that pencil, please.
(tekisuto)   Sono tekisuto o onegai shimasu.   I'd like that text, please.
(okashi)   Sono okashi o onegai shimasu.   I'd like that cake, please.
(chokoreeto) Sono chokoreeto o onegai shimasu.   I'd like that chocolate, please.
(hako)   Sono hako o onegai shimasu.   I'd like that box, please.
(zasshi)   Sono zasshi o onegai shimasu.   I'd like that magazine, please.
(shimbun)   Sono shimbun o onegai shimasu.   I'd like that newspaper, please.

7. Conversation

A. Sono okashi o onegai shimasu.   I'd like that cake, please.
B. Hai. Doozo.   Here you are.
A. Arigatoo gozaimasu.   Thank you.

(Use list in Drill 2 above.)

8. Substitution

Kinoo jidoosha o kaimashita.   I bought an automobile yesterday.

(fune)   Kinoo fune o kaimashita.   I bought a boat yesterday.
(hikooki)   Kinoo hikooki o kaimashita.   I bought a plane yesterday.
(uchi)   Kinoo uchi o kaimashita.   I bought a house yesterday.
(hako)   Kinoo hako o kaimashita.   I bought a box yesterday.
(isu)   Kinoo isu o kaimashita.   I bought a chair yesterday.
(tsukue)   Kinoo tsukue o kaimashita.   I bought a desk yesterday.

9. Substitution

Dono zasshi o kaimashita ka?   Which magazine did you buy?

(hon)   Dono hon o kaimashita ka?   Which book did you buy?
(empitsu)   Dono empitsu o kaimashita ka?   Which pencil did you buy?
(okashi)   Dono okashi o kaimashita ka?   Which cake did you buy?
(pan)   Dono pan o kaimashita ka?   Which bread did you buy?
(jidoosha)   Dono jidoosha o kaimashita ka?   Which automobile did you buy?
(shimbun)   Dono shimbun o kaimashita ka?   Which paper did you buy?

10. Response

Q. Dono okashi o kaimashita ka?   Which cake did you buy?
A. Kono okashi o kaimashita.   I bought this cake.

(Use list in Drill 9 above.)

11. Affirmative Response

Q. Ano jidoosha o kaimashita ka?   Did you buy that car (we were talking
                                                   about)?
A. Ee. Ano jidoosha o kaimashita.   Yes, I bought that car.

(Ano okashi o kaimashita ka?)   (Did you buy that cake?)
 Ee. Ano okashi o kaimashita.   Yes, I bought that cake.
(Ano okashi o kaimashoo ka?)   (Shall we buy that cake?)
 Ee. Ano okashi o kaimashoo.   Yes, let's buy that cake.
(Ano okashi o tabemashoo ka?)   (Shall we eat that cake?)
 Ee. Ano okashi o tabemashoo.   Yes, let's eat that cake.
(Ano chokoreeto o tabemashoo ka?)   (Shall we eat that chocolate?)
 Ee. Ano chokoreeto o tabemashoo.   Yes, let's eat that chocolate.
(Ano chokoreeto o kaimashita ka?)   (Did you buy that chocolate?)
 Ee. Ano chokoreeto o kaimashita.   Yes, I bought that chocolate.
(Ano shimbun o kaimashita ka?)   (Did you buy that newspaper?)
 Ee. Ano shimbun o kaimashita.   Yes, I bought that newspaper.
(Ano shimbun o onegai shimashita ka?)   (Did you order (request) that newspaper?)
 Ee. Ano shimbun o onegai shimashita.   Yes, I ordered that newspaper.
(Ano zasshi o onegai shimashita ka?)   (Did you order (request) that magazine?)
 Ee. Ano zasshi o onegai shimashita.   Yes, I ordered that magazine.
(Ano hon o onegai shimashita ka?)   (Did you order (request) that book?)
 Ee. Ano hon o onegai shimashita.   Yes, I ordered that book.

12. Repetition

juuen   ten yen
nijuuen   twenty yen
sanjuuen   thirty yen
yonjuuen   forty yen
gojuuen   fifty yen

rokujuuen	sixty yen
nanajuuen, shichijuuen	seventy yen
hachijuuen	eighty yen
kyuujuuen	ninety yen

13. Affirmative Response

Q. Juuen desu ka?	Is it ten yen?
A. Ee. Juuen desu.	Yes, it's ten yen.

(Use list in Drill 12 above.)

14. Affirmative Response

Q. Kono chokoreeto wa juuen desu ka?	Is this chocolate ten yen?
A. Ee. Sono chokoreeto wa juuen desu.	Yes, that chocolate is ten yen.

(Use list in Drill 12 above.)

15. Repetition (pointing to the numbers)

goen	five yen
juuen	ten yen
juu-goen	fifteen yen
nijuuen	twenty yen
nijuu-goen	twenty-five yen
sanjuuen	thirty yen
sanjuu-goen	thirty-five yen
yonjuuen	forty yen
yonjuu-goen	forty-five yen
gojuuen	fifty yen
gojuu-goen	fifty-five yen
rokujuuen	sixty yen
rokujuu-goen	sixty-five yen
nanajuuen, shichijuuen	seventy yen
nanajuu-goen	seventy-five yen
hachijuuen	eighty yen
hachijuu-goen	eighty-five yen
kyuujuuen	ninety yen
kyuujuu-goen	ninety-five yen

16. Response (pointing to the numbers)

Q. Ikura deshita ka?	How much was it?
A. Juuen deshita.	It was ten yen.

(Use list in Drill 15 above.)

17.   Response (answers being supplied)

Q. Okane wa ikura arimasu ka?   How much money do you have?
A. Goen arimasu.   I have five yen.

(Use list in Drill 15 above.)

18.   Substitution

Okane o juuen dashimashita.   He paid (presented) ten yen.

(Use list in Drill 15 above.)

19.   Progressive Substitution

Dare ni onegai shimashita ka?   Who did you request it of?

(Yukio-san)   Yukio-san ni onegai   Did you request it of Yukio?
                 shimashita ka?
(dashimashita)   Yukio-san ni dashima- Did you mail it to Yukio?
                 shita ka?
(tsukue no ue)   Tsukue no ue ni dashi- Did you put it out on the desk?
                 mashita ka?
(dashimashoo)   Tsukue no ue ni dashi- Shall I put it out on the desk?
                 mashoo ka?
(shimbun)   Shimbun ni dashimashoo Shall I put it in the newspapers?
                 ka?
(dashimasu)   Shimbun ni dashimasu   Are you going to put it in the newspa-
                 ka?   pers?
(dare)   Dare ni dashimasu ka? Who are you mailing it to?
(onegai shi-   Dare ni onegai shima- Who did you request it of?
 mashita)   shita ka?

CULTURAL NOTES

1. A greeting said by shopkeepers, innkeepers, etc.

2. Monetary unit in Japan. Today, about 360 yen is equal to one U. S. dollar.
One, five, ten, fifty, and one hundred-yen coins are in circulation. One hundred,
five hundred, one thousand, five thousand, and ten thousand-yen notes are in circulation. The yen sign is ¥.

3. Hai basically means "yes" and is closer to meaning "yes, sir" in contrast to
the more informal ee. In this instance, it has the meaning "here," when handing
something to someone.

4. Arigatoo gozaimasu means "thank you" and is used by everyone. The phrase preceded by maido is used only by shopkeepers, innkeepers, etc., to customers. Ari-

gatoo gozaimashita is said in thanking someone for a deed already finished, for example, if someone just mailed a letter for you.

EXERCISES

A. Do the exercises below on the basis of the following information.

Near the Customer   Near the Clerk

Chocolate	¥ 30
Newspaper	20
Pencil	10
Cake	40
Magazine	75

Chocolate	¥ 50
Newspaper	15
Pencil	5
Cake	60
Magazine	90

You are the customer. Ask for:

1. the chocolate near you.
2. the chocolate near the clerk.
3. the newspaper near the clerk.
4. the cake near you.
5. the magazine near you.
6. the newspaper near you.
7. the cake near the clerk.
8. the pencil near you.
9. the magazine near the clerk.
10. the pencil near the clerk.

You are the customer. Ask how much:

1. the chocolate near the clerk is.
2. the chocolate near you is.
3. the newspaper near the clerk is.
4. the newspaper near you is.
5. the pencil near you is.
6. the pencil near the clerk is.
7. the cake near you is.
8. the cake near the clerk is.
9. the magazine near the clerk is.
10. the magazine near you is.

You are the clerk. Answer how much:

1. the chocolate near you is.
2. the chocolate near the customer is.
3. the newspaper near you is.
4. the newspaper near the customer is.
5. the pencil near the customer is.
6. the pencil near you is.
7. the cake near the customer is.
8. the cake near you is.
9. the magazine near you is.
10. the magazine near the customer is.

Yukio is the customer. Ten'in is the word for "clerk." Tell where the following objects are located.

Example: Sanjuuen no chokoreeto wa Yukio-san no chikaku ni arimasu.

1. the fifty-yen chocolate
2. the twenty-yen newspaper
3. the fifteen-yen newspaper
4. the ten-yen pencil
5. the five-yen pencil

6. the forty-yen cake
7. the sixty-yen cake
8. the seventy-five-yen magazine
9. the ninety-yen magazine

B. You are talking with your friend.

1. Tell your friend that Yukio bought a cake.
2. Ask your friend how much that cake was.
3. Tell your friend that the cake was eighty yen.
4. Tell your friend that Yukio paid (put out) eighty yen.
5. Ask your friend if he has any money.
6. Ask your friend how much money he has.
7. Suggest buying chocolates.
8. Ask whether you should buy the thirty-yen chocolates or the fifty-yen choco-
       lates.
9. Suggest buying the sixty-yen cake.
10. Suggest eating that cake tomorrow.

Basu no teeryuujo wa sono omise no mae
 desu. Yukio-san wa soko de basu o
 machimashita ga sugu kimasen deshita.
 Roppun gurai machimashita.

The bus stop is in front of that store.
 Yukio waited there for the bus, but it
 didn't come immediately. He waited
 about six minutes.

GRAMMAR

I-6.1 Verbs (-masen deshita ending)

The -masen deshita ending is the negative of the -mashita ending and is the
negative perfective. It has the meaning "did not" do something.

EXAMPLES:

Chokoreeto wa kaimasen deshita.	He didn't buy the chocolates.
Sugu kimasen deshita.	He didn't come right away.
Kinoo wa tabemasen deshita.	I didn't eat yesterday.

I-6.2 Conjunction ga

The conjunction ga links two sentences and has the meaning "but" or "however."

EXAMPLES:

Kyoo wa ikimasen ga ashita wa ikimasu.	I'm not going today, but I am going tomorrow.
Omise wa arimasu ga depaato wa arimasen.	There are stores, but there isn't a department store.
Okashi o dashimashita ga tabemasen deshita.	I served (put out) some cakes, but they didn't eat them.

I-6.3 Particle de

The particle de indicates the place where an action occurs. (Also see 3.4)

EXAMPLES:

Uchi de tabemashita.	I ate at home.
Omise de kaimashoo.	Let's buy it at a store.
Gakkoo de benkyoo shimasu.	I study at school.
Gakkoo de wa asobimasen.	I don't play at school (meaning he plays elsewhere).

I-6.4 Gurai

Gurai occurring after units of time indicates "about how long" an action
takes. (Compare with goro, 2.4)

EXAMPLES:

Gofun gurai machimashita.	He waited about five minutes.
Nijippun gurai hanashimashita.	We talked for about twenty minutes.
Jippun gurai de kaerimasu.	He will return in about ten minutes.

In other occurrences, gurai has the meaning "about" or "about the extent of."

EXAMPLES:
>   Juuen gurai desu.   It's about ten yen.
>   Dono gurai kakarimasu ka?   About how long does it take?
>   About how much does it cost?
>
>   Tanaka-san gurai desu.   He's about Mr. Tanaka's [size].

I-6.5 Koko, soko, asoko, and doko
    Koko meaning "this place," soko meaning "that place," asoko meaning "that place (farther away)," and doko meaning "what place" have the same spatial and temporal references as the kono, sono, ano, and dono series. (See 5.3) Koko, soko, asoko, and doko function as nouns.

EXAMPLES:
>   Koko ni arimasu.   It's here. (It's at this place.)
>   Soko e ikimashoo ka?   Shall we go there? (The place has just
>   been mentioned.)
>
>   Asoko de machimashoo.   Let's wait over there.
>   Doko de kaimashita ka?   Where did you buy it?

DRILLS

1. Repetition (using a clock)

ippun	one minute
nifun	two minutes
sampun	three minutes
yompun	four minutes
gofun	five minutes
roppun	six minutes
nanafun, shichifun	seven minutes
happun, hachifun	eight minutes
kyuufun	nine minutes
jippun, juppun	ten minutes

2. Substitution

Ippun machimashita.   I waited one minute.

(nifun)	Nifun machimashita.	I waited two minutes.
(sampun)	Sampun machimashita.	I waited three minutes.
(yompun)	Yompun machimashita.	I waited four minutes.
(gofun)	Gofun machimashita.	I waited five minutes.
(roppun)	Roppun machimashita.	I waited six minutes.
(nanafun)	Nanafun machimashita.	I waited seven minutes.
(hachifun)	Hachifun machimashita.	I waited eight minutes.
(happun)	Happun machimashita.	I waited eight minutes.
(kyuufun)	Kyuufun machimashita.	I waited nine minutes.
(jippun)	Jippun machimashita.	I waited ten minutes.

3. Repetition

juu-ippun   eleven minutes
juu-nifun   twelve minutes
juu-sampun   thirteen minutes
juu-yompun   fourteen minutes
juu-gofun   fifteen minutes
juu-roppun   sixteen minutes
juu-nanafun   seventeen minutes
juu-happun   eighteen minutes
juu-kyuufun   nineteen minutes

4. Substitution

Juu-ippun hanashimashita.   We talked for eleven minutes.

(juu-nifun)   Juu-nifun hanashimashita.   We talked for twelve minutes.
(juu-sampun)   Juu-sampun hanashimashita.   We talked for thirteen minutes.
(juu-yompun)   Juu-yompun hanashimashita.   We talked for fourteen minutes.
(juu-gofun)   Juu-gofun hanashimashita.   We talked for fifteen minutes.
(juu-roppun)   Juu-roppun hanashimashita.   We talked for sixteen minutes.
(juu-nanafun)   Juu-nanafun hanashimashita.   We talked for seventeen minutes.
(juu-happun)   Juu-happun hanashimashita.   We talked for eighteen minutes.
(juu-kyuufun)   Juu-kyuufun hanashimashita.   We talked for nineteen minutes.

5. Substitution

Jippun benkyoo shimasu.   I'll study for ten minutes.

(nijippun)   Nijippun benkyoo shimasu.   I'll study for twenty minutes.
(sanjippun)   Sanjippun benkyoo shimasu.   I'll study for thirty minutes.
(yonjippun)   Yonjippun benkyoo shimasu.   I'll study for forty minutes.
(gojippun)   Gojippun benkyoo shimasu.   I'll study for fifty minutes.

6. Substitution

Nijuu-ippun machimashita.   We waited for twenty-one minutes.

(nijuu-nifun)   Nijuu-nifun machimashita.   We waited for twenty-two minutes.
(nijuu-sampun)   Nijuu-sampun machimashita.   We waited for twenty-three minutes.
(nijuu-yompun)   Nijuu-yompun machimashita.   We waited for twenty-four minutes.
(nijuu-gofun)   Nijuu-gofun machimashita.   We waited for twenty-five minutes.
(nijuu-roppun)   Nijuu-roppun machimashita.   We waited for twenty-six minutes.
(nijuu-nana-   Nijuu-nanafun machimashita.   We waited for twenty-seven minutes.
   fun)
(nijuu-happun)   Nijuu-happun machimashita.   We waited for twenty-eight minutes.
(nijuu-kyuu-   Nijuu-kyuufun machimashita.   We waited for twenty-nine minutes.
   fun)

7. Response

Q. Nampun hanashimashita ka?   How many minutes did you talk?
A. Ippun hanashimashita.   We talked for one minute.

(Review lists in Drills 1, 3, 5, and 6.)

8. Substitution

Gofun gurai kakarimasu.   It takes about five minutes.

(jippun gurai)   Jippun gurai kakarimasu.   It takes about ten minutes.
(juu-gofun   Juu-gofun gurai kakarimasu.   It takes about fifteen minutes.
  gurai)
(nijippun gu-   Nijippun gurai kakarimasu.   It takes about twenty minutes.
  rai)
(nijuu-gofun   Nijuu-gofun gurai kakari-   It takes about twenty-five minutes.
  gurai)   masu.
(sanjippun   Sanjippun gurai kakarimasu.   It takes about thirty minutes.
  gurai)
(sanjuu-gofun   Sanjuu-gofun gurai kakari-   It takes about thirty-five minutes.
  gurai)   masu.
(yonjippun   Yonjippun gurai kakarimasu.   It takes about forty minutes.
  gurai)
(yonjuu-gofun   Yonjuu-gofun gurai kakari-   It takes about forty-five minutes.
  gurai)   masu.
(gojippun gu-   Gojippun gurai kakarimasu.   It takes about fifty minutes.
  rai)
(gojuu-gofun   Gojuu-gofun gurai kakari-   It takes about fifty-five minutes.
  gurai)   masu.

9. Response

Q. Nampun gurai kakarimashita ka?   About how many minutes did it take?
A. Gofun gurai kakarimashita.   It took about five minutes.

(Use list in Drill 8 above.)

10. Response

Q. Dono gurai kakarimasu ka?   About how long does it take?
A. Gofun gurai kakarimasu.   It takes about five minutes.

Q. Dono gurai kakarimasu ka?   About how much does it cost?
A. Goen gurai kakarimasu.   It costs about five yen.

(jippun)   Jippun gurai kakari-   It takes about ten minutes.
                    masu.
(juuen)   Juuen gurai kakarimasu.   It costs about ten yen.

(juu-gofun)	Juu-gofun gurai kakarimasu.	It takes about fifteen minutes.
(juu-goen)	Juu-goen gurai kakarimasu.	It costs about fifteen yen.
(nijippun)	Nijippun gurai kakarimasu.	It takes about twenty minutes.
(nijuuen)	Nijuuen gurai kakarimasu.	It costs about twenty yen.
(nijuu-gofun)	Nijuu-gofun gurai kakarimasu.	It takes about twenty-five minutes.
(nijuu-goen)	Nijuu-goen gurai kakarimasu.	It costs about twenty-five yen.
(sanjippun)	Sanjippun gurai kakarimasu.	It takes about thirty minutes.
(sanjuuen)	Sanjuuen gurai kakarimasu.	It costs about thirty yen.

11. Substitution (using a clock)

Ippun mae desu.   It's one minute before the hour.

(nifun mae)	Nifun mae desu.	It's two minutes before the hour.
(sampun mae)	Sampun mae desu.	It's three minutes before the hour.
(yompun mae)	Yompun mae desu.	It's four minutes before the hour.
(gofun mae)	Gofun mae desu.	It's five minutes before the hour.
(roppun mae)	Roppun mae desu.	It's six minutes before the hour.
(nanafun mae)	Nanafun mae desu.	It's seven minutes before the hour.
(happun mae)	Happun mae desu.	It's eight minutes before the hour.
(kyuufun mae)	Kyuufun mae desu.	It's nine minutes before the hour.
(jippun mae)	Jippun mae desu.	It's ten minutes before the hour.
(juu-gofun mae)	Juu-gofun mae desu.	It's fifteen minutes before the hour.
(nijippun mae)	Nijippun mae desu.	It's twenty minutes before the hour.
(nijuu-gofun mae)	Nijuu-gofun mae desu.	It's twenty-five minutes before the hour.

12. Response (using a clock)

Q. Nanji desu ka?   What time is it?
A. Ichiji ippun mae desu.   It's one minute before one.

(Use list in Drill 11 above.)

13. Substitution (using a clock)

Ippun sugi desu.   It's one minute after the hour.

(nifun sugi)	Nifun sugi desu.	It's two minutes after the hour.
(sampun sugi)	Sampun sugi desu.	It's three minutes after the hour.
(yompun sugi)	Yompun sugi desu.	It's four minutes after the hour.
(gofun sugi)	Gofun sugi desu.	It's five minutes after the hour.
(roppun sugi)	Roppun sugi desu.	It's six minutes after the hour.
(nanafun sugi)	Nanafun sugi desu.	It's seven minutes after the hour.
(happun sugi)	Happun sugi desu.	It's eight minutes after the hour.
(kyuufun sugi)	Kyuufun sugi desu.	It's nine minutes after the hour.
(jippun sugi)	Jippun sugi desu.	It's ten minutes after the hour.

(juu-gofun sugi)	Juu-gofun sugi desu.	It's fifteen minutes after the hour.
(nijippun sugi)	Nijippun sugi desu.	It's twenty minutes after the hour.
(nijuu-gofun sugi)	Nijuu-gofun sugi desu.	It's twenty-five minutes after the hour.

14. Response (using a clock)

Q. Nanji desu ka?   What time is it?
A. Niji gofun sugi desu.   It's five minutes after two.

(Use list in Drill 13 above.)

15. Repetition (using a clock)

Ichiji ippun desu.   It's one minute after one.

(Use list in Drill 1 above.)

16. Progressive Substitution

Gogo yoji-han ni dekakemashita.		He started out at 4:30 p.m.
(gozen)	Gozen yoji-han ni dekakemashita.	He started out at 4:30 a.m.
(goji jippun)	Gozen goji jippun ni dekakema-shita.	He started out at 5:10 a.m.
(mimashita)	Gozen goji jippun ni mimashita.	He saw it at 5:10 a.m.
(gogo)	Gogo goji jippun ni mimashita.	He saw it at 5:10 p.m.
(kuji)	Gogo kuji ni mimashita.	He saw it at 9:00 p.m.
(kaerimashita)	Gogo kuji ni kaerimashita.	He returned at 9:00 p.m.
(gozen)	Gozen kuji ni kaerimashita.	He returned at 9:00 a.m.
(hachiji juu-gofun)	Gozen hachiji juu-gofun ni ka-erimashita.	He returned at 8:15 a.m.
(yasumima-shita)	Gozen hachiji juu-gofun ni ya-sumimashita.	He went to bed at 8:15 a.m.
(gogo)	Gogo hachiji juu-gofun ni yasu-mimashita.	He went to bed at 8:15 p.m.
(yoji-han)	Gogo yoji-han ni yasumimashita.	He went to bed at 4:30 p.m.
(dekakema-shita)	Gogo yoji-han ni dekakemashita.	He started out at 4:30 p.m.

17. Repetition

ichibyoo	one second
nibyoo	two seconds
sambyoo	three seconds
yombyoo	four seconds
gobyoo	five seconds

rokubyoo	six seconds
nanabyoo	seven seconds
hachibyoo	eight seconds
kyuubyoo	nine seconds
juubyoo	ten seconds
juu-gobyoo	fifteen seconds
nijuubyoo	twenty seconds
nijuu-gobyoo	twenty-five seconds
sanjuubyoo	thirty seconds
yonjuubyoo	forty seconds
gojuubyoo	fifty seconds

18. Substitution

Koko de machimashoo ka?   Shall we wait here?

(soko)	Soko de machimashoo ka?	Shall we wait there?
(asoko)	Asoko de machimashoo ka?	Shall we wait over there?
(doko)	Doko de machimashoo ka?	Where shall we wait?
(teeryuujo)	Teeryuujo de machimashoo ka?	Shall we wait at the bus (streetcar) stop?

19. Substitution

Doko de kakimashoo ka?   Where shall we write it?

(hanashimashoo)	Doko de hanashimashoo ka?	Where shall we talk?
(machimashoo)	Doko de machimashoo ka?	Where shall we wait?
(benkyoo shimashoo)	Doko de benkyoo shimashoo ka?	Where shall we study?
(yomimashoo)	Doko de yomimashoo ka?	Where shall we read it?
(kaimashoo)	Doko de kaimashoo ka?	Where shall we buy it?
(tabemashoo)	Doko de tabemashoo ka?	Where shall we eat?
(mimashoo)	Doko de mimashoo ka?	Where shall we look at it?
(asobimashoo)	Doko de asobimashoo ka?	Where shall we play?

20. Substitution

Itsu toshokan de kakimashita ka?   When did you write it at the library?

(yuubinkyoku)	Itsu yuubinkyoku de kakimashita ka?	When did you write it at the post office?
(kaisha)	Itsu kaisha de kakimashita ka?	When did you write it at the office?
(gakkoo)	Itsu gakkoo de kakimashita ka?	When did you write it at school?
(Yamada-san no uchi)	Itsu Yamada-san no uchi de kakimashita ka?	When did you write it at Mr. Yamada's home?
(uchi)	Itsu uchi de kakimashita ka?	When did you write it at home?

21. Substitution

Doko de mimashita ka?   Where did you see it?

(Amerika)   Amerika de mimashita ka?   Did you see it in America?
(Nihon)   Nihon de mimashita ka?   Did you see it in Japan?
(gakkoo)   Gakkoo de mimashita ka?   Did you see it at school?
(toshokan)   Toshokan de mimashita ka?   Did you see it at the library?
(kaisha)   Kaisha de mimashita ka?   Did you see it at the office?
(koko)   Koko de mimashita ka?   Did you see it here?
(soko)   Soko de mimashita ka?   Did you see it there?
(asoko)   Asoko de mimashita ka?   Did you see it over there?

22. Response

Yukio-san wa toshokan de hon o yomimasu.   Yukio reads books at the li-
                                                 brary.

(nani)   Nani o yomimasu ka?   What does he read?
              Hon o yomimasu.   He reads books.
(doko)   Doko de yomimasu ka?   Where does he read?
              Toshokan de yomimasu.   He reads at the library.
(dare)   Dare ga yomimasu ka?   Who reads?
              Yukio-san ga yomimasu.   Yukio reads.

Okaasan wa ban uchi de zasshi o yomimasu.   Mother reads magazines at home
                                                 in the evening.

(nani)   Nani o yomimasu ka?   What does she read?
              Zasshi o yomimasu.   She reads magazines.
(doko)   Doko de yomimasu ka?   Where does she read?
              Uchi de yomimasu.   She reads at home.
(itsu)   Itsu yomimasu ka?   When does she read?
              Ban yomimasu.   She reads in the evening.
(dare)   Dare ga yomimasu ka?   Who reads?
              Okaasan ga yomimasu.   Mother reads.

Yukio-san wa teeryuujo de tororii basu o machi-   Yukio waits for the trolley bus
    masu.   at the bus stop.

(nani)   Nani o machimasu ka?   What does he wait for?
              Tororii basu o machimasu.   He waits for the trolley bus.
(doko)   Doko de machimasu ka?   Where does he wait?
              Teeryuujo de machimasu.   He waits at the bus stop.
(dare)   Dare ga machimasu ka?   Who waits?
              Yukio-san ga machimasu.   Yukio waits.

Yukio-san wa ashita uchi de asobimasu.   Yukio will play at home tomor-
                                                 row.

(doko)   Doko de asobimasu ka?   Where will he play?
              Uchi de asobimasu.   He will play at home.

(itsu)	Itsu asobimasu ka?	When will he play?
	Ashita asobimasu.	He will play tomorrow.
(dare)	Dare ga asobimasu ka?	Who will play?
	Yukio-san ga asobimasu.	Yukio will play.

23. Substitution

Sugu kimasen deshita.   They didn't come right away.

(ikimasen deshita)	Sugu ikimasen deshita.	They didn't go right away.
(onegai shimasen deshita)	Sugu onegai shimasen deshita.	They didn't request it right away.
(benkyoo shimasen deshita)	Sugu benkyoo shimasen deshita.	They didn't study right away.
(kakimasen deshita)	Sugu kakimasen deshita.	They didn't write it right away.
(hanashimasen deshita)	Sugu hanashimasen deshita.	They didn't speak right away.
(yomimasen deshita)	Sugu yomimasen deshita.	They didn't read it right away.
(mimasen deshita)	Sugu mimasen deshita.	They didn't look at it right away.
(tabemasen deshita)	Sugu tabemasen deshita.	They didn't eat right away.

24. Negative Response

Q. Kinoo ikimashita ka?   Did you go yesterday?
A. Iie. Kinoo ikimasen deshita.   No, I didn't go yesterday.

(Hachiji goro ni yasumimashita ka?)   (Did you retire around eight o'clock?)
  Iie. Hachiji goro ni yasumimasen   No, I didn't retire around eight
  deshita.   o'clock.
(Rokuji-han goro ni dekakemashita ka?)   (Did you start out around six-thirty?)
  Iie. Rokuji-han goro ni dekakemasen   No, I didn't start out around six-
  deshita.   thirty.
(Shichiji jippun sugi ni okimashita   (Did you get up at ten past seven?)
  ka?)
  Iie. Shichiji jippun sugi ni okima-   No, I didn't get up at ten past seven.
  sen deshita.
(Yoji juu-gofun mae ni kaerimashita   (Did you return at a quarter of four?)
  ka?)
  Iie. Yoji juu-gofun mae ni kaerima-   No, I didn't return at a quarter of
  sen deshita.   four.
(Sampun hanashimashita ka?)   (Did you speak for three minutes?)
  Iie. Sampun hanashimasen deshita.   No, I didn't speak for three minutes.
(Nijippun machimashita ka?)   (Did you wait for twenty minutes?)
  Iie. Nijippun machimasen deshita.   No, I didn't wait for twenty minutes.
(Basu o machimashita ka?)   (Did you wait for the bus?)
  Iie. Basu o machimasen deshita.   No, I didn't wait for the bus.
(Hon o kakimashita ka?)   (Did you write a book?)
  Iie. Hon o kakimasen deshita.   No, I didn't write a book.

(Koko de benkyoo shimashita ka?)   (Did you study here?)
 Iie. Koko de benkyoo shimasen   No, I didn't study here.
   deshita.
(Kono zasshi o yomimashita ka?)   (Did you read this magazine?)
 Iie. Kono zasshi o yomimasen deshita.   No, I didn't read this magazine.
(Yuubinkyoku de mimashita ka?)   (Did you see it at the post office?)
 Iie. Yuubinkyoku de mimasen deshita.   No, I didn't see it at the post office.
(Asoko de asobimashita ka?)   (Did you amuse yourself there?)
 Iie. Asoko de asobimasen deshita.   No, I didn't amuse myself there.
(Teeryuujo no chikaku de mimashita ka?)   (Did you see it near the bus stop?)
 Iie. Teeryuujo no chikaku de mimasen   No, I didn't see it near the bus stop.
   deshita.
(Nijuu-gofun kakarimashita ka?)   (Did it take twenty-five minutes?)
 Iie. Nijuu-gofun kakarimasen deshita.   No, it didn't take twenty-five minutes.

25. Grammar (making one sentence out of two, using ga)

(Yuubinkyoku e ikimashita.)   (I went to the post office.)
(Mimasen deshita.)   (I didn't see it.)
 Yuubinkyoku e ikimashita ga mimasen   I went to the post office but I didn't
   deshita.   see it.

(Yamada-san o machimashita.)   (I waited for Mr. Yamada.)
(Kimasen deshita.)   (He didn't come.)
 Yamada-san o machimashita ga kimasen   I waited for Mr. Yamada, but he didn't
   deshita.   come.

(Eki no mae ni wa arimasu.)   (There is one in front of the station.)
(Eki no naka ni wa arimasen.)   (There isn't one inside the station.)
 Eki no mae ni wa arimasu ga eki no   There is one in front of the station,
   naka ni wa arimasen.   but there isn't one inside the sta-
     tion.

(Kinoo shimbun o kaimashita.)   (I bought a newspaper yesterday.)
(Yomimasen deshita.)   (I didn't read it.)
 Kinoo shimbun o kaimashita ga yomi-   I bought a newspaper yesterday but I
   masen deshita.   didn't read it.

(Kyoo okashi o dashimashita.)   (I served cakes today.)
(Tabemasen deshita.)   (They didn't eat them.)
 Kyoo okashi o dashimashita ga tabe-   I served cakes today, but they didn't
   masen deshita.   eat them.

EXERCISES

A. Give the following times in Japanese.

1. one-five   4. seven-twelve
2. five minutes past one   5. eleven twenty-nine
3. one-fifteen   6. seventeen minutes of four

7. twenty-five minutes past one
8. twenty minutes of nine
9. two-ten
10. forty-five minutes after two
11. fifteen minutes of three
12. one minute to eight
13. six minutes past three

14. three fifty-five
15. two minutes past four
16. nine minutes past four
17. three minutes of five
18. eight minutes past five
19. nine-eighteen
20. twenty-three minutes of six

B. In the following blanks, supply a particle, _gurai_, or _goro_.

1. Basu _____ machimashita.   He waited for the bus.
2. Jippun _____ machimashoo.   Let's wait about ten minutes.
3. Teeryuujo _____ machimashita.   I waited at the [bus] stop.
4. Sanjippun _____ benkyoo shimasu.   I'll study for about thirty minutes.
5. Nani _____ benkyoo shimashoo ka?   What shall we study?
6. Nan _____ kakimashoo ka?   What shall I write with?
7. Doko _____ asobimashoo ka?   Where shall we play?
8. Niji juu-gofun _____ deshita.   It was around two-fifteen.
9. Yamada-san _____ mimashita ka?   Did you see Mr. Yamada?
10. Yoji-han _____ ni mimashita.   I saw him around four-thirty.
11. Koko _____ tabemashoo.   Let's eat here.
12. Dono _____ kakarimasu ka?   About how long does it take?
13. Kono zasshi _____ yomimashita ka?   Did you read this magazine?
14. Yonjuu-en _____ kakarimasu.   It costs about forty yen.
15. Koko _____ arimasu ka?   Is it here?
16. Gakkoo no mae _____ gofun _____   We spoke for about five minutes in front
     hanashimashita.   of the school.

C. Give the negatives of the following, and the English meanings.

1. Yomimasu.
2. Yomimashita.
3. Benkyoo shimashita.
4. Onegai shimasu.
5. Kakimasu.
6. Hanashimashita.
7. Machimashita.
8. Kaerimasu.
9. Yorimashita.
10. Asobimashita.

11. Mimashita.
12. Tabemashita.
13. Kaimasu.
14. Kaimashita.
15. Machimasu.
16. Dekakemashita.
17. Yasumimashita.
18. Hanashimasu.
19. Ikimashita.
20. Kimashita.

D. Give appropriate answers to the following general questions.

1. Toshokan de nani o yomimasu ka?
2. Doko de basu o machimasu ka?
3. Gakkoo de asobimasu ka?
4. Ban doko e kaerimasu ka?
5. Nanji goro ni yasumimasu ka?
6. Denwa de nampun gurai hanashimasu ka?
7. Asa nanji goro ni gakkoo e dekakemasu ka?

8. Doko de hon o kaimasu ka?
9. Gogo nanji ni kaerimasu ka?

E. Listen to (or read) the following story. Then answer the questions based on
    the story.

    Machi ni hon'ya ga arimasu. Yukio-san wa gogo soko e ikimashita. Yonjippun
gurai hon o mimashita ga hon wa kaimasen deshita. Hachijuuen no zasshi o kaimashita. Basu no teeryuujo wa hon'ya no mae desu. Soko de Yukio-san wa basu o machimashita. Gofun gurai machimashita. Goji nijuu-gofun sugi ni uchi e kaerimashita.

1.   Machi ni hon'ya ga arimasu ka?
2.   Kono machi ni hon'ya wa arimasen ka?
3.   Yukio-san wa kyoo machi e ikimasen deshita ka?
4.   Itsu hon'ya e ikimashita ka?
5.   Nampun gurai hon o mimashita ka?
6.   Hon wa kaimasen deshita ka?
7.   Nani o kaimashita ka?
8.   Sono zasshi wa rokujuuen deshita ka?
9.   Aruite kaerimashita ka?
10. Basu no teeryuujo wa doko desu ka?
11. Doko de basu o machimashita ka?
12. Nampun gurai machimashita ka?
13. Nanji ni uchi e kaerimashita ka?
14. Nanji goro ni uchi e kaerimashita ka?

Soko ni Yamamoto-sensee[1] ga imashita. Mr. Yamamoto was there. He (the teacher)
  Sensee mo basu de gakkoo ni ikimasu. also goes to school by bus.

Yukio:	Sensee, ohayoo gozaimasu.	Yukio: Good morning, sir.
Sensee:	Ohayoo.	Teacher: Good morning.
Yukio:	Aa. Basu ga kimashita.	Yukio: Oh, the bus has come.
	Chigaimashita. Basu de wa	I was mistaken. It wasn't the
	arimasen deshita.	bus.
Sensee:	Moo kuru deshoo.	Teacher: It'll probably come soon.

GRAMMAR

I-7.1 Verbs (informal non-past)

In medium polite conversation, verb endings may be viewed as falling into two categories of politeness level, the informal and semi-formal. The various -masu forms learned to date all belong to the semi-formal category; they are polite forms used in daily conversation. Each of these -masu forms has a counterpart in the informal. Both categories have the same meaning but differ in the level of formality. In this text, the ending -masu, already taught, will be called the "semi-formal non-past" and its informal counterpart will be called the "informal non-past." (Formal language will be discussed later.)

EXAMPLES:

	Informal non-past	Semi-formal non-past	
First Conjugation:	tabe-ru	tabe-masu	I (he, etc.) eat; I (he, etc.) will eat
	dekake-ru	dekake-masu	I (he, etc.) start out; I (he, etc.) will start out
	mi-ru	mi-masu	I (he, etc.) see; I (he, etc.) will see
	oki-ru	oki-masu	I (he, etc.) get up; I (he, etc.) will get up
Second Conjugation:			
"t" group*	mat-su	machi-masu	I (he, etc.) wait; I (he, etc.) will wait
"r" group	kaer-u	kaer-imasu	I (he, etc.) return; I (he, etc.) will return
	yor-u	yor-imasu	I (he, etc.) drop in; I (he, etc.) will drop in
	kakar-u	kakar-imasu	it takes; it will take
"w" group**	ka(w)-u	ka(w)-imasu	I (he, etc.) buy; I (he, etc.) will buy
"m" group	yasum-u	yasum-imasu	I (he, etc.) rest; I (he, etc.) will rest

	Informal non-past	Semi-formal non-past	
"b" group	asob-u	asob-imasu	I (he, etc.) play; I (he, etc.) will play
"s" group***	hanas-u	hanash-imasu	I (he, etc.) speak; I (he, etc.) will speak
	das-u	dash-imasu	I (he, etc.) offer; I (he, etc.) will offer
"k" group	ik-u	ik-imasu	I (he, etc.) go; I (he, etc.) will go
	kak-u	kak-imasu	I (he, etc.) write; I (he, etc.) will write
"g" group	isog-u	isog-imasu	I (he, etc.) hurry; I (he, etc.) will hurry
Irregular Verbs:			
	ku-ru	ki-masu	I (he, etc.) come; I (he, etc.) will come
	onegai su-ru	onegai shi-masu	I (he, etc.) request; I (he, etc.) will request
	benkyoo su-ru	benkyoo shi-masu	I (he, etc.) study; I (he, etc.) will study

All the above verbs, with the exception of isogu, have already been introduced in the -masu form. The hyphens in the above examples separate the endings from the stems. In the first conjugation informal non-past, the ending is "ru" and the stem ends with a vowel, either "e" or "i". In the second conjugation informal non-past, the ending is "u" and the stem ends with a consonant. Note that there is an "i" between the stem and -masu endings in second-conjugation verbs.

Various uses of the informal forms will be introduced later.

* Note that the "t" ending of the stem is "ch" in the -masu forms. (The separation between "t" and "su" is an unnatural spelling; it is written thus to show that the stem ends with a "t".)
** Note that the "w" ending is silent in these forms.
*** Note that the "s" ending of the stem is "sh" in the -masu forms.

I-7.2 Verb iru
The verb imasu (a first-conjugation verb) indicates existence and occurs in reference to animate objects. (Compare with arimasu, 4.2)

EXAMPLES:

Yamada-san wa doko ni imasu ka?	Where is Mr. Yamada?
Sensee mo imashita.	The teacher was there also.
Dare ga imasu ka?	Who's there?
Koko ni wa imasen.	He isn't here.

I-7.3 Semi-formal negative forms of the copula
The negative of desu (1.1) is de wa arimasen, meaning "is not" or "are not." The negative of deshita is de wa arimasen deshita, meaning "was not" or "were not."

EXAMPLES:

Depaato de wa arimasen.   It isn't a department store.

Gakkoo no chikaku de wa arimasen.   It isn't near the school.

Yamada-san de wa arimasen.   It isn't Mr. Yamada.

Yuubinkyoku no soba de wa arima-   It wasn't near the post office.
sen deshita.

I-7.4 Semi-formal tentative form of the copula

Deshoo is the tentative form of the copula and it expresses probability.
Deshoo ka has a feeling of contemplation, "I wonder." A noun plus deshoo and the
informal non-past verb plus deshoo are possible uses of deshoo at this point.
(Other uses will be taught later.) The combination of a non-past verb plus deshoo
is not used for the first person singular. It never means "I'll probably . . ."
It may mean "We'll probably . . ."

EXAMPLES:

Gakkoo deshoo.   It's probably a school.

Yamada-san no deshoo.   It's probably Mr. Yamada's.

Watakushi deshoo.   It's probably I (that they mean).

Iku deshoo.   They'll probably go.

Ashita kaku deshoo.   They'll probably write it tomorrow.

I-7.5 Particle mo

The particle mo occurring after a noun (or a noun followed by another particle) has the meaning "too" or "also."

EXAMPLES:

Watakushi mo ikimasu.   I'm also going.

Empitsu mo arimasu.   There is also a pencil.

Okashi mo tabemashoo.   Let's eat cakes also.

Koko ni mo arimasu.   There is one here also.

Note that mo occurs in positions where particles o, ga, and wa occur and not
in combination with them.

I-7.6 Particles . . . mo . . . mo

A series of noun plus mo may occur. A mo B mo (C mo) . . . means "A and also
B (and also C)." A series of two has a meaning similar to the English "both A and
B" or "neither A nor B" depending on whether the verb is positive or negative.

EXAMPLES:

Sensee mo seeto mo imasu.   Both teachers and pupils are there.

Nihon ni mo Amerika ni mo arima-   There isn't one in Japan or in America.
sen.

Pan mo okashi mo tabemasen.   He eats neither bread nor cake.

I-7.7 Particle to

The particle to links nouns and has the meaning "and."

EXAMPLES:

Hon to empitsu ga arimasu.   There is a book and a pencil.

Yukio-san to sensee ga ikima-   Yukio and the teacher went.
shita.

Anata no to watakushi no o yomi-   He read yours and mine.
mashita.
Uchi no mae to ushiro ni arimasu.   It's in front and in back of the house.

DRILLS

1. Repetition

taberu	I'll eat
dekakeru	I'll start out
iru	I'll be here
miru	I'll look
okiru	I'll get up
matsu	I'll wait
kaeru	I'll return
yoru	I'll drop by
kakaru	it'll take
wakaru	I'll understand
aru	there will be
kau	I'll buy
chigau	it'll differ
yasumu	I'll rest
yomu	I'll read
asobu	I'll play
hanasu	I'll speak
dasu	I'll put it out
iku	I'll go
kaku	I'll write
isogu	I'll hurry
kuru	I'll come
suru	I'll do it
onegai suru	I'll request it
benkyoo suru	I'll study

2. Substitution

Kuru deshoo.   He'll probably come.

(taberu)	Taberu deshoo.	He'll probably eat it.
(dekakeru)	Dekakeru deshoo.	He'll probably start out.
(iru)	Iru deshoo.	He'll probably be there.
(miru)	Miru deshoo.	He'll probably see it.
(okiru)	Okiru deshoo.	He'll probably get up.
(matsu)	Matsu deshoo.	He'll probably wait.
(kaeru)	Kaeru deshoo.	He'll probably return.
(yoru)	Yoru deshoo.	He'll probably drop by.
(kakaru)	Kakaru deshoo.	It'll probably take (that long).
(aru)	Aru deshoo.	There probably is.
(kau)	Kau deshoo.	He'll probably buy it.
(chigau)	Chigau deshoo.	It's probably different.

(yasumu)	Yasumu deshoo.	He'll probably rest.
(yomu)	Yomu deshoo.	He'll probably read it.
(asobu)	Asobu deshoo.	He'll probably play.
(hanasu)	Hanasu deshoo.	He'll probably speak.
(dasu)	Dasu deshoo.	He'll probably serve it.
(iku)	Iku deshoo.	He'll probably go.
(kaku)	Kaku deshoo.	He'll probably write it.
(isogu)	Isogu deshoo.	He'll probably hurry.
(suru)	Suru deshoo.	He'll probably do it.
(onegai suru)	Onegai suru deshoo.	He'll probably request it.
(benkyoo suru)	Benkyoo suru deshoo.	He'll probably study.

3. Response

Q. Tabemasu ka?   Does he eat it?
A. Taberu deshoo.   He probably eats it.

(Shichiji ni dekakemasu ka?)   (Does he start out at seven o'clock?)
 Shichiji ni dekakeru deshoo.   He probably starts out at seven o'clock.
(Rokuji goro ni okimasu ka?)   (Does he get up around six o'clock?)
 Rokuji goro ni okiru deshoo.   He probably gets up around six o'clock.
(Fune de ikimasu ka?)   (Is he going by ship?)
 Fune de iku deshoo.   He'll probably go by ship.
(Hon o kakimasu ka?)   (Will he write a book?)
 Hon o kaku deshoo.   He'll probably write a book.
(Ohiru goro ni kaerimasu ka?)   (Will he return around noon?)
 Ohiru goro ni kaeru deshoo.   He'll probably return around noon.
(Yonjippun gurai kakarimasu ka?)   (Does it take about forty minutes?)
 Yonjippun gurai kakaru deshoo.   It probably takes about forty minutes.
(Gogo toshokan ni yorimasu ka?)   (Will he drop by the library in the af-
                                              ternoon?)
 Gogo toshokan ni yoru deshoo.   He'll probably drop by the library in
                                              the afternoon.

(Eki de shimbun o kaimasu ka?)   (Does he buy the paper at the station?)
 Eki de shimbun o kau deshoo.   He probably buys the paper at the sta-
                                              tion.

(Chigaimasu ka?)   (Is it wrong?)
 Chigau deshoo.   It's probably wrong.
(Shimbun ni dashimasu ka?)   (Will he put it in the newspapers?)
 Shimbun ni dasu deshoo.   He'll probably put it in the newspapers.
(Gofun gurai machimasu ka?)   (Will he wait about five minutes?)
 Gofun gurai matsu deshoo.   He'll probably wait about five minutes.
(Kuruma de kimasu ka?)   (Will he come by car?)
 Kuruma de kuru deshoo.   He'll probably come by car.
(Tanaka-san ni onegai shimasu ka?)   (Will he request it of Mr. Tanaka?)
 Tanaka-san ni onegai suru deshoo.   He'll probably request it of Mr. Tanaka.

4. Substitution

Moo kuru deshoo.   He'll probably come any moment.

(Use list in Drill 2 above.)

5. Substitution

Kodomo deshoo.   It's probably a child.

(otona)   Otona deshoo.   It's probably an adult.
(hito)   Hito deshoo.   It's probably a person.
(sensee)   Sensee deshoo.   It's probably a teacher.
(seeto)   Seeto deshoo.   It's probably a pupil.
(toshokan)   Toshokan deshoo.   It's probably a library.
(takushii)   Takushii deshoo.   It's probably a taxi.
(basu)   Basu deshoo.   It's probably a bus.
(ohiru)   Ohiru deshoo.   It's probably noon.
(tokee)   Tokee deshoo.   It's probably a clock.
(gakkoo)   Gakkoo deshoo.   It's probably a school.
(chikatetsu)   Chikatetsu deshoo.   It's probably a subway.

6. Substitution

Yukio-san wa imasu ka?   Is Yukio there?

(sensee)   Sensee wa imasu ka?   Is the teacher there?
(Yamamoto-   Yamamoto-sensee wa   Is Mr. (teacher) Yamamoto there?
  sensee)   imasu ka?
(seeto)   Seeto wa imasu ka?   Are the pupils there?
(ano hito)   Ano hito wa imasu ka?   Is that person there?
(kodomo)   Kodomo wa imasu ka?   Are the children there?

7. Substitution

Dare ga imashita ka?   Who was there?

(sensee)   Sensee ga imashita ka?   Was the teacher there?
(ano seeto-   Ano seeto-san ga ima-   Was that pupil there?
  san)   shita ka?
(sono hito)   Sono hito ga imashita   Was that person (whom you just mentioned)
                     ka?   there?
(otomodachi)   Otomodachi ga imashita   Was your friend there?
                     ka?
(kodomo)   Kodomo ga imashita ka?   Were there children there?
(otona)   Otona ga imashita ka?   Were there adults there?

8. Expansion

(Okaasan ga imasu.)	Okaasan ga imasu.	The mother is there.
(Yukio to)	Yukio to okaasan ga imasu.	Yukio and his mother are there.
(Seeto ga imasu.)	Seeto ga imasu.	The pupils are there.
(sensee to)	Sensee to seeto ga imasu.	The teacher and the pupils are there.
(Watakushi ga imasu.)	Watakushi ga imasu.	I am here.
(anata to)	Anata to watakushi ga imasu.	You and I are here.
(Otona ga imasu.)	Otona ga imasu.	The adults are there.
(kodomo to)	Kodomo to otona ga imasu.	Children and adults are there.
(Watakushi ga imasu.)	Watakushi ga imasu.	I am here.
(tomodachi to)	Tomodachi to watakushi ga imasu.	My friends and I are here.

9. Correlation Substitution (imasu, arimasu)

Yukio-san to sensee ga imasu.		Yukio and the teacher are there.
(kaisha to gakkoo)	Kaisha to gakkoo ga arimasu.	There is a company and a school.
(empitsu to booru pen)	Empitsu to booru pen ga arimasu.	There is a pencil and a ballpoint pen.
(otona to kodomo)	Otona to kodomo ga imasu.	There is an adult and a child.
(densha to basu)	Densha to basu ga arimasu.	There is an electric train and a bus.
(yaoya to pan'ya)	Yaoya to pan'ya ga arimasu.	There is a greengrocery and a bakery.
(sensee to seeto)	Sensee to seeto ga imasu.	There is a teacher and a pupil.

10. Progressive Substitution

Nan to nani o kaimashita ka?		What (and what) did you buy?
(ano shimbun to zasshi)	Ano shimbun to zasshi o kaimashita ka?	Did you buy that newspaper and magazine?
(yomimashita ka)	Ano shimbun to zasshi o yomimashita ka?	Did you read that newspaper and magazine?
(ano hon to tekisuto)	Ano hon to tekisuto o yomimashita ka?	Did you read that book and text?
(onegai shimashita ka)	Ano hon to tekisuto o onegai shimashita ka?	Did you request that book and text?

(nan to nani)   Nan to nani o onegai shi-   What (and what) did you
                               mashita ka?   request?
(kaimashita ka)   Nan to nani o kaimashita   What (and what) did you
                               ka?   buy?

11.   Grammar (ga, wa to mo)

(Watakushi ga imashita.)   (I was there.)
 Watakushi mo imashita.   I was also there.
(Anata wa imasen deshita.)   (You weren't there.)
 Anata mo imasen deshita.   You weren't there either.
(Tomodachi ga imashita.)   (A friend was there.)
 Tomodachi mo imashita.   A friend was also there.
(Kodomo ga imasu.)   (The children are there.)
 Kodomo mo imasu.   The children are also there.
(Ano hito ga iru deshoo.)   (That person is probably there.)
 Ano hito mo iru deshoo.   That person is probably also there.
(Sensee wa imasen.)   (The teacher isn't there.)
 Sensee mo imasen.   The teacher isn't there either.
(Otona ga iru deshoo.)   (There are probably adults there.)
 Otona mo iru deshoo.   There are probably adults there also.
(Sono seeto wa imasen deshita.)   (That pupil wasn't there.)
 Sono seeto mo imasen deshita.   That pupil wasn't there either.

12.   Grammar (o to mo)

(Shimbun o kaimashita.)   (I bought a newspaper.)
 Shimbun mo kaimashita.   I bought a newspaper, too.
(Kokuban o kaimashoo.)   (Let's buy a blackboard.)
 Kokuban mo kaimashoo.   Let's buy a blackboard, too.
(Okashi o tabemasu.)   (I eat cakes.)
 Okashi mo tabemasu.   I eat cakes, too.
(Chokoreeto o taberu deshoo.)   (He probably eats chocolates.)
 Chokoreeto mo taberu deshoo.   He probably eats chocolates, too.
(Pan o onegai shimashita.)   (I requested bread.)
 Pan mo onegai shimashita.   I requested bread, too.
(Okane o kudasai.)   (Please give me some money.)
 Okane mo kudasai.   Please give me some money, too.

13.   Affirmative Response

Q.   Yaoya ni mo yorimashoo ka?   Shall we drop by the greengrocery, also?
A.   Ee. Yaoya ni mo yorimashoo.   Yes, let's drop by the greengrocery,
                                        also.

(Yuubinkyoku no chikaku ni mo arimasu   (Is there one near the post office,
   ka?)   also?)
(Machi e mo ikimashita ka?)   (Did you go downtown, also?)
(Sensee ni mo onegai shimashoo ka?)   (Shall we request it of the teacher,
                                            also?)

(Otona ni mo dashimashita ka?)   (Did you serve it to the adults, also?)
(Kaisha e mo iku deshoo ka?)   (I wonder if they'll go to the office, also?)

(Uchi de mo benkyoo shimasu ka?)   (Does he study at home, also?)
(Toshokan de mo mimashita ka?)   (Did you see it at the library, also?)

14. Progressive Substitution

Tomodachi mo watakushi mo benkyoo shimashita.   Both my friend and I studied.

(Yukio-san mo watakushi mo)	Yukio-san mo watakushi mo benkyoo shimashita.	Both Yukio and I studied.
(mimashita)	Yukio-san mo watakushi mo mimashita.	Both Yukio and I saw it.
(hikooki mo jettoki mo)	Hikooki mo jettoki mo mimashita.	We saw both (propeller) planes and jet planes.
(arimashita)	Hikooki mo jettoki mo arimashita.	There were both (propeller) planes and jet planes.
(tsukue mo isu mo)	Tsukue mo isu mo arimashita.	There were both desks and chairs.
(kaimashita)	Tsukue mo isu mo kaimashita.	I bought both a desk and a chair.
(tomodachi mo watakushi mo)	Tomodachi mo watakushi mo kaimashita.	Both my friend and I bought it.
(benkyoo shimashita)	Tomodachi mo watakushi mo benkyoo shimashita.	Both my friend and I studied.

15. Affirmative Response to a Negative Question

Q. Hako no naka ni mo shita ni mo   There isn't any either in the box or un-
   arimasen ka?   der it?
A. Ee. Hako no naka ni mo shita ni   No, there isn't any either in or under
   mo arimasen.   the box.

(Yamada-sensee mo Yamamoto-sensee mo   (Is neither Mr. Yamada nor Mr. Yamamoto
   kimasen ka?)   coming?)
(Kyoo mo ashita mo yasumimasen ka?)   (You're not taking a holiday either today
                                             or tomorrow?)

(Asa no shimbun mo ban no shimbun mo   (You read neither the morning newspaper
   yomimasen ka?)   nor the evening newspaper?)
(Kodomo mo otona mo wakarimasen ka?)   (Do neither children nor adults under-
                                             stand it?)

(Gakkoo e mo kaisha e mo ikimasen ka?)   (He goes neither to school nor to the of-
                                             fice?)

16. Response (placing objects)

Q. Nan to nani no aida desu ka?   It's between what and what?
A. _____ to _____ no aida desu.   It's between _____ and _____.

17. Response (referring to members of the class)

Q. _____ -san wa dare to dare no _____ is between who and who?
   aida desu ka?
A. _____ -san wa _____ to _____ _____ is between _____ and _____.
   no aida desu.

18. Substitution

Tonari de wa arimasen deshita.   It wasn't next door.

(ushiro)   Ushiro de wa arimasen deshita.   It wasn't in back.
(chikaku)   Chikaku de wa arimasen deshita.   It wasn't near by.
(soba)   Soba de wa arimasen deshita.   It wasn't near by.
(kinoo)   Kinoo de wa arimasen deshita.   It wasn't yesterday.
(tomodachi) Tomodachi de wa arimasen deshita.   It wasn't a friend
(ano hito)   Ano hito de wa arimasen deshita.   It wasn't that person.
(seeto)   Seeto de wa arimasen deshita.   It wasn't a pupil.

19. Substitution

Hako de wa arimasen.   It isn't a box.

(aida)   Aida de wa arimasen.   It isn't in between.
(hoh'ya to   Hoh'ya to pan'ya no aida de wa arima-   It isn't between the book-
  pan'ya no   sen.   store and the bakery.
  aida)
(yoko)   Yoko de wa arimasen.   It isn't beside it.
(uchi no yoko)   Uchi no yoko de wa arimasen.   It isn't beside the house.
(soba)   Soba de wa arimasen.   It isn't near.
(kuruma no so-   Kuruma no soba de wa arimasen.   It isn't near the car.
  ba)
(Yukio-san)   Yukio-san de wa arimasen.   It isn't Yukio.
(otona)   Otona de wa arimasen.   It isn't an adult.
(teeryuujo)   Teeryuujo de wa arimasen.   It isn't a stop.
(kyoo)   Kyoo de wa arimasen.   It isn't today.
(yoru)   Yoru de wa arimasen.   It isn't at night.
(gogo)   Gogo de wa arimasen.   It isn't in the afternoon.

CULTURAL NOTES

1. Sensee, by itself, means "teacher." As a suffix after personal names, it is
a term showing respect; it is used in addressing and referring to doctors, den-
tists, etc., as well as to members of the teaching profession.

EXERCISES

A. Give the informal equivalents of the following:

1.   ikimasu
2.   kakimasu
3.   isogimasu
4.   machimasu
5.   kaerimasu
6.   yorimasu
7.   kakarimasu
8.   arimasu
9.   wakarimasu
10. kaimasu
11. chigaimasu
12. yasumimasu
13. yomimasu
14. asobimasu
15. hanashimasu
16. dashimasu
17. tabemasu
18. dekakemasu
19. imasu
20. mimasu
21. okimasu
22. kimasu
23. onegai shimasu
24. benkyoo shimasu
25. shimasu

B. Insert a suitable form of _iru_ or _aru_ in the following blanks.

1. Sensee ga _____ deshoo ka?   Is the teacher there?
2. Empitsu ga _____ deshoo ka?   Do you have a pencil?
3. Yamamoto-sensee wa _____.   Mr. Yamamoto wasn't there.
4. Kodomo ga _____ ka?   Were the children there?
5. Kodomo mo _____ deshoo.   The children are probably also there.
6. Depaato ni wa _____.   They didn't have it at the department
                                            store.
7. Sono hito wa _____.   That person isn't here.
8. Hako wa _____.   I don't have a box.
9. _____ ka?   Aren't they (people) there?
10. Uchi ni _____.   It was at home.

C. Supply suitable particles for the following blanks.

1. Koko _____ _____ imasen.   He isn't here.
2. Gakkoo _____ _____ yorimashita.   He also dropped by the school.
3. Tsukue no ue _____ _____ arimasu.   There's one on top of the desk, also.
4. Sono omise _____ _____ kaimasen   I didn't buy it at that store.
       deshita.

5. Kuruma _____ _____ ikimasen   We didn't go by car.
       deshita.
6. Yamada-san _____ _____ kakimasen   I didn't write to Mr. Yamada.
       deshita.
7. Sensee _____ _____ hanashimashoo.   Let's also speak of it to the teacher.
8. Kono hon _____ yomimashoo.   Let's also read this book.
9. Pan _____ tabemashita.   He also ate some bread.
10. Yamamoto-sensee _____ isogima-   Mr. Yamamoto also hurried.
       shita.
11. Tanaka-san _____ Yamada-san _____   Neither Mr. Tanaka nor Mr. Yamada is
       kimasen.   coming.
12. Shimbun _____ zasshi _____ ari-   There are both newspapers and magazines.
       masu.
13. Shimbun _____ zasshi _____ ari-   There is a newspaper and a magazine.
       masu.
14. Chokoreeto _____ okashi _____   Let's buy both chocolates and cakes.
       kaimashoo.
15. Tanaka-san _____ Yamada-san _____   Mr. Tanaka and Mr. Yamada came.
       kimashita.
16. Kono chokoreeto _____ sono choko-   Please give me this chocolate [bar] and
       reeto _____ kudasai.   that chocolate [bar].
17. Yaoya _____ pan'ya _____ aida   It's between the greengrocery and the
       desu.   bakery.
18. Eki _____ depaato _____ soba desu.   It's near the station and the department
                                            store.
19. Yamada-sensee _____ Yukio-san   Mr. Yamada is the person between Yukio
       _____ Yamamoto-sensee _____ aida   and Mr. Yamamoto.
       _____ hito desu.
20. Hon'ya _____ pan'ya _____ eki   The bookstore is between the bakery and
       _____ aida _____ arimasu.   the station.

D. Tell your friend:

1. that Mr. Yamamoto is not Yukio's teacher.
2. that Yukio is not an adult.
3. that a friend of yours will probably go to America.
4. that that friend will probably return soon.
5. that you wonder whether Yukio will get up at five-thirty.
6. that it wasn't Mr. Yamada's.
7. that Mr. Yamada will probably buy it.
8. that you saw Mr. Yamada's car.
9. that the bus will probably come soon.
10. that they'll probably eat soon.

E. Make single sentences from the following pairs of sentences, using to between
       the nouns.

Example: Tsukue ga arimasu.
           Isu ga arimasu.
           Tsukue to isu ga arimasu.

1. Yukio-san ga imasu.
    Sensee ga imasu.
2. Kuruma o kaimashita.
    Fune o kaimashita.
3. Basu de kimasu.
    Chikatetsu de kimasu.
4. Kono hako ni iremasu.
    Sono hako ni iremasu.
5. Yuubinkyoku no mae ni arimasu.
    Toshokan no mae ni arimasu.
6. Shimbun o yomimashoo.
    Zasshi o yomimashoo.
7. Sensee ni kikimashita.
    Seeto ni kikimashita.
8. Yukio wa isogimashita.
    Watakushi wa isogimashita.
9. Anata no o kudasai.
    Watakushi no o kudasai.
10. Yamada-san ni miseru deshoo.
    Yamamoto-sensee ni miseru deshoo.

F. Listen to (or read) the following story. Then answer the questions based on
      the story.

        Kyoo gozen juuji goro ni tomodachi ga uchi e kimasu. Sono tomodachi wa Ya-
mada-san no uchi e mo, Tanaka-san no uchi e mo ikimasu. Uchi ni wa nijippun gurai iru deshoo.

1. Kyoo dare ga kimasu ka?
2. Asa kimasu ka?
3. Nanji goro ni kuru deshoo ka?
4. Doko e ikimasu ka?
5. Yamada-san no uchi e mo iku deshoo ka?
6. Tanaka-san no uchi e mo iku deshoo ka?
7. Uchi ni wa dono gurai iru deshoo ka?
8. Ohiru wa uchi de taberu deshoo ka?

Yukio-san ya sensee wa ima basu no teeryuujo ni imasu. Kono chikaku wa basu shika toorimasen. Basu wa Yukio-san no mae ni tomarimashita.

Yukio-san wa, "Sensee, doozo osaki ni," to iimashita.

Suru to, sensee wa, "Doomo arigatoo," to kotaemashita.

Sensee mo Yukio-san mo basu ni norimashita. Kyoo wa Yukio-san wa sensee to gakkoo e iku deshoo.

Yukio and the teacher are now at the bus stop. Only buses run near here. The bus stopped in front of Yukio.

Yukio said, "Please go first, sir."

Then the teacher replied, "Thank you."

Both the teacher and Yukio boarded the bus. Yukio will probably go to school with the teacher today.

GRAMMAR

I-8.1 Particle ya

The particle ya links two nouns and has the meaning "[such things as] _____ and _____." It usually occurs in a partial listing of similar objects.

EXAMPLES:

Hon'ya ya yaoya ga arimasu.

There are [such things as] a bookstore and a greengrocery.

Sensee ya tomodachi ni kikimashoo.

Let's ask [such people as] the teacher and friends.

Empitsu ya hon o kaimashita.

He bought [such things as] pencils and books.

I-8.2 to yuu*, to kiku, to omou, etc.

Verbs with meanings such as "say," "ask," "think," "reply," etc., are preceded by to in indicating what one "said," "asked," "thought," etc.

EXAMPLES:

Ashita iku to omoimasu.
Kyoo ikimasen to iimashita.

Ashita iku deshoo ka to kikimashita.

I think that they'll go tomorrow.
He said, "I'm not going today."
He said that he wasn't going today.**
He asked, "I wonder if they'll go tomorrow?"
He wondered if they would go tomorrow.**

* Yuu is also transcribed iuu or iu.
** There is no definite distinction between direct and indirect quotations. In ordinary daily semi-formal level speech, one uses informal endings for the final verb (copula, etc.) within the "quotation."

I-8.3 Particle to

The particle to has the meaning "with [someone]" when it occurs with verbs of motion such as "go" and "return," and other verbs such as "speak."

EXAMPLES:
>   Sensee to gakkoo e iku deshoo.   He'll probably go to school with the
>   teacher.
>
>   Tanaka-san to gofun gurai hana-   I spoke for about five minutes with
>   shimashita.   Mr. Tanaka.

I-8.4 Particles dake, shika, dake shika
   (a) The particle dake, meaning "only," singles out the noun it follows.
Empitsu dake arimasu means "I (he, etc.) have only a pencil." Empitsu dake arimasen means "The only thing I (he, etc.) don't have is a pencil." Dake usually
occurs alone in slots where o, ga, wa, or mo would occur, but it also occurs with
other particles in combinations such as ni dake, dake ni, e dake, dake e.

EXAMPLES:
>   Yukio-san dake kotaemashita.   Only Yukio replied.
>   Depaato dake de mimashita.   I saw it only at the department store.
>   Tanaka-san dake kimasen deshita.   The only one who didn't come was Mr. Ta-
>   naka.

   (b) The particles shika and dake shika also single out the nouns which they
follow, with the meaning "nothing more than" or "nothing but." Of the two, the
latter, dake shika, is more emphatic. The verb which follows is always in the
negative form.

EXAMPLES:
>   Q. Gojuuen arimasu ka?   Do you have fifty yen?
>   A. Yonjuuen shika arimasen.   I have only (no more than) forty yen.
>   Q. Chikatetsu ni mo norimasu ka?   Does he also ride the subway?
>   A. Basu ni shika norimasen.   He doesn't ride anything but buses.
>   Pan dake shika tabemasen.   He doesn't eat anything other than bread.

I-8.5 Transitive and intransitive verbs
   Many Japanese verbs occur in transitive and intransitive pairs, transitives
being those which take objects and intransitives, those not taking objects. In
such pairs, the transitive and intransitive may have a common base.

EXAMPLES:
>   Denwa ga kakarimashita. (intr.)   There was a telephone [call].
>   Sensee ga denwa o kakemashita.   The teacher telephoned.
>   (tr.)
>   Sono koto wa shimbun ni dema-   That item appeared in the newspapers.
>   shita. (intr.)
>   Tanaka-san wa sono koto o shimbun   Mr. Tanaka put that item in the newspa-
>   ni dashimashita. (tr.)   pers.

   It is recommended that effort be made to learn verbs in transitive and intransitive pairs.

I-8.6 Particle o
   The particle o followed by a verb of motion indicates the route of the motion.

EXAMPLES:
>   Kono machi o toorimasu.   We pass through this town.
>   Yuubinkyoku no soba o toorimasu Do you go (pass) near the post office?
>   ka?

DRILLS

1. Repetition

Kotaeru deshoo.   He'll probably reply.
Ireru deshoo.   He'll probably put it in.
Miseru deshoo.   He'll probably show it.
Kakeru deshoo.   He'll probably telephone.
                                 He'll probably sit (in a chair).
                                 He'll probably hang it up.
Deru deshoo.   He'll probably attend.
Tomeru deshoo.   He'll probably stop it.
Tomaru deshoo.   He'll probably stop.
Noru deshoo.   He'll probably board it.
Suwaru deshoo.   He'll probably sit.
Tooru deshoo.   He'll probably pass by.
Hairu deshoo.   He'll probably enter.
Kiku deshoo.   He'll probably ask.
Yuu deshoo.   He'll probably say.
Soo omou deshoo.   He'll probably think so.
Au deshoo.   He'll probably meet him.

2. Grammar (informal to semi-formal non-past)

(deru)   Demasu.   I'll attend.
(miseru)   Misemasu.   I'll show it.
(kotaeru)   Kotaemasu.   I'll answer.
(kakeru)   Kakemasu.   I'll telephone.
(tomeru)   Tomemasu.   I'll stop it.
(ireru)   Iremasu.   I'll put it in.
(hairu)   Hairimasu.   I'll enter.
(tooru)   Toorimasu.   I'll pass by.
(noru)   Norimasu.   I'll board it.
(suwaru)   Suwarimasu.   I'll sit down.
(tomaru)   Tomarimasu.   I'll stop.
(yuu)   Iimasu.   I'll say it.
(omou)   Omoimasu.   I'll think so.
(au)   Aimasu.   I'll meet them.
(kiku)   Kikimasu.   I'll ask.

3. Repetition

Sensee ga sono koto o shimbun ni da-   The teacher put that matter in the news-
  shimashita.   paper.

Sono koto ga shimbun ni demashita.   That matter appeared in the newspaper.
Yukio-san ga denwa o kakemashita.   Yukio telephoned.
Denwa ga kakarimashita.   There was a telephone call.
Tanaka-san ga takushii o tomemashita.   Mr. Tanaka stopped the taxi.
Takushii ga tomarimashita.   The taxi stopped.
Tanaka-san ga pan o iremashita.   Mr. Tanaka put in the bread.
Pan ga hairimashita.   The bread fitted in.

4. Affirmative Response

Q. Rajio o kakemasu ka?   Do you turn on the radio?
A. Ee. Rajio o kakemasu.   Yes, I turn on the radio.

(Denwa o kakemashoo ka?)   (Shall we telephone?)
(Sensee ni denwa o kakemashita ka?)   (Did you telephone the teacher?)
(Koko ni kakemashoo ka?)   (Shall we sit here?)
(Rajio ga kakarimashita ka?)   (Did the radio work?)
(Okashi o dasu deshoo ka?)   (I wonder if they'll serve cakes?)
(Fune o dashimasu ka?)   (Will they put out a boat?)
(Shimbun ni dashimashoo ka?)   (Shall we put it in the newspapers?)
(Okashi ga deru deshoo ka?)   (I wonder if cakes will be served?)
(Kyoo fune ga demasu ka?)   (Does the boat leave today?)
(Yamada-san no koto ga shimbun ni de-   (Did that matter about Mr. Yamada appear
   mashita ka?)   in the papers?)
(Takushii o tomemashoo ka?)   (Shall we stop a taxi?)
(Ano jidoosha no ushiro ni tomema-   (Did you park in back of that car?)
   shita ka?)
(Basu ga sono chikaku ni tomarimasu   (Does the bus stop near there?)
   ka?)
(Yukio-san no uchi ni tomarimasu ka?)   (Will you stay at Yukio's home?)
(Okashi o iremashita ka?)   (Did you put in the cakes?)
(Sono hako ni hon o iremashoo ka?)   (Shall we put the books in that box?)
(Fune ga hairimashita ka?)   (Has the ship come in?)
(Gakkoo ni hairimasu ka?)   (Will he enter school?)

5. Grammar (intransitive to transitive)

(Hako ni shimbun ga hairimashita.)   (The newspapers fitted into the box.)
 Hako ni shimbun o iremashita.   I put the newspapers into the box.
(Denwa ga kakarimasu.)   (There are telephone calls.)
 Denwa o kakemasu.   I telephone.
(Zasshi ni Nihon no koto ga demashita.)   (Things about Japan appeared in the maga-
                                              zine.)
 Zasshi ni Nihon no koto o dashima-   I put things about Japan in the maga-
   shita.   zine.
(Densha ga tomarimasu.)   (The streetcar stops.)
 Densha o tomemasu.   I stop the streetcar.

6. Substitution

Dare ni iimashoo ka?   To whom shall we tell it?

(kikimashoo)   Dare ni kikimashoo ka?   Whom shall we ask?
(kotaemashoo)   Dare ni kotaemashoo ka?   To whom shall we reply?
(aimashoo)   Dare ni aimashoo ka?   Whom shall we meet?
(misemashoo)   Dare ni misemashoo ka?   To whom shall we show it?
(kakemashoo)   Dare ni kakemashoo ka?   Whom shall we telephone?
(onegai shi-   Dare ni onegai shimashoo ka?   Of whom shall we request it?
  mashoo)
(dashimashoo)   Dare ni dashimashoo ka?   To whom shall we mail it?
(hanashima-   Dare ni hanashimashoo ka?   To whom shall we speak?
  shoo)
(kakimashoo)   Dare ni kakimashoo ka?   To whom shall we write?

7. Progressive Substitution

Tomodachi dake ni misemashita.   He showed it only to his
                                                               friends.

(sensee)   Sensee dake ni misemashita.   He showed it only to the teach-
                                                               er.
(kikimashita)   Sensee dake ni kikimashita.   He asked only the teacher.
(watakushi)   Watakushi dake ni kikimashita.   He asked only me.
(iimashita)   Watakushi dake ni iimashita.   He told it only to me.
(otona)   Otona dake ni iimashita.   He told it only to the adults.
(aimashita)   Otona dake ni aimashita.   He met only the adults.
(tomodachi)   Tomodachi dake ni aimashita.   He met only his friends.
(misemashita)   Tomodachi dake ni misemashita.   He showed it only to his
                                                               friends.

8. Substitution

Dare to kimashita ka?   With whom did you come?

(ikimashita)   Dare to ikimashita ka?   With whom did you go?
(kaerimashita)   Dare to kaerimashita ka?   With whom did you return?
(hanashima-   Dare to hanashimashita ka?   With whom did you speak?
  shita)
(demashita)   Dare to demashita ka?   With whom did you appear?

9. Grammar

Okaasan to shika kimasen.   He won't come with anyone but
                                                               his mother.

(iku)   Okaasan to shika ikimasen.   He won't go with anyone but his
                                                               mother.

(kaeru)	Okaasan to shika kaerimasen.	He won't return with anyone but his mother.
(iru)	Okaasan to shika imasen.	He won't remain with anyone but his mother.
(matsu)	Okaasan to shika machimasen.	He won't wait with anyone but his mother.
(noru)	Okaasan to shika norimasen.	He won't ride with anyone but his mother.
(asobu)	Okaasan to shika asobimasen.	He won't play with anyone but his mother.
(dekakeru)	Okaasan to shika dekakemasen.	He won't go out with anyone but his mother.

10. Substitution

Jidoosha ni shika norimasen. — He won't ride in anything other than a car.

(kuruma)	Kuruma ni shika norimasen.	He won't ride in anything other than a car.
(basu)	Basu ni shika norimasen.	He won't ride in anything other than a bus.
(chikatetsu)	Chikatetsu ni shika norimasen.	He won't ride in anything other than the subway.
(takushii)	Takushii ni shika norimasen.	He won't ride in anything other than a taxi.

11. Grammar (inserting dake)

(Chokoreeto o tabemasen.) — (I don't eat chocolate.)
Chokoreeto dake tabemasen. — The only thing I don't eat is chocolate.
(Rajio o kakemasen.) — (I don't turn on the radio.)
Rajio dake kakemasen. — The only thing I don't turn on is the radio.

(Hikooki o kaimasen.) — (I won't buy an airplane.)
Hikooki dake kaimasen. — The only thing I won't buy is an airplane.

(Kyoo wa ikimasen.) — (I'm not going today.)
Kyoo dake ikimasen. — Today's the only day I'm not going.
(Tanaka-san wa asobimasen.) — (Mr. Tanaka doesn't play.)
Tanaka-san dake asobimasen. — Mr. Tanaka's the only one who doesn't play.

(Ano hito wa kimasen deshita.) — (That person didn't come.)
Ano hito dake kimasen deshita. — That person's the only one who didn't come.

(Kono hon wa yomimasen deshita.) — (I didn't read this book.)
Kono hon dake yomimasen deshita. — This book is the only one I didn't read.
(Kono hon wa yomimashita.) — (I read this book.)
Kono hon dake yomimashita. — I read only this book.
(Kinoo wa yasumimashita.) — (I took a holiday yesterday.)
Kinoo dake yasumimashita. — I took a holiday yesterday only.

(Booru pen o kaimasu.)   (I'll buy a ballpoint pen.)
 Booru pen dake kaimasu.   I'll buy only a ballpoint pen.
(Isu ga arimasu.)   (There are **chairs**.)
 Isu dake arimasu.   There are only chairs.

12. Expansion

(isu ga arimasu)   Isu ga arimasu.   There are chairs.
(tsukue ya)   Tsukue ya isu ga arimasu.   There are such things as desks
                                                            and chairs.

(rajio mo arimasu)   Rajio mo arimasu.   There is also a radio.
(denwa ya)   Denwa ya rajio mo arimasu.   There are also such things as a
                                                            telephone and a radio.
(koko ni wa)   Koko ni wa denwa ya rajio   There are also such things as a
                         mo arimasu.   telephone and a radio here.

(tomodachi ni mi-   Tomodachi ni misemashita.   He showed it to his friends.
  semashita)
(sensee ya)   Sensee ya tomodachi ni mi-   He showed it to such people as
                         semashita.   the teacher and his friends.
(hon o)   Hon o sensee ya tomodachi   He showed the book to such peo-
                         ni misemashita.   ple as the teacher and his
                                                            friends.
(Yukio-san wa)   Yukio-san wa hon o sensee   Yukio showed the book to such
                         ya tomodachi ni misema-   people as the teacher and his
                         shita.   friends.

(Tanaka-sensee shi-   Tanaka-sensee shika waka-   No one other than Prof. Tanaka
  ka wakarimasen   rimasen deshita.   understood.
  deshita)
(Yamamoto-sensee   Yamamoto-sensee ya Tanaka-   No one other than people like
  ya)   sensee shika wakarimasen   Prof. Yamamoto and Prof. Ta-
                         deshita.   naka understood.
(ano koto wa)   Ano koto wa Yamamoto-sensee   No one other than people like
                         ya Tanaka-sensee shika   Prof. Yamamoto and Prof. Ta-
                         wakarimasen deshita.   naka understood that matter.

(hon dake irema-   Hon dake iremashoo.   Let's put in the books only.
  shoo)
(tekisuto ya)   Tekisuto ya hon dake ire-   Let's put in only such things
                         mashoo.   as texts and books.
(kono hako ni wa)   Kono hako ni wa tekisuto ya   Let's put only such things as
                         hon dake iremashoo.   texts and books in this box.

(densha ni shika   Densha ni shika norimasen.   He won't ride anything but the
  norimasen)   electric train.
(basu ya)   Basu ya densha ni shika no-   He won't ride things other than
                         rimasen.   buses and electric trains.
(Yukio-san wa)   Yukio-san wa basu ya densha   Yukio won't ride things other
                         ni shika norimasen.   than buses and electric
                                                            trains.

(Nihon to wa chi-gaimasu)	Nihon to wa chigaimasu.	It's different from Japan.
(Amerika ya)	Amerika ya Nihon to wa chigaimasu.	It's different from such places as America and Japan.
(koko wa)	Koko wa Amerika ya Nihon to wa chigaimasu.	This place is different from such places as America and Japan.

13. Guided Response

(Amerika, Nihon)	(Doko to chigaimasu ka?)	(With what places does it differ?)
	Amerika ya Nihon to chi-gaimasu.	It differs from such places as America and Japan.
(tororii basu, chikatetsu)	(Nani ni norimasu ka?)	(What do you ride?)
	Tororii basu ya chikatetsu ni norimasu.	I ride such things as trolley buses and subways.
(ohiru, ban)	(Itsu tabemasu ka?)	(When do you eat it?)
	Ohiru ya ban tabemasu.	I eat it at such times as noon and evening.
(eki no mae, eki no soba)	(Doko ni tomemasu ka?)	(Where do you park it?)
	Eki no mae ya eki no soba ni tomemasu.	I park in such places as in front or near the station.
(okaasan, tomoda-chi)	(Dare ni iimasu ka?)	(Who will you tell it to?)
	Okaasan ya tomodachi ni iimasu.	I'll tell such people as my mother and friends.
(gojuuen no, roku-juuen no)	(Ikura no ga arimasu ka?)	(How much are the ones you have?)
	Gojuuen no ya rokujuuen no ga arimasu.	I have fifty-yen ones and six-ty-yen ones [and others].
(kono hako, sono hako)	(Dono hako ni iremashoo ka?)	(What box shall I put it in?)
	Kono hako ya sono hako ni iremashoo.	Let's put it in such boxes as this one and that one.

14. Substitution

Soo omoimasen deshita.		I didn't think so.
(kikimasen)	Soo kikimasen deshita.	I didn't ask that. I didn't hear it thus.
(kotaemasen)	Soo kotaemasen deshita.	I didn't answer thus.
(iimasen)	Soo iimasen deshita.	I didn't say so.
(kakimasen)	Soo kakimasen deshita.	I didn't write it thus.

15. Progressive Substitution

Doo omoimasu ka?	What do you think?

(soo)	Soo omoimasu ka?	Do you think so?
(kakimashita)	Soo kakimashita ka?	Did they write it that way?
(koo)	Koo kakimashita ka?	Did they write it this way?
(iimashita)	Koo iimashita ka?	Did they say it this way?
(soo)	Soo iimashita ka?	Did they say that?
(kikimashoo)	Soo kikimashoo ka?	Shall I ask it that way?
(doo)	Doo kikimashoo ka?	How shall we ask it?
(omoimasu)	Doo omoimasu ka?	What do you think?

16. Substitution

Ohayoo gozaimasu to iimashita.   He said, "Good morning."

(osaki ni doozo)	Osaki ni doozo to iimashita.	He said, "Please go first."
(itte mairimasu)	Itte mairimasu to iimashita.	He said, "Goodbye."
(itte irasshai)	Itte irasshai to iimashita.	He said, "Goodbye."
(gochisoo-sama)	Gochisoo-sama to iimashita.	He said, "Gochisoo-sama."
(doomo arigatoo)	Doomo arigatoo to iimashita.	He said, "Thank you very much."

17. Substitution

Kikimashoo ka to kikimashita.   He asked, "Shall we ask?"

(yasumimashoo ka)	Yasumimashoo ka to kikima-shita.	He asked, "Shall we rest?"
(norimashoo ka)	Norimashoo ka to kikima-shita.	He asked, "Shall we get on board?"
(iremashoo ka)	Iremashoo ka to kikimashita.	He asked, "Shall we put it in?"
(hairimashoo ka)	Hairimashoo ka to kikima-shita.	He asked, "Shall we go in?"
(suwarimashoo ka)	Suwarimashoo ka to kikima-shita.	He asked, "Shall we sit down?"
(toorimashoo ka)	Toorimashoo ka to kikima-shita.	He asked, "Shall we pass through?"

18. Negative Response

Q. Itsu desu ka?   When is it?
A. Itsu ka kikimasen deshita.   I didn't ask when it would be.

(nan)	Nan desu ka?	What is it?
	Nani ka kikimasen deshita.	I didn't ask what it was.
(doko)	Doko desu ka?	Where is it?
	Doko ka kikimasen deshita.	I didn't ask where it was.
(dare)	Dare desu ka?	Who is it?
	Dare ka kikimasen deshita.	I didn't ask who it was.
(ikura)	Ikura desu ka?	How much is it?
	Ikura ka kikimasen deshita.	I didn't ask how much it was.

19. Response

Q. Yukio-san dake kuru deshoo ka?   I wonder if only Yukio is coming?
A. Ee. Yukio-san dake kuru to kiki-   Yes, I heard that only Yukio is coming.
        mashita.

(Yamamoto-san ya Yamada-san ni au   (I wonder if he'll be seeing such people
    deshoo ka?)   as Mr. Yamamoto and Mr. Yamada?)
Ee.   Yamamoto-san ya Yamada-san ni   Yes, I heard that he would be seeing
    au to kikimashita.   such people as Mr. Yamamoto and
                                                Mr. Yamada.
(Seeto to iku deshoo ka?)   (I wonder if he's going with the pupils?)
Ee.   Seeto to iku to kikimashita.   Yes, I heard that he's going with the
                                                pupils.
(Kyoo no shimbun ni deru deshoo ka?)   (I wonder if it's going to appear in to-
                                                day's paper?)
Ee.   Kyoo no shimbun ni deru to kiki-   Yes, I heard that it's going to appear
    mashita.   in today's paper.
(Ashita Tanaka-san ni kotaeru deshoo   (I wonder if he's going to give Mr. Ta-
    ka?)   naka an answer tomorrow?)
Ee. Ashita Tanaka-san ni kotaeru to   Yes, I heard that he's going to give
    kikimashita.   Mr. Tanaka an answer tomorrow.

20. Substitution

Nan to kotaemashita ka?   What did he reply?

(iku)   Iku to kotaemashita ka?   Did he reply that he would go?
(iru)   Iru to kotaemashita ka?   Did he reply that he would be there?
(aru)   Aru to kotaemashita ka?   Did he reply that there was some?
(wakaru)   Wakaru to kotaemashita ka?   Did he reply that he understood?
(nampun)   Nampun to kotaemashita ka?   How many minutes did he reply [that it
                                                would be]?
(itsu)   Itsu to kotaemashita ka?   When did he reply [it would be]?

21. Substitution

Kono mae o tooru to omoimasu ka?   Do you think it will pass in front of
                                                here?

(chikaku)   Kono chikaku o tooru to   Do you think it will pass near here?
                omoimasu ka?
(machi)   Kono machi o tooru to omoi-   Do you think it will pass through this
                masu ka?   town?
(naka)   Kono naka o tooru to omoi-   Do you think it will pass through here?
                masu ka?
(shita)   Kono shita o tooru to omoi-   Do you think it will pass under here?
                masu ka?
(ue)   Kono ue o tooru to omoimasu   Do you think it will pass overhead?
                ka?

EXERCISES

A. Combine the following pairs of sentences into single sentences.

Example: Yamamoto-sensee wa ashita ikimasu.
          Soo iimashita.
          Yamamoto-sensee wa ashita iku to iimashita.

  1. Kono hako ni hairimasu.
      Soo omoimasu.
  2. Yukio-san no tonari ni suwarimasu.
      Soo iimashita.
  3. Ashita aimasu.
      Soo kotaemashita.
  4. Tanaka-san ni misemasu.
      Soo kikimashita.
  5. Koko ni tomarimasu.
      Soo iimashita.
  6. Ima kono hako ni iremasu.
      Soo iimashita.
  7. Watakushi ga kotaemasu.
      Soo iimashita.
  8. Ima sensee ni kikimasu.
      Soo omoimasu.
  9. Doko ni suwaru deshoo ka?
      Soo kikimashita.
 10. Hikooki de ikimasu.
      Soo kakimashita.

B. Supply the missing particles.

  1. Okashi _____ chokoreeto _____   He eats such things as cakes and choco-
      tabemasu.   lates.
  2. Okashi _____ chokoreeto _____   He eats cakes and chocolates.
      tabemasu.
  3. Okashi _____ chokoreeto _____   He eats both cakes and chocolates.
      tabemasu.
  4. Sensee _____ aimashita.   I saw the teacher.
  5. Sensee _____ aimashita.   The teacher saw him.
  6. Sensee _____ aimashita.   I, together with the teacher, met him.
  7. Koko _____ toorimasu ka?   Does it pass by here?
  8. Koko _____ norimashoo.   Let's board it here.
  9. Kono densha _____ norimashoo.   Let's board this streetcar.
 10. Dare _____ kikimashita ka?   Who did you ask?
 11. Doko _____ kikimashita ka?   Where did you ask?
 12. Doko _____ tomarimasu ka?   Where does it stop?
 13. Nan _____ kotaemashita ka?   What did he reply?
 14. Kono yuubinkyoku _____ hairima-   Let's go in this post office.
      shoo.
 15. Tanaka-san _____ denwa _____   Did you telephone Mr. Tanaka?
      kakemashita ka?

16. Tanaka-san _____ denwa _____   Did Mr. Tanaka telephone?
    kakemashita ka?
17. Denwa _____ kakarimashita.   There was a telephone call.
18. Yukio-san _____ sensee _____   He sat down between Yukio and the teach-
    aida _____ suwarimashita.   er.
19. Shimbun _____ demashita ka?   Did it appear in the papers?
20. Tomodachi _____ kuru deshoo.   He'll probably come with his friends.

C. Select the verb which best completes the sentence.

1. Ano koto o shimbun ni (demashita, dashimashita).
2. Tanaka-san no koto ga shimbun ni (demashita, dashimashita).
3. Ashita fune ga (deru, dasu) deshoo.
4. Hon o hako ni (hairimashoo, iremashoo).
5. Hon ga hako ni (hairu, ireru) deshoo ka?
6. Tanaka-san ni denwa ga (kakarimashita, kakemashita).
7. Tanaka-san ni denwa o (kakarimashita, kakemashita).
8. Rajio ga (kakaru, kakeru) deshoo ka?
9. Doko ni kuruma o (tomarimashoo, tomemashoo) ka?
10. Basu wa koko ni (tomaru, tomeru) deshoo ka?

D. Insert dake or shika in the following blanks.

1. Rajio _____ kaimashita.   I bought only a radio.
2. Rajio _____ kaimasen deshita.   The only thing I didn't buy was a radio.
3. Rajio _____ kaimasen deshita.   I bought only a radio [and nothing more].
4. Sono koto _____ kikimasen deshita. That's the only thing I didn't hear.
5. Sensee _____ wakarimasen.   No one but the teacher understands.
6. Watakushi _____ wakarimasen.   I'm the only one who doesn't understand.
7. Basu _____ toorimasu.   Only a bus passes by.
8. Depaato _____ de mimashita.   I saw it only at the department store.
9. Depaato ni _____ arimasen.   They don't have it anyplace but at the
                                          department store.
10. Sensee ni _____ kikimashita.   I asked only the teacher.

E. Ask your friend:

1. if he saw (met) Yukio.
2. where he saw (met) Yukio.
3. when he will be seeing Yukio.
4. whether he thinks Mr. Yamada will show it to the teacher.
5. whether it will fit into the box.
6. if he doesn't think so.
7. if he won't sit next to Mr. Yamada.
8. of whom he asked it.
9. where the streetcar stops.
10. whether Yukio boarded the ship.
11. how he answered Mr. Yamada.
12. whether you should sit next to Mr. Yamada.
13. what you should do.

14. if you should put it in this way.
15. whether the bus passes in front of here.

F. Listen to (or read) the following passage, then answer the questions which
    follow.

    Kyoo gozen juuji goro ni, Yukio-san wa otomodachi ni denwa o kakemashita.
Yukio-san wa asa no shimbun de sono otomodachi no koto o yomimashita.
    "Jiroo-san wa Amerika e iku to shimbun de yomimashita ga, itsu desu ka?" to
kikimashita.
    Suru to, tomodachi wa, "Fune de ikimasu ga, itsu no fune ka wakarimasen," to
kotaemashita.

1.   Yukio-san ni denwa ga kakarimashita ka?
2.   Yukio-san wa dare ni denwa o kakemashita ka?
3.   Nanji goro ni kakemashita ka?
4.   Yukio-san wa kyoo no shimbun o mimashita ka?
5.   Asa no shimbun deshita ka, ban no shimbun deshita ka?
6.   Yukio-san no otomodachi wa dare desu ka?
7.   Shimbun ni Jiroo-san no koto ga demashita ka?
8.   Yukio-san ga sono koto o shimbun ni dashimashita ka?
9.   Jiroo-san wa doko e ikimasu ka?
10. Yukio-san wa Jiroo-san ni nan to kikimashita ka?
11. Sono otomodachi wa hikooki de ikimasu ka, fune de ikimasu ka?
12. Tomodachi wa nan to kotaemashita ka?

REVIEW

A. Respond to the following questions.

1. Ohayoo gozaimasu.
2. Ima nanji desu ka?
3. Kyoo wa nanji ni okimashita ka?
4. Asa wa nanji ni tabemasu ka?
5. Kyoo wa nanji ni tabemashita ka?
6. Kyoo wa nanji ni dekakemashita ka?
7. Nanji ni gakkoo ni kimashita ka?
8. Aruite kimashita ka?
9. Dono gurai kakarimashita ka?
10. Ohiru wa nanji ni tabemasu ka?
11. Gogo nanji ni kaerimasu ka?
12. Ban wa nanji ni tabemasu ka?
13. Nanji ni yasumimasu ka?
14. Kinoo wa nanji ni yasumimashita ka?

B. Listen to the following passage and then respond to the questions.

Yukio-san wa rokuji-han goro ni okimashita. Shita e ikimashita. Okaasan ni, "Nanji desu ka?" to kikimashita. Okaasan wa, "Shichiji desu," to kotaemashita. Yukio-san wa sugu tabemashita. Shichiji-han goro ni dekakemashita. Jippun gurai teeryuujo de machimashita. Suru to, basu ga kimashita. Kono chikaku wa basu shika toorimasen. Basu no teeryuujo de Yamamoto-sensee ni aimashita. Yukio-san to Yamamoto-sensee wa basu de gakkoo e ikimashita. Nijippun gurai kakarimashita.

1. Yukio-san wa rokuji goro ni wa uchi ni imashita ka?
2. Yukio-san wa nanji ni okimashita ka?
3. Yukio-san wa ue de yasumimasu ka?
4. Yukio-san wa asa gakkoo de tabemashita ka?
5. Asa nanji ni tabemashita ka?
6. Okaasan ga, "Nanji desu ka?" to kikimashita ka?
7. Okaasan wa nan to iimashita ka?
8. Yukio-san wa nanji goro ni dekakemashita ka?
9. Gakkoo e aruite iku deshoo ka?
10. Doko de basu o machimasu ka?
11. Dono gurai machimashita ka?
12. Kono chikaku wa densha mo toorimasu ka?
13. Basu no teeryuujo de dare ni aimashita ka?
14. Sensee mo Yukio-san mo basu ni norimashita ka?
15. Basu de nampun gurai kakarimasu ka?
16. Kyoo wa sensee to gakkoo e iku deshoo ka?

C. Give the following times in Japanese.

1. 7:30   2. around 7:30

3. 7:45678   15. 1:15
4. 1:16   16. 2:10
5. 2:20   17. 15 minutes of 3:00
6. 3:40   18. 4:00
7. 10 minutes of 5:00   19. around 5:00
8. 3 minutes after 6:00   20. 6:04
9. 6:08   21. 8:05
10. 6 minutes after 8:00   22. 8:12
11. 8:14   23. 8:15
12. 9:18   24. 9:19
13. 9:23   25. 10:35
14. around 11:30

D. Identification of various slides.

1. Nan desu ka?
2. Nihon no _____ desu ka?

E. Respond to the following questions on the basis of Slide 13.

1. Tsukue ga arimasu ka?
2. Isu mo arimasu ka?
3. Isu mo tsukue mo arimasu ka?
4. Isu wa doko ni arimasu ka?
5. Isu no ue ni nani ga arimasu ka?
6. Tsukue no ue ni nani ga arimasu ka?
7. Tsukue no ue ni tokee ya rajio ga arimasu ka?
8. Rajio ya tokee ya denwa ga arimasu ka?
9. Hako no naka ni nani ga aru ka wakarimasu ka?
10. Empitsu wa doko ni arimasu ka?
11. Tokee wa nanji desu ka?
12. Rajio wa nani no soba desu ka?
13. Booru pen mo empitsu mo arimasu ka?
14. Ima Yukio-san ga imasu ka?
15. Yukio-san wa koko de nani o suru deshoo ka?

F. Listen to the following passage and then respond to the questions.

Jiroo-san wa Yukio-san no tomodachi desu. Jiroo-san no uchi wa tonari desu. Yukio-san to Jiroo-san no uchi no soba ni toshokan ga arimasu. Yukio-san wa ban rokuji ni tabemashita. Jiroo-san mo rokuji ni tabemashita. Rokuji-han ni toshokan e dekakemashita. Toshokan de benkyoo shimashita. Hachiji goro ni aruite kaerimashita.

1. Jiroo-san wa dare desu ka?
2. Sono Jiroo-san no uchi wa doko desu ka?
3. Jiroo-san wa kodomo deshoo ka, otona deshoo ka?
4. Jiroo-san to Yukio-san no uchi no soba ni nani ga arimasu ka?
5. Yukio-san wa ban nanji ni tabemashita ka?
6. Jiroo-san wa rokuji jippun mae ni tabemashita ka?

7. Gogo rokuji-han ni doko e dekakemashita ka?
8. Sugu kaerimashita ka?
9. Toshokan de nani o shimashita ka?
10. Toshokan ni wa nani ga aru deshoo?
11. Nanji ni uchi e kaerimashita ka?
12. Yukio-san to Jiroo-san wa basu de kaerimashita ka?

G. Listen to the following story. Repeat the story in your own way.

   Basu no teeryuujo wa omise no mae desu. Soko de Yukio-san wa basu ni norimasu. Kyoo wa teeryuujo no mae no omise ni yorimashita. Soko de chokoreeto o
kaimashita. Gojuuen no chokoreeto mo rokujuuen no chokoreeto mo arimashita. Gojuuen no chokoreeto o kaimashita. Sono chokoreeto wa gakkoo de taberu deshoo.

LESSON 1

Yukio-san no uchi wa Tookyoo ni arimasu. Furui uchi desu ga, ookii
desu. Tonari no Jiroo-san no uchi
yori ookii desu.

Yukio's home is in Tokyo. It's an old
house, but it's large. It's larger
than Jiro's home next door.

GRAMMAR

II-1.1 Verbal adjectives

A verbal adjective, in its non-past form, ends with an "i" and that "i" is
immediately preceded by another vowel. (Note, however, that words with this ending are not all verbal adjectives.) The verbal adjective is conjugated. In this
lesson it occurs only in the informal and semi-formal non-past form.

EXAMPLES:

Informal	Semi-formal	
Ookii.	Ookii desu.	It's large.
Takai.	Takai desu.	It's expensive.
		It's high.
Hikui.	Hikui desu.	It's low.
Tooi.	Tooi desu.	It's far away.
Yasui.	Yasui deshoo.	It's probably inexpensive.
Osoi.	Osoi deshoo.	It's probably late.

The informal non-past form occurs before nouns.

EXAMPLES:

Ookii uchi desu.   It's a large house.
Ookii, furui uchi desu.   It's a large, old house.
Atarashii jidoosha o kaimashita.   He bought a new car.

II-1.2 Comparison using yori

In the construction A wa (B yori) ookii desu, A wa ookii desu is the main
element, meaning "A is big." B yori adds the comparative element, meaning "[more]
than B."

EXAMPLES:

Yukio-san no uchi wa tonari no   Yukio's home is larger than the home next
  uchi yori ookii desu.   door.
Mae no kisha wa kono kisha yori   The earlier train is faster than this
  hayai desu.   one.

II-1.3 Comparative (positive)

To express the idea that A is better (faster, etc.) without mentioning B,
one says "the side of A is good (fast, etc.)." One might think of a scale with A
on one side and B on the other. By saying "A's side is heavy" one implies that
A is heavier. Side (or direction) in Japanese is hoo. It functions as a noun.

84

     Yukio-san no hoo ga . . .
       (noun modifying hoo) ·
     Ooki'i hoo ga . . .
       (non-past verbal adjective modifying hoo)
     Iku hoo ga . . .
       (non-past verb modifying hoo)

EXAMPLES:

Kono hoo ga takai desu.	This is more expensive.
Chiisai hoo ga takai desu.	The smaller one is more expensive.
Takai hoo o kudasai.	Please give me the more expensive one.
Iku hoo ga hayai desu.	It's faster to go. (This form will be discussed again later.)

II-1.4 Kore, sore, are, and dore

    Kore meaning "this one" or "these," sore meaning "that one" or "those," are meaning "that one over there" or "those over there," and dore meaning "which one (of more than two things)" have the same spatial and temporal references as the kono, sono series, the koko, soko series, and the koo, soo series.

EXAMPLES:

Kore wa hikui desu.	This one is low.
Sore wa furui deshoo.	That one is probably old.
Dore ga Yukio-san no desu ka?	Which one is Yukio's?

II-1.5 Ka meaning "or"

    Between two nouns, ka has an "either _____ or _____" meaning.

EXAMPLES:

Hon ka zasshi desu.	It's either a book or a magazine.
Jettoki ka hikooki o kaimashita.	He bought either a jet plane or a propeller plane.

II-1.6 Final particle ne

    Ne at the end of an utterance has the meaning "isn't it?" or "isn't it!"

EXAMPLES:

Tanaka-san desu ne.	You're Mr. Tanaka, aren't you? (You're Mr. Tanaka, isn't that so?)
Osoi desu ne.	It's late, isn't it!
Koko de kaimashoo ne.	Let's buy it here, all right?
Kinoo ikimashita ne.	You went yesterday, didn't you?

II-1.7 Final particle yo

    The final particle yo, said on a higher note than the remainder of the sentence, has the meaning "you know." On a lower tone, it is more emphatic and has a note of warning, anger, etc.

EXAMPLES:

Kore desu yo.	It's this one, [you know].
Ooki'i desu yo.	It's large, [you know].
Ikimasen yo. (low)	I'm not going!

II-1.8 N desu

N desu after an informal ending of a verb, verbal adjective or noun plus na makes the statement emphatic. It has a meaning like "it's a fact that . . ."

EXAMPLES:
Iku n desu.   I'm going!
Takai n desu.   It's expensive!

II-1.9 Shiru and wakaru

The verb shiru in the positive form means "learn [of something]."

EXAMPLE:
Kinoo shirimashita.   I learned of it yesterday.

In its other forms, including the negative, it means to "know [a fact or a person]." Thus, shirimasen means "I don't know [that fact]," but wakarimasen means "It's not clear" or "I don't understand."

EXAMPLES:
(Do you know how much it is?)
Iie. Shirimasen.   No, I don't know.
(Do you know Mr. Tanaka?)
Iie. Shirimasen.   No, I don't know him.

(Do you know if you're going to-
   morrow?)
Iie. Wakarimasen.   No, it isn't clear.
(Do you understand it?)
Iie. Wakarimasen.   No, I don't understand it.

DRILLS

1. Repetition

Ookii desu.   It's large.
Chiisai desu.   It's small.
Nagai desu.   It's long.
Mijikai desu.   It's short.
Takai desu.   It's expensive.
Yasui desu.   It's inexpensive.
Takai desu.   It's tall.
Hikui desu.   It's low.
Tooi desu.   It's far away.
Chikai desu.   It's near by.
Atarashii desu.   It's new.
Furui desu.   It's old.
Hayai desu.   It's early.
                                         It's fast.

Osoi desu.   It's late.
                                         It's slow.

Īi desu.   It's good.
Warui desu.   It's bad.
Hiroi desu.   It's wide.
Semai desu.   It's narrow.

2. Affirmative Response

Q. Ookii desu ka?   Is it large?
A. Ee. Ookii desu.   Yes, it's large.

(Chiisai desu ka?)   (Is it small?)
 Ee. Chiisai desu.   Yes, it's small.
(Nagai desu ka?)   (Is it long?)
 Ee. Nagai desu.   Yes, it's long.
(Mijikai desu ka?)   (Is it short?)
 Ee. Mijikai desu.   Yes, it's short.
(Takai desu ka?)   (Is it expensive?)
 Ee. Takai desu.   Yes, it's expensive.
(Yasui desu ka?)   (Is it inexpensive?)
 Ee. Yasui desu.   Yes, it's inexpensive.
(Hikui desu ka?)   (Is it low?)
 Ee. Hikui desu.   Yes, it's low.
(Tooi desu ka?)   (Is it far?)
 Ee. Tooi desu.   Yes, it's far.
(Chikai desu ka?)   (Is it near?)
 Ee. Chikai desu.   Yes, it's near.
(Atarashii desu ka?)   (Is it new?)
 Ee. Atarashii desu.   Yes, it's new.
(Furui desu ka?)   (Is it old?)
 Ee. Furui desu.   Yes, it's old.
(Hayai desu ka?)   (Is it fast?)
 Ee. Hayai desu.   Yes, it's fast.
(Osoi desu ka?)   (Is it slow?)
 Ee. Osoi desu.   Yes, it's slow.
(Īi desu ka?)   (Is it good?)
 Ee. Īi desu.   Yes, it's good.
(Warui desu ka?)   (Is it bad?)
 Ee. Warui desu.   Yes, it's bad.
(Hiroi desu ka?)   (Is it wide?)
 Ee. Hiroi desu.   Yes, it's wide.
(Semai desu ka?)   (Is it narrow?)
 Ee. Semai desu.   Yes, it's narrow.

3. Opposite Response

Q. Ookii desu ka?   Is it large?
A. Iie. Chiisai desu.   No, it's small.

(Chiisai desu ka?)   (Is it small?)
 Iie. Ookii desu.   No, it's large.

(Nagai desu ka?)   (Is it long?)
 Iie. Mijikai desu.   No, it's short.
(Mijikai desu ka?)   (Is it short?)
 Iie. Nagai desu.   No, it's long.
(Takai desu ka?)   (Is it expensive?)
 Iie. Yasui desu.   No, it's inexpensive.
(Yasui desu ka?)   (Is it inexpensive?)
 Iie. Takai desu.   No, it's expensive.
(Takai desu ka?)   (Is it tall?)
 Iie. Hikui desu.   No, it's low.
(Hikui desu ka?)   (Is it low?)
 Iie. Takai desu.   No, it's tall.
(Tooi desu ka?)   (Is it far?)
 Iie. Chikai desu.   No, it's near.
(Chikai desu ka?)   (Is it near?)
 Iie. Tooi desu.   No, it's far.
(Atarashii desu ka?)   (Is it new?)
 Iie. Furui desu.   No, it's old.
(Furui desu ka?)   (Is it old?)
 Iie. Atarashii desu.   No, it's new.
(Hayai desu ka?)   (Is it early?)
 Iie. Osoi desu.   No, it's late.
(Osoi desu ka?)   (Is it late?)
 Iie. Hayai desu.   No, it's early.
(Ii desu ka?)   (Is it good?)
 Iie. Warui desu.   No, it's bad.
(Warui desu ka?)   (Is it bad?)
 Iie. Ii desu.   No, it's good.
(Hiroi desu ka?)   (Is it wide?)
 Iie. Semai desu.   No, it's narrow.
(Semai desu ka?)   (Is it narrow?)
 Iie. Hiroi desu.   No, it's wide.

4. Progressive Substitution

Nagai empitsu desu ne.   Isn't it a long pencil!

(mijikai)   Mijikai empitsu desu ne.   Isn't it a short pencil!
(booru pen)   Mijikai booru pen desu   Isn't it a short ballpoint pen!
                   ne.
(ii)   Ii booru pen desu ne.   Isn't it a good ballpoint pen!
(rajio)   Ii rajio desu ne.   Isn't it a good radio!
(furui)   Furui rajio desu ne.   Isn't it an old radio!
(uchi)   Furui uchi desu ne.   Isn't it an old house!
(takai)   Takai uchi desu ne.   Isn't it an expensive house!
(tsukue)   Takai tsukue desu ne.   Isn't it a high desk!
(hikui)   Hikui tsukue desu ne.   Isn't it a low desk!
(isu)   Hikui isu desu ne.   Isn't it a low chair!
(warui)   Warui isu desu ne.   Isn't it a bad chair!
(kaisha)   Warui kaisha desu ne.   Isn't it a bad company!
(atarashii)   Atarashii kaisha desu ne.   Isn't it a new company!
(kuruma)   Atarashii kuruma desu ne.   Isn't it a new car!

(nagai)   Nagai kuruma desu ne.   Isn't it a long car!
(empitsu)   Nagai empitsu desu ne.   Isn't it a long pencil!

5. Substitution

Kore wa takai n desu.   This one is expensive!

(yasui)   Kore wa yasui n desu.   This one is inexpensive!
(ookii)   Kore wa ookii n desu.   This one is large!
(chiisai)   Kore wa chiisai n desu.   This one is small!
(nagai)   Kore wa nagai n desu.   This one is long!
(mijikai)   Kore wa mijikai n desu.   This one is short!
(atarashii)   Kore wa atarashii n desu.   This one is new!
(furui)   Kore wa furui n desu.   This one is old!

6. Substitution

Sore yori takai desu yo.   It's higher than that!

(hikui)   Sore yori hikui desu yo.   It's lower than that!
(mijikai)   Sore yori mijikai desu yo.   It's shorter than that!
(nagai)   Sore yori nagai desu yo.   It's longer than that!
(furui)   Sore yori furui desu yo.   It's older than that!
(atarashii)   Sore yori atarashii desu yo.   It's newer than that!
(hiroi)   Sore yori hiroi desu yo.   It's wider than that!
(semai)   Sore yori semai desu yo.   It's narrower than that!
(ii)   Sore yori ii desu yo.   It's better than that!
(warui)   Sore yori warui desu yo.   It's worse than that!
(chikai)   Sore yori chikai desu yo.   It's nearer than that!
(tooi)   Sore yori tooi desu yo.   It's farther than that!

7. Substitution and Affirmative Response

Q. Ano heya yori hiroi deshoo ka?   I wonder if it's more spacious
                                                   than that room?

A. Ee. Are yori wa hiroi desu yo.   Yes, it's more spacious than
                                                   that one!

(ano heya,   Ano heya yori semai deshoo ka?   I wonder if it's smaller (less
  semai)   spacious) than that room?

               Ee. Are yori wa semai desu yo. Yes, it's smaller than that
                                                   one!

(ano jidoo-   Ano jidoosha yori hayai deshoo ka?   I wonder if it's faster than
  sha, hayai)   that car?

               Ee. Are yori wa hayai desu yo. Yes, it's faster than that one!

(ano densha,   Ano densha yori osoi deshoo ka? I wonder if it's slower than
  osoi)   that electric train?

               Ee. Are yori wa osoi desu yo.   Yes, it's slower than that one!

(ano tsukue, hikui)	Ano tsukue yori hikui deshoo ka?	I wonder if it's lower than that desk?
	Ee. Are yori wa hikui desu yo.	Yes, it's lower than that one!
(ano gakkoo, chikai)	Ano gakkoo yori chikai deshoo ka?	I wonder if it's closer than that school?
	Ee. Are yori wa chikai desu yo.	Yes, it's closer than that one!
(ano omise, tooi)	Ano omise yori tooi deshoo ka?	I wonder if it's farther than that store?
	Ee. Are yori wa tooi desu yo.	Yes, it's farther than that one!
(ano tokee, ii)	Ano tokee yori ii deshoo ka?	I wonder if it's better than that clock?
	Ee. Are yori wa ii desu yo.	Yes, it's better than that one!
(ano kaisha, furui)	Ano kaisha yori furui deshoo ka?	I wonder if it's older than that company?
	Ee. Are yori wa furui desu yo.	Yes, it's older than that one!
(ano fune, mijikai)	Ano fune yori mijikai deshoo ka?	I wonder if it's shorter than that boat?
	Ee. Are yori wa mijikai desu yo.	Yes, it's shorter than that one!

8. Substitution

Kore wa sore yori hikui to iimashita.		He said that this one is lower than that one.
(takai)	Kore wa sore yori takai to iimashita.	He said that this one is more expensive than that one.
(yasui)	Kore wa sore yori yasui to iimashita.	He said that this one is cheaper than that one.
(ookii)	Kore wa sore yori ookii to iimashita.	He said that this one is larger than that one.
(furui)	Kore wa sore yori furui to iimashita.	He said that this one is older than that one.
(atarashii)	Kore wa sore yori atarashii to iimashita.	He said that this one is newer than that one.
(nagai)	Kore wa sore yori nagai to iimashita.	He said that this one is longer than that one.
(mijikai)	Kore wa sore yori mijikai to iimashita.	He said that this one is shorter than that one.

9. Response and Grammar

Q. Kore yori atarashii hon ga arimasu ka?	Is there a newer book than this?
A. Ee. Kono hon wa sore yori atarashii to omoimasu.	Yes, I think this book is newer than that one.

(ookii, kokuban)	Kore yori ookii kokuban ga arimasu ka?	Is there a larger blackboard than this?
	Ee. Kono kokuban wa sore yori ookii to omoimasu.	Yes, I think this blackboard is larger than that one.
(hikui, tsukue)	Kore yori hikui tsukue ga arimasu ka?	Is there a lower desk than this?
	Ee. Kono tsukue wa sore yori hikui to omoimasu.	Yes, I think this desk is lower than that one.
(yasui, isu)	Kore yori yasui isu ga arimasu ka?	Is there a cheaper chair than this?
	Ee. Kono isu wa sore yori yasui to omoimasu.	Yes, I think this chair is cheaper than that one.
(ii, choko-reeto)	Kore yori ii chokoreeto ga arimasu ka?	Is there better chocolate than this?
	Ee. Kono chokoreeto wa sore yori ii to omoimasu.	Yes, I think this chocolate is better than that.
(chiisai, hako)	Kore yori chiisai hako ga arimasu ka?	Is there a smaller box than this?
	Ee. Kono hako wa sore yori chiisai to omoimasu.	Yes, I think this box is smaller than that one.
(hiroi, heya)	Kore yori hiroi heya ga arimasu ka?	Is there a more spacious room than this?
	Ee. Kono heya wa sore yori hiroi to omoimasu.	Yes, I think this room is more spacious than that one.

10. Substitution

Dotchi no hoo ga furui desu ka?	Which one is older?
(atarashii)	Dotchi no hoo ga atarashii desu ka?	Which one is newer?
(mijikai)	Dotchi no hoo ga mijikai desu ka?	Which one is shorter?
(warui)	Dotchi no hoo ga warui desu ka?	Which one is worse?
(ii)	Dotchi no hoo ga ii desu ka?	Which one is better?
(hiroi)	Dotchi no hoo ga hiroi desu ka?	Which one is wider?
(semai)	Dotchi no hoo ga semai desu ka?	Which one is narrower?
(hayai)	Dotchi no hoo ga hayai desu ka?	Which one is faster?
(osoi)	Dotchi no hoo ga osoi desu ka?	Which one is slower?
(chikai)	Dotchi no hoo ga chikai desu ka?	Which one is nearer?
(tooi)	Dotchi no hoo ga tooi desu ka?	Which one is farther?

11. Substitution

Kotchi to sotchi to, dotchi no hoo ga ii desu ka?	Between this one and that one, which one is better?

(Use list in Drill 10 above.)

12. Response (using objects)

Q. Kotchi to sotchi to, dotchi no hoo ga   Between this one and that one,
       chiisai desu ka?   which one is smaller?
A. Sotchi no hoo ga chiisai deshoo.   That one is probably smaller.
A. Kotchi no hoo ga chiisai deshoo.   This one is probably smaller.

13. Progressive Substitution

Kono hoo ga takai desu yo.   This is more expensive, you
                                                    know.

(kono hon no)   Kono hon no hoo ga takai desu yo.   This book is more expensive,
                                                      you know.

(atarashii)   Kono hon no hoo ga atarashii   This book is newer, you know.
                  desu yo.

(kore no)   Kore no hoo ga atarashii desu yo.   This one is newer, you know.
(ii)   Kore no hoo ga ii desu yo.   This one is better, you know.
(kotchi no)   Kotchi no hoo ga ii desu yo.   This one is better, you know.
(chiisai)   Kotchi no hoo ga chiisai desu yo.   This one is smaller, you know.
(sono)   Sono hoo ga chiisai desu yo.   That's smaller, you know.
(hikui)   Sono hoo ga hikui desu yo.   That's lower, you know.
(sono isu no)   Sono isu no hoo ga hikui desu yo.   That chair's lower, you know.
(yasui)   Sono isu no hoo ga yasui desu yo.   That chair's cheaper, you know.
(sore no)   Sore no hoo ga yasui desu yo.   That one is cheaper, you know.
(ookii)   Sore no hoo ga ookii desu yo.   That one is larger, you know.
(sotchi no)   Sotchi no hoo ga ookii desu yo.   That one is larger, you know.
(tooi)   Sotchi no hoo ga tooi desu yo.   That one is farther away, you
                                                      know.

(atchi no)   Atchi no hoo ga tooi desu yo.   That one over there is farther
                                                      away, you know.

(furui)   Atchi no hoo ga furui desu yo.   That one over there is older,
                                                      you know.

(kono)   Kono hoo ga furui desu yo.   This is older, you know.
(takai)   Kono hoo ga takai desu yo.   This is more expensive, you
                                                      know.

14. Substitution (using three or more objects for each example)

Dore ga atarashii no desu ka?   Which one (of more than two)
                                                    is the new one?

(furui)   Dore ga furui no desu ka?   Which one is the old one?
(yasui)   Dore ga yasui no desu ka?   Which one is the inexpensive
                                                      one?
(takai)   Dore ga takai no desu ka?   Which one is the expensive one?
(ookii)   Dore ga ookii no desu ka?   Which one is the large one?
(chiisai)   Dore ga chiisai no desu ka?   Which one is the small one?

15. Affirmative Response

A. Kore wa ookii, ii uchi desu ne.   This is a nice, large house, isn't it!
B. Ee. Ookii, ii uchi desu ne.   Yes, it's a nice, large house, isn't it!

(Are wa furui, ii kaisha desu ne.)   (That's an old, good company, isn't it!)
Ee. Furui, ii kaisha desu ne.   Yes, it's an old, good company, isn't
                                              it!
(Kore wa semai, warui heya desu ne.)   (This is a narrow, bad room, isn't it!)
Ee. Semai, warui heya desu ne.   Yes, it's a narrow, bad room, isn't it!
(Are wa atarashii, hayai kisha desu ne.)   (That's a new, fast train, isn't it!)
Ee. Atarashii, hayai kisha desu ne.   Yes, it's a new, fast train, isn't it!
(Sore wa furui, takai tsukue desu ne.)   (That's an old, expensive desk, isn't
                                              it!)
Ee. Furui, takai tsukue desu ne.   Yes, it's an old, expensive desk, isn't
                                              it!
(Kore wa osoi, furui basu desu ne.)   (This is an old, slow bus, isn't it!)
Ee. Osoi, furui basu desu ne.   Yes, it's an old, slow bus, isn't it!

16. Substitution

Sono chiisai, yasui no o kudasai.   Please give me that small, in-
                                             expensive one.

(furui, ookii)   Sono furui, ookii no o kudasai.   Please give me that old, large
                                                       one.
(nagai, ii)   Sono nagai, ii no o kudasai.   Please give me that long, good
                                                       one.
(warui, furui)   Sono warui, furui no o kudasai.   Please give me that bad, old
                                                       one.
(chiisai, ata-   Sono chiisai, atarashii no o   Please give me that small, new
rashii)   kudasai.   one.
(ookii, takai)   Sono ookii, takai no o kudasai.   Please give me that large, ex-
                                                       pensive one.

17. Expansion

(Yamada-san no   Yamada-san no deshoo.   It's probably Mr. Yamada's.
 deshoo)
(Tanaka-san no   Tanaka-san no ka Yamada-san no   It's probably either Mr. Tanaka)   deshoo.   ka's or Mr. Yamada's.
(sono ookii,   Sono ookii, ii uchi wa Tanaka-   That large, nice house is pro-
 ii uchi wa)   san no ka Yamada-san no deshoo.   bably either Mr. Tanaka's or
                                                      Mr. Yamada's.

(kaisha   Kaisha deshoo.   It's probably a company.
 deshoo)
(toshokan ka)   Toshokan ka kaisha deshoo.   It's probably a library or a
                                                      company.

(ano ookii, furui no wa)	Ano ookii, furui no wa to-shokan ka kaisha deshoo.	That large, old one over there is probably a library or a company。
(yaoya deshoo)	Yaoya deshoo.	It's probably a greengrocery。
(pan'ya ka)	Pan'ya ka yaoya deshoo.	It's probably a bakery or a greengrocery.
(ano chiisai omise wa)	Ano chiisai omise wa pan'ya ka yaoya deshoo.	That small store is probably a bakery or a greengrocery.
(aru deshoo)	Aru deshoo.	It's probably there.
(isu no ue ni)	Isu no ue ni aru deshoo.	It's probably on the chair.
(tsukue ka)	Tsukue ka isu no ue ni aru deshoo.	It's probably either on the desk or the chair.
(ano atarashii zasshi wa)	Ano atarashii zasshi wa tsukue ka isu no ue ni aru deshoo.	That new magazine is probably either on the desk or the chair.
(yuubinkyoku de mimashita)	Yuubinkyoku de mimashita.	I saw it at the post office.
(gakkoo ka)	Gakkoo ka yuubinkyoku de mimashita.	I saw it either at school or at the post office.
(sono furui, takai no wa)	Sono furui, takai no wa gakkoo ka yuubinkyoku de mimashita.	I saw that old, high one either at school or at the post office.

18. Response

Q. Sanji desu ka, yoji desu ka?

A. Sanji ka yoji ka shirimasen.

Is it [at] three o'clock or is it [at] four o'clock?

I don't know whether it's [at] three or [at] four.

(Amerika no desu, Nihon no desu)	Amerika no desu ka, Nihon no desu ka?	Is it an American one or is it a Japanese one?
	Amerika no ka Nihon no ka shirimasen.	I don't know if it's an American one or a Japanese one.
(Tanaka-san no desu, Yamamoto-san no desu)	Tanaka-san no desu ka, Yamamoto-san no desu ka?	Is it Mr. Tanaka's or is it Mr. Yamamoto's?
	Tanaka-san no ka, Yamamoto-san no ka shirimasen.	I don't know whether it's Mr. Tanaka's or Mr. Yamamoto's.
(takushii de kimasu, chikatetsu de kimasu)	Takushii de kimasu ka, chikatetsu de kimasu ka?	Does he come by taxi or does he come by subway?
	Takushii de kuru ka, chikatetsu de kuru ka shirimasen.	I don't know whether he comes by taxi or by subway.

(hon'ya no tonari ni arimasu, yaoya no tonari ni arimasu)	Hon'ya no tonari ni arimasu ka, yaoya no tonari ni arimasu ka?	Is it next door to the book-store or is it next door to the greengrocery?
	Hon'ya no tonari ni aru ka, yaoya no tonari ni aru ka shirimasen.	I don't know whether it's next door to the bookstore or the greengrocery.
(ookii desu, chiisai desu)	Ookii desu ka, chiisai desu ka?	Is it large or is it small?
	Ookii ka chiisai ka shiri-masen.	I don't know whether it's large or small.

19. Substitution

Jidoosha ka basu ka wakarimasen.		I can't tell whether it's a car or a bus.
(otona, kodomo)	Otona ka kodomo ka wakari-masen.	I can't tell whether it's an adult or a child.
(hikooki, jettoki)	Hikooki ka jettoki ka wa-karimasen.	I can't tell whether it's a propeller plane or a jet.
(atarashii, furui)	Atarashii ka furui ka wa-karimasen.	I can't tell whether it's new or old.
(tokee, nani)	Tokee ka nani ka wakarima-sen.	I can't tell whether it's a watch or what [it is].

20. Response (using diagram of a town)

	Q. Doko ni chikai desu ka?	Where is it near?
(gakkoo)	A. Gakkoo ni chikai desu.	It's near the school.
(depaato)	Depaato ni chikai desu.	It's near the department store.
(yuubinkyoku)	Yuubinkyoku ni chikai desu.	It's near the post office.
(toshokan)	Toshokan ni chikai desu.	It's near the library.
(eki)	Eki ni chikai desu.	It's near the station.
(Tanaka-san no uchi)	Tanaka-san no uchi ni chi-kai desu.	It's near Mr. Tanaka's house.
(sensee no uchi)	Sensee no uchi ni chikai desu.	It's near the teacher's house.
(tomodachi no uchi)	Tomodachi no uchi ni chi-kai desu.	It's near my friend's house.

EXERCISES

A. Supply the proper verbal adjective.

1. _____ desu ne.   It's large, isn't it.
2. _____ desu ka?   Is it near?

3. _____ hon desu.   It's an inexpensive book.
4. _____ no o kudasai.   Please give me the expensive one.
5. _____ deshoo?   It's far, isn't it?
6. _____ hako deshita.   It was a small box.
7. _____ desu ne.   It's expensive, isn't it.
8. _____ kisha desu.   It's a slow train.
9. _____ desu yo.   It's near, you know.
10. _____ desu ka, _____ desu ka?   Is it long or short?
11. _____ desu ka, _____ desu ka?   Is it narrow or wide?
12. _____ desu ka, _____ desu ka?   Is it good or bad?

B. Give the opposites in meaning.

   1. Nagai desu.
   2. Chiisai desu.
   3. Chikai desu.
   4. Hikui desu.
   5. Yasui desu.
   6. Osoi desu.
   7. Furui desu.
   8. Warui desu.
   9. Hiroi desu.

C. Change the following into the comparative so that they will have the meaning
    "more _____." (There are at least two possible ways for each.)

   1. Kore wa furui desu.
   2. Sore wa atarashii desu ka?
   3. Sono teeryuujo wa tooi desu.
   4. Are wa takai desu ne.
   5. Kore wa hikui deshoo.
   6. Are ga yasui to omoimasu.
   7. Sono kisha wa hayai desu ka?
   8. Yukio-san no uchi wa ookii to iimashita.
   9. Kono tsukue wa nagai deshoo.
   10. Kono depaato wa chikai desu.
   11. Kore wa mijikai desu ka?
   12. Sono hako wa chiisai desu.

D. Insert a suitable particle.

   1. Machi _____ chikai desu.   The town is near by.
   2. Machi _____ chikai desu.   It's near the town.
   3. Ookii hako _____ arimasu ka?   Do you have a large box?
   4. Hayai kisha _____ kaerimashoo.   Let's return by the fast train.
   5. Yasui no _____ kudasai.   Please give me the inexpensive one.
   6. Hikui tsukue _____ dare no desu   Whose is the low desk?
       ka?
   7. Atarashii jidoosha _____ tonari   It's next to the new car.
       desu.

8. Sono takai isu no shita _____   It's under that high chair.
    arimasu.

9. Booru pen _____ empitsu deshoo.   It's probably a ballpoint pen or a pen-
    cil.

10. Ii _____ warui _____ shirimasen.   I don't know whether it's good or bad.

11. Yukio-san _____ Jiroo-san _____   Let's ask either Yukio or Jiro.
    kikimashoo.

12. Yamamoto-sensee _____ Tanaka-   Either Mr. Yamamoto or Mr. Tanaka will
    sensee _____ kimasu.   come.

13. Ookii desu _____.   It's large, isn't it!

14. Ookii desu _____.   It's large, you know.

15. Kore _____ kau n desu.   I'm going to buy this!

16. Kore _____ hoo _____ ii deshoo.   This one is probably better.

17. Kono hoo _____ ii _____ omoimasu.   I think this is better.

18. Amerika no jidoosha _____ Nihon   American cars are larger than Japanese
    no jidoosha _____ ookii desu   ones!
    _____.

19. Kore _____ nagai no _____ ari-   Is there a longer one than this?
    masu ka?

20. Jiroo-san _____ Yukio-san _____   Both Jiro and Yukio said that chocolates
    okashi _____ chokoreeto no hoo   would be better than cakes.
    _____ ii _____ iimashita.

E. Tell (ask) your friend:

1. whether the school is near or far away.
2. that you don't know whether the office (company) is near or far.
3. that you can't tell whether it's a bus or an automobile.
4. that you don't know whether Yukio will do it or whether Jiro will do it.
5. that either Yukio or Jiro will probably do it.
6. that it's either a pencil or a ballpoint pen.
7. which is more expensive, this book or that book.
8. which (of three things) he thinks is a good one.
9. which (of the two) is fresher.
10. that the subway is faster than the electric train.

F. Listen to the following conversation, then answer the questions which follow.

Tanaka-san: Kono uchi wa doo omoimasu ka?
Yamada-san: Atarashii uchi de wa arimasen ga, ookii desu ne.
Tanaka-san: Gakkoo ni mo chikai deshoo?
Yamada-san: Ee. Chikai to omoimasu. Basu mo chikaku o toorimasu.
Tanaka-san: Ue no heya wa semai desu ne.
Yamada-san: Shita no heya yori semai desu ga...
Tanaka-san: Watakushi no ima no uchi yori ii desu ne.
Yamada-san: Sore wa wakarimasen ne.
Tanaka-san: Kaimasu yo.

1. Tanaka-san wa dare to imasu ka?
2. Nani o mimashita ka?
3. Dare ga uchi o kau n desu ka?

4. Chiisai uchi desu ka?
5. Kono uchi o kau deshoo ka?
6. Tanaka-san no ima no uchi wa kono uchi yori ii desu ka?
7. Kono uchi wa doko ni chikai desu ka?
8. Densha ga chikaku o toorimasu ka?
9. Ue no heya to shita no heya to dotchi no hoo ga hiroi desu ka?
10. Atarashii uchi desu ne.

Yukio-san no otoosan wa kyoo Kyooto kara kaerimasu. Kyooto kara Tookyoo made sonna ni tooku arimasen. Shinkansen de sanjikan gurai kakarimasu. Mae hodo kakarimasen. Mae wa roku-shichijikan kakarimashita.	Yukio's father will return from Kyoto to-day. It isn't so far from Kyoto to Tokyo. It takes about three hours by the Shinkansen ("the new trunk line"). It doesn't take as long as before. Before, it took six or seven hours.

GRAMMAR

II-2.1 Verbal adjectives (-ku arimasen, -ku nai desu endings)

The semi-formal negative of the verbal adjective form ends with -ku arimasen. This -ku arimasen ending follows the stem of the verbal adjective, that is, the verbal adjective without the final "i". For example, the stem of ookii is ooki-, the stem of chiisai is chiisa-, etc. The -ku arimasen form has the meaning "is not _____."

EXAMPLES:

Positive	Negative	Meaning of negative form
Chiisai desu.	Chiisaku arimasen.	It isn't small.
Ookii desu.	Ookiku arimasen.	It isn't large.
Furui desu.	Furuku arimasen.	It isn't old.
Tooi desu.	Tooku arimasen.	It isn't far.

There is an alternate semi-formal negative for the verbal adjective form. This is the ending -ku nai desu, which also follows the stem of the verbal adjective. Stem plus -ku nai, without the desu, is the informal negative.

EXAMPLES:

Positive		Negative	
Informal	Semi-formal	Informal	Semi-formal
Chiisai.	Chiisai desu.	Chiisaku nai.	Chiisaku nai desu.
Ookii.	Ookii desu.	Ookiku nai.	Ookiku nai desu.
Furui.	Furui desu.	Furuku nai.	Furuku nai desu.
Tooi.	Tooi desu.	Tooku nai.	Tooku nai desu.

II-2.2 Hodo

The construction A wa B hodo . . . means that "A is not _____ to the extent that B is" or "A is not as _____ as B." The predicate is usually negative.

EXAMPLES:

Jidoosha wa hikooki hodo takaku arimasen.	Cars are not as expensive as planes.
Nagoya wa Kyooto hodo Tookyoo kara tooku arimasen.	Nagoya is not as far from Tokyo as Kyoto.

99

Compare the following:

Sore hodo kakaru deshoo.	It probably costs about that [much].
	(It probably costs to that extent.)
Sono gurai kakaru deshoo.	It probably costs about that.

II-2.3 Particle kara
The particle kara occurs after a noun with the meaning "from." It occurs with both spatial and temporal meanings of "from."

EXAMPLES:

Kyooto kara kaerimasu.	He will return from Kyoto.
Basu no naka kara mimashita.	I saw him from (inside) the bus.
Gakkoo kara tooi desu.	It's far from the school.
Hachiji kara benkyoo shimasu.	I study from eight o'clock.
Kyoo kara ikimasu.	I'm going from today on.

II-2.4 Made
The particle made follows a noun and has the meaning "as far as _____" or "up to (and including) _____." It occurs with both a spatial and temporal meaning.

EXAMPLES:

Oosaka made ikimashoo.	Let's go as far as Ōsaka.
Yuubinkyoku made tooi desu ka?	Is it far to the post office?
Ashita made kakarimasu.	It'll take until tomorrow.

Made also occurs after a non-past verb with the same "until" meaning.

EXAMPLES:

Tanaka-san ga kuru made machimasu.	I'll wait until Mr. Tanaka comes.
Kiku made wakarimasen.	I won't know until I ask.

The particle made after a noun also occurs with the meaning "even (including)."

EXAMPLES:

Sensee made wakarimasen.	(No one understands.) Even the teacher doesn't understand.
Yukio-san made kimashita.	(Everyone came.) Even Yukio came.

II-2.5 Konna, sonna, anna, donna
The konna, sonna series modifies nouns.

EXAMPLES:

konna hon	this kind of book
sonna hon	that kind of book
	such a book
anna hon	that kind of book
donna hon	what kind of book

Members of the konna, sonna series plus ni are modifiers of verbs or verbal adjectives, with the meaning "this much," "that much," etc.

EXAMPLES:

Sonna ni tabemashita ka?	Did he eat that much?
Sonna ni ookii desu ka?	Is it so big?
Anna ni benkyoo shimasu.	He studies that much (seeing him studying).

II-2.6 Particle mo

The particle mo after a number (with or without a counter) has the meaning "as many (long, etc.) as _____."

EXAMPLES:

| Gojikan mo kakarimashita. | It took as long as five hours. |
| Gojuuen mo shimasu. | It costs as much as fifty yen. |

DRILLS

1. Repetition

Kyooto kara kaerimashita.	He returned from Kyoto.
Koobe kara kaerimashita.	He returned from Kobe.
Nagoya kara kaerimashita.	He returned from Nagoya.
Nagasaki kara kaerimashita.	He returned from Nagasaki.
Oosaka kara kaerimashita.	He returned from Osaka.
Tookyoo kara kaerimashita.	He returned from Tokyo.
Hiroshima kara kaerimashita.	He returned from Hiroshima.
Yokohama kara kaerimashita.	He returned from Yokohama.
Hakone kara kaerimashita.	He returned from Hakone.
Sapporo kara kaerimashita.	He returned from Sapporo.

2. Substitution

| Koobe kara kisha de kaerimashita. | He returned from Kobe by train. |

(hikooki)	Koobe kara hikooki de kaerimashita.	He returned from Kobe by plane.
(fune)	Koobe kara fune de kaerimashita.	He returned from Kobe by boat.
(basu)	Koobe kara basu de kaerimashita.	He returned from Kobe by bus.
(jidoosha)	Koobe kara jidoosha de kaerimashita.	He returned from Kobe by automobile.
(kuruma)	Kobbe kara kuruma de kaerimashita.	He returned from Kobe by car.

3. Substitution

| Sensee to Oosaka kara kimashita. | He came from Osaka with the teacher. |

| (Yokohama) | Sensee to Yokohama kara kimashita. | He came from Yokohama with the teacher. |
| (Hakone) | Sensee to Hakone kara kimashita. | He came from Hakone with the teacher. |

(Sapporo)	Sensee to Sapporo kara kimashita.	He came from Sapporo with the teacher.
(Tookyoo)	Sensee to Tookyoo kara kimashita.	He came from Tokyo with the teacher.

4. Substitution

Nagoya made ikimashita.   He went as far as Nagoya.

(Kyooto)	Kyooto made ikimashita.	He went as far as Kyoto.
(Koobe)	Koobe made ikimashita.	He went as far as Kobe
(Nagasaki)	Nagasaki made ikimashita.	He went as far as Nagasaki.
(Oosaka)	Oosaka made ikimashita.	He went as far as Ōsaka.
(Hiroshi-ma)	Hiroshima made ikimashita.	He went as far as Hiroshima.
(Yokohama)	Yokohama made ikimashita.	He went as far as Yokohama.
(Hakone)	Hakone made ikimashita.	He went as far as Hakone.
(Sapporo)	Sapporo made ikimashita.	He went as far as Sapporo.
(Tookyoo)	Tookyoo made ikimashita.	He went as far as Tokyo.

5. Repetition

Tookyoo kara Yokohama made jidoosha de ikimashita.	He went from Tokyo to Yokohama by auto-mobile.
Yokohama kara Hakone made basu de ikimashita.	He went from Yokohama to Hakone by bus.
Hakone kara Nagoya made kisha de ikimashita.	He went from Hakone to Nagoya by train.
Nagoya kara Kyooto made kisha de ikimashita.	He went from Nagoya to Kyoto by train.
Kyooto kara Oosaka made kuruma de ikimashita.	He went from Kyoto to Ōsaka by car.
Oosaka kara Koobe made fune de ikimashita.	He went from Ōsaka to Kobe by boat.
Koobe kara Hiroshima made kisha de ikimashita.	He went from Kobe to Hiroshima by train.
Hiroshima kara Nagasaki made kuruma de ikimashita.	He went from Hiroshima to Nagasaki by car.

6. Response

Tookyoo kara Yokohama made jidoosha de ikimashita.	He went from Tokyo to Yokohama by auto-mobile.
(a) Q. Nan de ikimashita ka?	How did he go?
A. Jidoosha de ikimashita.	He went by automobile.
(b) Q. Doko made ikimashita ka?	How far did he go?
A. Yokohama made ikimashita.	He went as far as Yokohama.

(c) Q. Doko kara doko made ikimashita   From where to where did he go?
        ka?

    A. Tookyoo kara Yokohama made   He went from Tokyo as far as Yokohama.
        ikimashita.

(Use statements in Drill 5 above.)

7. Repetition

Ookiku arimasen.	It's not large.
Chiisaku arimasen.	It's not small.
Nagaku arimasen.	It's not long.
Mijikaku arimasen.	It's not short.
Takaku arimasen.	It's not expensive.
Yasuku arimasen.	It's not cheap.
Hikuku arimasen.	It's not low.
Atarashiku arimasen.	It's not new.
Furuku arimasen.	It's not old.
Chikaku arimasen.	It's not near by.
Hayaku arimasen.	It's not early.
Yoku arimasen.	It's not good.
Waruku arimasen.	It's not bad.
Hiroku arimasen.	It's not spacious.
Semaku arimasen.	It's not narrow.
Osoku arimasen.	It's not late.
Tooku arimasen.	It's not far.

8. Negative Response

Q. Ookii desu ka?   Is it large?
A. Iie. Ookiku arimasen.   No, it isn't large.

(Chiisai desu ka?)	(Is it small?)
Iie. Chiisaku arimasen.	No, it isn't small.
(Nagai desu ka?)	(Is it long?)
Iie. Nagaku arimasen.	No, it isn't long.
(Mijikai desu ka?)	(Is it short?)
Iie. Mijikaku arimasen.	No, it isn't short.
(Ii desu ka?)	(Is it good?)
Iie. Yoku arimasen.	No, it isn't good.
(Warui desu ka?)	(Is it bad?)
Iie. Waruku arimasen.	No, it isn't bad.
(Hiroi desu ka?)	(Is it spacious?)
Iie. Hiroku arimasen.	No, it isn't spacious.
(Semai desu ka?)	(Is it narrow?)
Iie. Semaku arimasen.	No, it isn't narrow.
(Takai desu ka?)	(Is it expensive?)
Iie. Takaku arimasen.	No, it isn't expensive.
(Yasui desu ka?)	(Is it cheap?)
Iie. Yasuku arimasen.	No, it isn't cheap.

(Hikui desu ka?)	(Is it low?)
Iie. Hikuku arimasen.	No, it isn't low.
(Atarashii desu ka?)	(Is it new?)
Iie. Atarashiku arimasen.	No, it isn't new.
(Furui desu ka?)	(Is it old?)
Iie. Furuku arimasen.	No, it isn't old.
(Chikai desu ka?)	(Is it near?)
Iie. Chikaku arimasen.	No, it isn't near.
(Hayai desu ka?)	(Is it early?)
Iie. Hayaku arimasen.	No, it isn't early.
(Osoi desu ka?)	(Is it late?)
Iie. Osoku arimasen.	No, it isn't late.
(Tooi desu ka?)	(Is it far?)
Iie. Tooku arimasen.	No, it isn't far.

9.   Negative Response

Q. Sono empitsu wa takai desu ka?	Is that pencil expensive?
A. Iie. Kore wa takaku arimasen.	No, this isn't expensive.

(Sono tsukue wa hikui desu ka?)	(Is that desk low?)
Iie. Kore wa hikuku arimasen.	No, this isn't low.
(Sono tokee wa yasui desu ka?)	(Is that clock inexpensive?)
Iie. Kore wa yasuku arimasen.	No, this isn't inexpensive.
(Sono hako wa nagai desu ka?)	(Is that box long?)
Iie. Kore wa nagaku arimasen.	No, this isn't long.
(Sono booru pen wa mijikai desu ka?)	(Is that ballpoint pen short?)
Iie. Kore wa mijikaku arimasen.	No, this isn't short.
(Sono chokoreeto wa furui desu ka?)	(Is that chocolate old?)
Iie. Kore wa furuku arimasen.	No, this isn't old.
(Sono pan wa atarashii desu ka?)	(Is that bread fresh?)
Iie. Kore wa atarashiku arimasen.	No, this isn't fresh.
(Sono uchi wa ookii desu ka?)	(Is that house large?)
Iie. Kore wa ookiku arimasen.	No, this isn't large.
(Sono kokuban wa chiisai desu ka?)	(Is that blackboard small?)
Iie. Kore wa chiisaku arimasen.	No, this isn't small.

10.   Grammar

(Kono machi wa ookiku arimasen.)	Kono machi wa ookiku nai desu.	This town isn't large.
(Kono hako wa chiisaku arimasen.)	Kono hako wa chiisaku nai desu.	This box isn't small.
(Kono isu wa hikuku arimasen.)	Kono isu wa hikuku nai desu.	This chair isn't low.
(Kono tsukue wa takaku arimasen.)	Kono tsukue wa takaku nai desu.	This desk isn't high.
(Kono tokee wa yasuku arimasen.)	Kono tokee wa yasuku nai desu.	This clock isn't inexpensive.
(Sono omise wa chikaku arimasen.)	Sono omise wa chikaku nai desu.	That store isn't near by.

(Sono uchi wa furuku arimasen.)	Sono uchi wa furuku nai desu.	That house isn't old.
(Sono pan wa atarashiku arimasen.)	Sono pan wa atarashiku nai desu.	That bread isn't fresh.
(Sono kisha wa osoku arimasen.)	Sono kisha wa osoku nai desu.	That train isn't slow.
(Sono gakkoo wa tooku arimasen.)	Sono gakkoo wa tooku nai desu.	That school isn't far.

11. Negative Response

Q. Sore wa takai empitsu desu ka?   Is that an expensive pencil?
A. Iie. Takai empitsu de wa arimasen. No, it isn't an expensive pencil.

(Sore wa yasui tokee desu ka?)   (Is that an inexpensive clock?)
 Iie. Yasui tokee de wa arimasen.   No, it isn't an inexpensive clock.
(Sore wa atarashii jidoosha desu ka?)   (Is that a new car?)
 Iie. Atarashii jidoosha de wa arima-   No, it isn't a new car.
sen.
(Sore wa furui hon desu ka?)   (Is that an old book?)
 Iie. Furui hon de wa arimasen.   No, it isn't an old book.
(Sore wa ookii uchi desu ka?)   (Is that a large house?)
 Iie. Ookii uchi de wa arimasen.   No, it isn't a large house.
(Sore wa chiisai machi desu ka?)   (Is that a small town?)
 Iie. Chiisai machi de wa arimasen.   No, it isn't a small town.
(Sore wa hayai kisha desu ka?)   (Is that a fast train?)
 Iie. Hayai kisha de wa arimasen.   No, it isn't a fast train.
(Sore wa osoi kisha desu ka?)   (Is that a slow train?)
 Iie. Osoi kisha de wa arimasen.   No, it isn't a slow train.
(Sore wa mijikai booru pen desu ka?)   (Is that a short ballpoint pen?)
 Iie. Mijikai booru pen de wa arima-   No, it isn't a short ballpoint pen.
sen.
(Sore wa nagai tsukue desu ka?)   (Is that a long desk?)
 Iie. Nagai tsukue de wa arimasen.   No, it isn't a long desk.

12. Grammar

(Nagoya kara Kyooto made sonna ni tooku nai desu.)	Nagoya kara Kyooto made sonna ni tooku arimasen.	It isn't so far from Nagoya to Kyoto.
(Tookyoo kara Nagoya made sonna ni tooku nai desu.)	Tookyoo kara Nagoya made sonna ni tooku arimasen.	It isn't so far from Tokyo to Nagoya.
(Koobe kara Nagoya made sonna ni tooku nai desu.)	Koobe kara Nagoya made sonna ni tooku arimasen.	It isn't so far from Kobe to Nagoya.
(Nagasaki kara Hiroshima made sonna ni tooku nai desu.)	Nagasaki kara Hiroshima made sonna ni tooku arimasen.	It isn't so far from Nagasaki to Hiro-shima.
(Hiroshima kara Koobe made sonna ni tooku nai desu.)	Hiroshima kara Koobe made sonna ni tooku arimasen.	It isn't so far from Hiroshima to Kobe.
(Tookyoo kara Oosaka made sonna ni tooku nai desu.)	Tookyoo kara Oosaka made sonna ni tooku arimasen.	It isn't so far from Tokyo to Osaka.

13. Substitution

Ichijikan kakarimasu.   It takes an hour.

(nijikan)   Nijikan kakarimasu.   It takes two hours.
(sanjikan)   Sanjikan kakarimasu.   It takes three hours.
(yojikan)   Yojikan kakarimasu.   It takes four hours.
(gojikan)   Gojikan kakarimasu.   It takes five hours.
(rokujikan)   Rokujikan kakarimasu.   It takes six hours.
(shichijikan)   Shichijikan kakarimasu.   It takes seven hours.
(hachijikan)   Hachijikan kakarimasu.   It takes eight hours.
(kujikan)   Kujikan kakarimasu.   It takes nine hours.
(juujikan)   Juujikan kakarimasu.   It takes ten hours.
(juu-ichijikan)   Juu-ichijikan kakarimasu.   It takes eleven hours.
(juu-nijikan)   Juu-nijikan kakarimasu.   It takes twelve hours.
(juu-sanjikan)   Juu-sanjikan kakarimasu.   It takes thirteen hours.
(juu-yojikan)   Juu-yojikan kakarimasu.   It takes fourteen hours.
(juu-gojikan)   Juu-gojikan kakarimasu.   It takes fifteen hours.
(nijuujikan)   Nijuujikan kakarimasu.   It takes twenty hours.

14. Negative Response

Q. Ichijikan kakarimasu ka?   Does it take an hour?
A. Iie. Ichijikan-han kakarimasu.   No, it takes an hour and a half.

(nijikan)   Nijikan kakarimasu ka?   Does it take two hours?
                     Iie. Nijikan-han kakari-   No, it takes two and a half hours.
                     masu.
(sanjikan)   Sanjikan kakarimasu ka?   Does it take three hours?
                     Iie. Sanjikan-han kakari-   No, it takes three and a half hours.
                     masu.
(yojikan)   Yojikan kakarimasu ka?   Does it take four hours?
                     Iie. Yojikan-han kakari-   No, it takes four and a half hours.
                     masu.
(gojikan)   Gojikan kakarimasu ka?   Does it take five hours?
                     Iie. Gojikan-han kakari-   No, it takes five and a half hours.
                     masu.
(rokujikan)   Rokujikan kakarimasu ka?   Does it take six hours?
                     Iie. Rokujikan-han kaka-   No, it takes six and a half hours.
                     rimasu.
(shichijikan)   Shichijikan kakarimasu ka?   Does it take seven hours?
                     Iie. Shichijikan-han kaka-   No, it takes seven and a half hours.
                     rimasu.
(hachijikan)   Hachijikan kakarimasu ka?   Does it take eight hours?
                     Iie. Hachijikan-han kaka-   No, it takes eight and a half hours.
                     rimasu.
(kujikan)   Kujikan kakarimasu ka?   Does it take nine hours?
                     Iie. Kujikan-han kakari-   No, it takes nine and a half hours.
                     masu.
(juujikan)   Juujikan kakarimasu ka?   Does it take ten hours?
                     Iie. Juujikan-han kakari-   No, it takes ten and a half hours.
                     masu.

15. Substitution

Mae wa gojikan mo kakarimashita.   It used to take as many as five
                                                    hours before.

(rokujikan)   Mae wa rokujikan mo kakari-   It used to take as many as six
                      mashita.   hours before.
(kujikan)   Mae wa kujikan mo kakari-   It used to take as many as nine
                      mashita.   hours before.
(juu-nijikan)   Mae wa juu-nijikan mo kakari-   It used to take as many as
                      mashita.   twelve hours before.
(nijuujikan)   Mae wa nijuujikan mo kakari-   It used to take as many as
                      mashita.   twenty hours before.

16. Negative Response

(Tookyoo kara Yokohama made ichijikan   (Does it take an hour from Tokyo to Yoko-
    kakarimasu ka?)   hama?)
  Iie. Ichijikan mo kakarimasen.   No, it doesn't take as long as an hour.
(Oosaka kara Kyooto made nijikan kaka-   (Does it take two hours from Osaka to
    rimasu ka?)   Kyooto?)
  Iie. Nijikan mo kakarimasen.   No, it doesn't take as long as two
                                               hours.

(Nagoya kara Oosaka made sanjikan ka-   (Does it take three hours from Nagoya to
    karimasu ka?)   Osaka?)
  Iie. Sanjikan mo kakarimasen.   No, it doesn't take as long as three
                                               hours.

(Tookyoo kara Oosaka made yojikan ka-   (Does it take four hours from Tokyo to
    karimasu ka?)   Osaka?)
  Iie. Yojikan mo kakarimasen.   No, it doesn't take as long as four
                                               hours.

(Tookyoo kara Koobe made gojikan ka-   (Does it take five hours from Tokyo to
    karimasu ka?)   Kobe?)
  Iie. Gojikan mo kakarimasen.   No, it doesn't take as long as five
                                               hours.

(Nagasaki kara Hiroshima made nijuu-   (Does it take twenty hours from Nagasaki
    jikan kakarimasu ka?)   to Hiroshima?)
  Iie. Nijuujikan mo kakarimasen.   No, it doesn't take as long as twenty
                                               hours.

17. Expansion

(nijikan gurai   Nijikan gurai kakarimasu.   It takes about two hours.
    kakarimasu)
(hikooki de)   Hikooki de nijikan gurai   It takes about two hours by
                      kakarimasu.   plane.
(Sapporo made)   Sapporo made hikooki de   It takes about two hours by
                      nijikan gurai kakarimasu.   plane to Sapporo.
(Tookyoo kara)   Tookyoo kara Sapporo made   It takes about two hours by
                      hikooki de nijikan gurai   plane from Tokyo to Sapporo.
                      kakarimasu.

(sanjippun gurai kakarimasu)	Sanjippun gurai kakarimasu.	It takes about thirty minutes.
(densha de)	Densha de sanjippun gurai kakarimasu.	It takes about thirty minutes by electric train.
(Yokohama made)	Yokohama made densha de sanjippun gurai kakarimasu.	It takes about thirty minutes to Yokohama by electric train.
(Tookyoo kara)	Tookyoo kara Yokohama made densha de sanjippun gurai kakarimasu.	It takes about thirty minutes from Tokyo to Yokohama by electric train.
(sanjikan gurai kakarimasu)	Sanjikan gurai kakarimasu.	It takes about three hours.
(Shinkansen de)	Shinkansen de sanjikan gurai kakarimasu.	It takes about three hours by the Shinkansen.
(Oosaka made)	Oosaka made Shinkansen de sanjikan gurai kakarimasu.	It takes about three hours to Osaka by the Shinkansen.
(Tookyoo kara)	Tookyoo kara Oosaka made Shinkansen de sanjikan gurai kakarimasu.	It takes about three hours from Tokyo to Osaka by the Shinkansen.
(nijikan-han gurai kakarimasu)	Nijikan-han gurai kakarimasu.	It takes about two and a half hours.
(Shinkansen de)	Shinkansen de nijikan-han gurai kakarimasu.	It takes about two and a half hours by the Shinkansen.
(Kyooto made)	Kyooto made Shinkansen de nijikan-han gurai kakarimasu.	It takes about two and a half hours to Kyoto by the Shinkansen.
(Tookyoo kara)	Tookyoo kara Kyooto made Shinkansen de nijikan-han gurai kakarimasu.	It takes about two and a half hours from Tokyo to Kyoto by the Shinkansen.
(nijikan gurai kakarimasu)	Nijikan gurai kakarimasu.	**It takes** about two hours.
(Shinkansen de)	Shinkansen de nijikan gurai kakarimasu.	It takes about two hours by the Shinkansen.
(Nagoya made)	Nagoya made Shinkansen de nijikan gurai kakarimasu.	It takes about two hours to Nagoya by the Shinkansen.
(Tookyoo kara)	Tookyoo kara Nagoya made Shinkansen de nijikan gurai kakarimasu.	It takes about two hours from Tokyo to Nagoya by the Shinkansen.

18. Factual Response

(Tookyoo, Nagoya)	Q. Tookyoo kara Nagoya made Shinkansen de dono gurai kakarimasu ka?	About how long does it take from Tokyo to Nagoya by the Shinkansen?
	A. _____ gurai kakarimasu.	It takes about _____.
(Tookyoo, Kyooto)	Tookyoo kara Kyooto made Shinkansen de dono gurai kakarimasu ka?	About how long does it take from Tokyo to Kyoto by the Shinkansen?

(Nagoya, Kyooto)	Nagoya kara Kyooto made Shinkansen de dono gurai kakarimasu ka?	About how long does it take from Nagoya to Kyoto by the Shin- kansen?
(Kyooto, Oosaka)	Kyooto kara Oosaka made Shinkansen de dono gurai kakarimasu ka?	About how long does it take from Kyoto to Osaka by the Shinkan- sen?
(Tookyoo, Oosaka)	Tookyoo kara Oosaka made Shinkansen de dono gurai kakarimasu ka?	About how long does it take from Tokyo to Osaka by the Shinkan- sen?

19. Negative Response

Q. Ichijikan-han kakarimashita ka?   Did it take an hour and a half?
A. Iie. Sonna ni kakarimasen deshita.   No, it didn't take that long.

(nijikan-han)	Nijikan-han kakarimashita ka?	Did it take two and a half hours?
(sanjikan-han)	Sanjikan-han kakarimashita ka?	Did it take three and a half hours?
(yojikan-han)	Yojikan-han kakarimashita ka?	Did it take four and a half hours?
(gojikan-han)	Gojikan-han kakarimashita ka?	Did it take five and a half hours?
(rokujikan-han)	Rokujikan-han kakarimashita ka?	Did it take six and a half hours?
(shichijikan-han)	Shichijikan-han kakarima- shita ka?	Did it take seven and a half hours?

20. Response

Q. Dono gurai ookii desu ka?   How large is it?
A. Konna ni ookii desu.   It's this large.

(chiisai)	Dono gurai chiisai desu ka? Konna ni chiisai desu.	How small is it? It's this small.
(furui)	Dono gurai furui desu ka? Konna ni furui desu.	How old is it? It's this old.
(takai)	Dono gurai takai desu ka? Konna ni takai desu.	How expensive is it? It's this expensive.
(nagai)	Dono gurai nagai desu ka? Konna ni nagai desu.	How long is it? It's this long.
(semai)	Dono gurai semai desu ka? Konna ni semai desu.	How narrow is it? It's this narrow.

21. Substitution

Anna ni benkyoo suru to wa omoimasen   I didn't think he would study
  deshita.   that much.

(kau)	Anna ni kau to wa omoimasen deshita.	I didn't think he would buy that much.
(taberu)	Anna ni taberu to wa omoimasen deshita.	I didn't think he would eat that much.
(dasu)	Anna ni dasu to wa omoimasen deshita.	I didn't think he would serve that much.
(kakaru)	Anna ni kakaru to wa omoimasen deshita.	I didn't think it would cost that much.
(chigau)	Anna ni chigau to wa omoimasen deshita.	I didn't think it would differ that much.

22. Substitution

Donna tokoro ka shirimasen.		I don't know what kind of place it is.
(mono)	Donna mono ka shirimasen.	I don't know what kind of thing it is.
(no)	Donna no ka shirimasen.	I don't know what kind of thing it is.
(hito)	Donna hito ka shirimasen.	I don't know what kind of person he is.
(kisha)	Donna kisha ka shirimasen.	I don't know what kind of train it is.

23. Progressive Substitution

Donna mono ga ii desu ka?		What kind of thing is good? What kind of thing would you like?
(konna)	Konna mono ga ii desu ka?	Is this kind of thing good?
(terebi)	Konna terebi ga ii desu ka?	Is this kind of television [set] good?
(sonna)	Sonna terebi ga ii desu ka?	Is that kind of television [set] good?
(kuruma)	Sonna kuruma ga ii desu ka?	Is that kind of car good?
(anna)	Anna kuruma ga ii desu ka?	Is a car like that one over there good?
(kaisha)	Anna kaisha ga ii desu ka?	Is a company like that good?
(donna)	Donna kaisha ga ii desu ka?	What kind of company is good?
(mono)	Donna mono ga ii desu ka?	What kind of thing is good?

24. Substitution

Okaasan wa otoosan hodo tabemasen.		My mother doesn't eat as much as my father.
(ookiku arimasen)	Okaasan wa otoosan hodo ookiku arimasen.	My mother isn't as big as my father.
(hanashimasen)	Okaasan wa otoosan hodo hanashimasen.	My mother doesn't talk as much as my father.
(takaku arimasen)	Okaasan wa otoosan hodo takaku arimasen.	My mother isn't as tall as my father.
(dekakemasen)	Okaasan wa otoosan hodo dekakemasen.	My mother doesn't go out as much as my father.
(hayaku arimasen)	Okaasan wa otoosan hodo hayaku arimasen.	My mother isn't as fast as my father.

25. Factual Response (using objects)

Q. Onaji desu ka?   Are they the same?
A. Ee. Onaji desu.   Yes, they're the same.
A. Iie. Onaji de wa arimasen.   No, they're not the same.

26. Factual Response

Q. Uchi mo jidoosha mo takai desu ka?   Are both houses and cars expensive?
A. Ee. Uchi mo jidoosha mo takai   Yes, both houses and cars are expensive,
      desu ga, jidoosha wa uchi hodo   but cars are not as expensive as
      takaku arimasen.   houses.

(Rajio mo terebi mo takai desu ka?)   (Are both radios and television [sets]
                                              expensive?)
  Ee. Rajio mo terebi mo takai desu   Yes, both radios and television [sets]
    ga, rajio wa terebi hodo takaku   are expensive, but radios are not as
    arimasen.   expensive as television [sets].
(Hiroshima mo Nagasaki mo Tookyoo   (Are both Hiroshima and Nagasaki far from
    kara tooi desu ka?)   Tokyo?)
  Ee. Hiroshima mo Nagasaki mo Tookyoo   Yes, both Hiroshima and Nagasaki are far
    kara tooi desu ga, Hiroshima wa Na-   from Tokyo, but Hiroshima is not as far
    gasaki hodo tooku arimasen.   as Nagasaki.
(Gozen rokuji mo shichiji mo hayai   (Are both 6 a.m. and 7 a.m. early?)
    desu ka?)
  Ee. Gozen rokuji mo shichiji mo   Yes, both 6 a.m. and 7 a.m. are early,
    hayai desu ga, shichiji wa rokuji   but 7 a.m. is not as early as 6 a.m.
    hodo hayaku arimasen.
(Hachijikan mo kujikan mo nagai desu   (Are both eight hours and nine hours
    ka?)   long?)
  Ee. Hachijikan mo kujikan mo nagai   Yes, both eight hours and nine hours are
    desu ga, hachijikan wa kujikan   long, but eight hours is not as long
    hodo nagaku arimasen.   as nine hours.
(Tookyoo mo Oosaka mo ookii desu ka?)   (Are both Tokyo and Osaka big?)
  Ee. Tookyoo mo Oosaka mo ookii desu   Yes, both Tokyo and Osaka are big, but
    ga, Oosaka wa Tookyoo hodo ookiku   Osaka is not as big as Tokyo.
    arimasen.

(Continue, using objects.)

27. Progressive Substitution

Otoosan made shirimasen deshita.   Even Father didn't know.

(sensee)   Sensee made shirimasen deshita.   Even the teacher didn't know.
(kimasen   Sensee made kimasen deshita.   Even the teacher didn't come.
  deshita)
(ano hito)   Ano hito made kimasen deshita.   Even that person didn't come.
(kikimasen   Ano hito made kikimasen deshita.   Even that person didn't ask.
  deshita)

(otoosan)   Otoosan made kikimasen deshita.   Even Father didn't ask.
(shirimasen   Otoosan made shirimasen deshita.   Even Father didn't know.
  deshita)

28. Substitution

Ashita made kakarimasu.   It will take through tomorrow.

(machimasu)   Ashita made machimasu.   I'll wait through tomorrow.
(yasumimasu)   Ashita made yasumimasu.   I'll take a holiday through
                                                         tomorrow.
(benkyoo   Ashita made benkyoo shimasu.   I'll study through tomorrow.
  shimasu)
(imasu)   Ashita made imasu.   He'll be there through tomor-
                                                         row.
(arimasu)   Ashita made arimasu.   It'll be there through tomor-
                                                         row.

CULTURAL NOTE

1. The Shinkansen or New Trunk Line runs on special tracks between Tokyo Station
in Tokyo and the Shin-Osaka station, Osaka. This train makes only two or three
stops en route. It was inaugurated in 1964.

EXERCISES

A. Give the negatives of the following. (two possibilities for each)

 1. Ookii desu.
 2. Nagai desu.
 3. Tooi desu.
 4. Chikai desu.
 5. Chiisai desu.
 6. Mijikai desu.
 7. Atarashii desu.
 8. Takai desu.
 9. Furui desu.
10. Yasui desu.
11. Hikui desu.
12. Osoi desu.
13. Hayai desu.
14. Ii desu.
15. Warui desu.
16. Hiroi desu.
17. Semai desu.

B. Supply the missing particles.

1. Oosaka _____ Kyooto _____ nan   How shall we go from Ōsaka to Kyōto?
        _____ ikimashoo ka?
2. Shinkansen _____ dono gurai ka-   How long does it take by the Shinkansen?
        karimasu ka?
3. Sanjippun _____ ikimashita.   We got there in thirty minutes.
4. Densha _____ hoo _____ hayai _____   I heard that the electric train is fas-
        kikimashita.   ter.
5. Ashita _____ benkyoo shimasu.   I'll start studying from tomorrow.
6. Hachijikan _____ kakaru _____   Do you think it will take as many as
        omoimasu ka?   eight hours?
7. Ashita _____ machimashoo.   Let's wait through tomorrow.
8. Tanaka-san wa Hakone _____ ki-   Mr. Tanaka came from Hakone.
        mashita.
9. Hakone _____ Tanaka-san ga ki-   The Mr. Tanaka from Hakone came.
        mashita.
10. Kono kisha _____ doko _____ iki-   How far does this train go?
        masu ka?
11. Oosaka _____ _____ kisha desu.   It's a train from Ōsaka (a "from Ōsaka"
                                                 train).
12. Otoosan _____ wakarimasen.   Even Father doesn't understand it.
13. Juujikan _____ kakarimasu.   It takes as many as ten hours.
14. Sonna _____ takaku arimasen.   It isn't so expensive.

C. Select the one which best completes the sentence.

1. (Sonna) (Sonna ni) yoku arimasen.   It isn't so good.
2. (Donna) (Dono) jidoosha o kai-   What kind of car did you buy?
        mashita ka?
3. (Konna) (Konna ni) mono o tabemasu   Do you eat this kind of thing?
        ka?
4. (Konna) (Konna ni) tabemasu ka?   Do you eat this much?
5. (Sonna) (Sonna ni) jidoosha wa   That kind of car isn't good.
        yoku arimasen.
6. (Anna) (Anna ni) arimasu!   There is [all] that!

D. Insert _tokoro_, _mono_, _koto_, or _hito_ in the following blanks.

1. Kyooto wa ii _____ desu.
2. Terebi wa sonna ni takai _____ de wa arimasen.
3. Sumisu-san wa ookii _____ desu.
4. Hayai _____ wa jettoki desu.
5. Amerika no _____ wa shimbun ni demasen deshita.
6. Shimbun wa yasui _____ desu.
7. Tanaka-san hodo hikui _____ de wa arimasen.
8. Nagasaki no _____ wa shirimasen.

E.   Answer the following questions.

1.   Tookyoo kara Oosaka made Shinkansen de dono gurai kakarimasu ka?
2.   Tookyoo kara Nagoya made Shinkansen de dono gurai kakarimasu ka?
3.   Kyooto kara Tookyoo made Shinkansen de dono gurai kakarimasu ka?
4.   Nagoya kara Kyooto made Shinkansen de dono gurai kakarimasu ka?
5.   Kyooto kara Oosaka made Shinkansen de dono gurai kakarimasu ka?
6.   Oosaka kara Nagoya made Shinkansen de dono gurai kakarimasu ka?

F.   Give replies using <u>hoo</u> and <u>hodo</u>.

1.   Hikooki to jettoki to dotchi no hoo ga hayai deshoo ka?
2.   Uchi mo jidoosha mo takai desu ka?
3.   Koobe to Nagasaki to dotchi no hoo ga Tookyoo kara tooi desu ka?
4.   Gogo juu-ichiji to gogo juu-niji to dotchi no hoo ga osoi desu ka?
5.   Depaato to eki to dotchi no hoo ga ookii deshoo ka?
6.   Otoosan to okaasan to dotchi no hoo ga ookii deshoo ka?
7.   Chikatetsu to basu to dotchi no hoo ga hayai deshoo ka?

G.   Listen to the following story, then answer the questions which follow.

     Sumisu-san wa Amerika kara kinoo kimashita. Sonna ni jikan wa kakarimasen
deshita. Jettoki de kujikan gurai de kimashita. Ima Tookyoo no tomodachi no uchi
ni imasu ga, ashita kara Kyooto e iku to kikimashita. Itsu made Kyooto ni iru ka
watakushi wa shirimasen.

1.   Dare ga Amerika kara kimashita ka?
2.   Itsu kimashita ka?
3.   Nan de kimashita ka?
4.   Dono gurai kakarimashita ka?
5.   Jikan wa kakarimashita ka?
6.   Ima doko ni imasu ka?
7.   Ashita mo soko ni iru deshoo ka?
8.   Ashita wa doko kara doko made ikimasu ka?
9.   Sumisu-san wa Kyooto ni dono gurai iru deshoo ka?
10. Sumisu-san wa watakushi ni sono koto o iimashita ka?

Otoosan:	Tadaima.[1]	Father:	Hello.
Yukio, Oka-asan, Oba-asan:	Okaeri nasai.[2]	Yukio, Mother, Grand-mother:	Welcome back!
Obaasan:	Hayakatta desu ne. Kaisha kara wa kaeri wa ashita da to kikimashita ga...	Grandmother:	You're early, aren't you! From the office, we heard you would be returning tomorrow (your return would be tomorrow)...
Otoosan:	Ee. Ichinichi hayaku na-rimashita.	Father:	Yes, it turned out to be a day earlier.

GRAMMAR

II-3.1 Verbal adjective (-katta desu ending)

The stem of the verbal adjective plus -katta desu is the semi-formal perfective of the verbal adjective, with the meaning "was (were) _____." It is the perfective of -i desu. The informal perfective is the ending -katta without the desu.

EXAMPLES:

"is _____"		"was _____"	
Informal	Semi-formal	Informal	Semi-formal
Ookii.	Ookii desu.	Ookikatta.	Ookikatta desu.
Takai.	Takai desu.	Takakatta.	Takakatta desu.
Furui.	Furui desu.	Furukatta.	Furukatta desu.
Tooi.	Tooi desu.	Tookatta.	Tookatta desu.

(Note: There is another semi-formal perfective form in use today, with deshita replacing desu. Example: Ookii deshita.

II-3.2 Verbal adjective (-ku form)

(a) The -ku form, or the stem of the verbal adjective plus the ending -ku, occurs as a modifier of verbs, telling "how" or "under what conditions" an action occurs.

EXAMPLES:

Ookiku kakimashita.	He wrote it large.
Chiisaku shimashoo.	Let's make it small (smaller).
Takaku narimasu.	It'll become expensive.
Hayaku tabemasu.	He eats quickly.
Osoku narimashita.	I am late. (It has become late.)

(b) Verbal adjectives in their -ku form function as nouns. Tooku (tooi) and chikaku (chikai) are examples.

115

EXAMPLES:

Chikaku ni arimasu.	It's near by.
Sono chikaku no omise de kaima- shita.	I bought it in a store near there.
Tooku e ikimashita.	He went to a distant place.

II-3.3 Suffix -sa

The stem of a verbal adjective plus the suffix -sa forms an abstract noun of that verbal adjective.

EXAMPLES:

Ookisa wa shirimasen.	I don't know the size.
Nagasa wa dono gurai desu ka?	About what is the length?

II-3.4 Nominal form of verbs

(a) In first-conjugation verbs, the stem is the nominal form. In second-conjugation verbs, it is the stem plus i* (or the -masu form without the -masu).

EXAMPLES:

Odekake desu.	She's out.
Hanashi* desu.	It's a story.

*Note that the "s" stem ends in "shi" and the "t" stem ends in "chi".

(b) The nominal form of verbs combines with nouns in forming "compound" nouns.

EXAMPLES:

Tabemono ga arimasen.	There isn't any food.
Yomimono o kaimashoo.	Let's buy some reading matter.

II-3.5 Informal non-past positive of the copula

Da is the informal non-past positive of the copula and it occurs after a noun.

EXAMPLES:

Informal	Semi-formal	
Hon da.	Hon desu.	It's a book
Tanaka-san da.	Tanaka-san desu.	It's Mr. Tanaka.

DRILLS

1. Repetition

ichinichi	one day
futsuka	two days
mikka	three days
yokka	four days
itsuka	five days
muika	six days

nanoka	seven days
yooka	eight days
kokonoka	nine days
tooka	ten days
juu-ichinichi	eleven days
juu-ninichi	twelve days
juu-sannichi	thirteen days
juu-yokka	fourteen days
juu-gonichi	fifteen days
hatsuka	twenty days

2. Substitution

Ichinichi imasu.   I'll be here one day.

(futsuka)	Futsuka imasu.	I'll be here two days.
(mikka)	Mikka imasu.	I'll be here three days.
(yokka)	Yokka imasu.	I'll be here four days.
(itsuka)	Itsuka imasu.	I'll be here five days.
(muika)	Muika imasu.	I'll be here six days.
(nanoka)	Nanoka imasu.	I'll be here seven days.
(yooka)	Yooka imasu.	I'll be here eight days.
(kokonoka)	Kokonoka imasu.	I'll be here nine days.
(tooka)	Tooka imasu.	I'll be here ten days.
(juu-ichinichi)	Juu-ichinichi imasu.	I'll be here eleven days.
(juu-ninichi)	Juu-ninichi imasu.	I'll be here twelve days.
(juu-sannichi)	Juu-sannichi imasu.	I'll be here thirteen days.
(juu-yokka)	Juu-yokka imasu.	I'll be here fourteen days.
(juu-gonichi)	Juu-gonichi imasu.	I'll be here fifteen days.
(hatsuka)	Hatsuka imasu.	I'll be here twenty days.

3. Progressive Substitution

Nannichi kakarimashita ka?   How many days did it take?

(futsuka)	Futsuka kakarimashita ka?	Did it take two days?
(yasumimashita)	Futsuka yasumimashita ka?	Did you take a two-day holiday?
(itsuka)	Itsuka yasumimashita ka?	Did you take a five-day holi-day?
(benkyoo shi-masu)	Itsuka benkyoo shimasu ka?	Do you study five days?
(muika)	Muika benkyoo shimasu ka?	Do you study six days?
(asobimasu)	Muika asobimasu ka?	Do you play six days?
(mikka)	Mikka asobimasu ka?	Do you play three days?
(dashimashoo)	Mikka dashimashoo ka?	Shall we put it [in the papers] for three days?
(ichinichi)	Ichinichi dashimashoo ka?	Shall we put it [in the papers] for one day?
(yorimashita)	Ichinichi yorimashita ka?	Did you drop by for one day?
(yokka)	Yokka yorimashita ka?	Did you drop by for four days?
(machimashoo)	Yokka machimashoo ka?	Shall we wait four days?

(hatsuka)   Hatsuka machimashoo ka?   Shall we wait twenty days?
(shimashita)   Hatsuka shimashita ka?   Did you do it for twenty days?
(nannichi)   Nannichi shimashita ka?   How many days did you do it?
(kakarima-   Nannichi kakarimashita ka?   How many days did it take?
  shita)

4. Repetition

isshuukan   one week
nishuukan   two weeks
sanshuukan   three weeks
yonshuukan   four weeks
goshuukan   five weeks
rokushuukan   six weeks
nanashuukan   seven weeks
hasshuukan   eight weeks
kyuushuukan   nine weeks
jisshuukan   ten weeks

5. Substitution

Nanshuukan benkyoo shimashita ka?   How many weeks did you study?

(isshuukan)   Isshuukan benkyoo shimashita ka?   Did you study one week?
(nishuukan)   Nishuukan benkyoo shimashita ka?   Did you study two weeks?
(sanshuukan)   Sanshuukan benkyoo shimashita ka?   Did you study three weeks?
(yonshuukan)   Yonshuukan benkyoo shimashita ka?   Did you study four weeks?
(goshuukan)   Goshuukan benkyoo shimashita ka?   Did you study five weeks?
(rokushuukan)   Rokushuukan benkyoo shimashita   Did you study six weeks?
                    ka?
(nanashuukan)   Nanashuukan benkyoo shimashita   Did you study seven weeks?
                    ka?
(hasshuukan)   Hasshuukan benkyoo shimashita ka?   Did you study eight weeks?

6. Substitution

Hayaku kaerimashoo.   Let's hurry home.

(ikimashoo)   Hayaku ikimashoo.   Let's go quickly.
(kaimashoo)   Hayaku kaimashoo.   Let's buy it quickly.
(okimashoo)   Hayaku okimashoo.   Let's get up early.
(yasumimashoo)   Hayaku yasumimashoo.   Let's get to bed early.
(tabemashoo)   Hayaku tabemashoo.   Let's eat quickly.
(onegai shi-   Hayaku onegai shimashoo.   Let's request it early.
  mashoo)
(kotaemashoo)   Hayaku kotaemashoo.   Let's reply quickly.
(dekakemashoo)   Hayaku dekakemashoo.   Let's start out quickly.
(yomimashoo)   Hayaku yomimashoo.   Let's read quickly.

7. Substitution and Conversation

A. Hayaku kaerimashita ne.   My, you've come home early,
                                               haven't you!

B. Ee. Ichinichi hayaku kaerimashita.   Yes, I've come home one day
                                               earlier.

(futsuka)   Ee. Futsuka hayaku kaerimashita.   Yes, I've come home two days
                                                           earlier.

(mikka)   Ee. Mikka hayaku kaerimashita.   Yes, I've come home three days
                                                           earlier.

(yokka)   Ee. Yokka hayaku kaerimashita.   Yes, I've come home four days
                                                           earlier.

(itsuka)   Ee. Itsuka hayaku kaerimashita.   Yes, I've come home five days
                                                           earlier.

(muika)   Ee. Muika hayaku kaerimashita.   Yes, I've come home six days
                                                           earlier.

(isshuukan)   Ee. Isshuukan hayaku kaerima-   Yes, I've come home one week
                      shita.   earlier.

(nishuukan)   Ee. Nishuukan hayaku kaerima-   Yes, I've come home two weeks
                      shita.   earlier.

(yonshuukan)   Ee. Yonshuukan hayaku kaerima-   Yes, I've come home four weeks
                      shita.   earlier.

8. Substitution

Yoku kakimashita.   He wrote it well.

(yomimashita)   Yoku yomimashita.   He read it well.
(kotaemashita)   Yoku kotaemashita.   He replied well.
(benkyoo shimashita) Yoku benkyoo shimashita.   He studied well.
(shimashita)   Yoku shimashita.   He did it well.

9. Grammar

(Yoofuku o nagaku shimasu.)   (I'll make my dress long.)
 Yoofuku o motto nagaku shimasu.   I'll make my dress longer.
(Yoofuku o mijikaku shimasu.)   (I'll make my dress short.)
 Yoofuku o motto mijikaku shimasu.   I'll make my dress shorter.
(Yoofuku o ookiku shimasu.)   (I'll make my dress large.)
 Yoofuku o motto ookiku shimasu.   I'll make my dress larger.
(Heya o hiroku shimasu.)   (I'll make my room large.)
 Heya o motto hiroku shimasu.   I'll make my room larger.
(Fune o yasuku shimasu.)   (I'll make the boat cheap.)
 Fune o motto yasuku shimasu.   I'll make the boat cheaper.
(Isu o hikuku shimasu.)   (I'll make the chair low.)
 Isu o motto hikuku shimasu.   I'll make the chair lower.
(Uchi o waruku shimasu.)   (They'll spoil the house.)
 Uchi o motto waruku shimasu.   They'll make the house worse.
(Benkyoo o hayaku shimasu.)   (I'll do my studying quickly.)
 Benkyoo o motto hayaku shimasu.   I'll do my studying more quickly.

10. Substitution

Mijikaku narimashita.   It's become short.

(yoku)   Yoku narimashita.   He's become well.
                                                     It's become good.

(waruku)   Waruku narimashita.   It's become bad.
(nagaku)   Nagaku narimashita.   It's become long.
(chiisaku)   Chiisaku narimashita.   It's become small.
(ookiku)   Ookiku narimashita.   It's become large.
(takaku)   Takaku narimashita.   It's become expensive.
(yasuku)   Yasuku narimashita.   It's become inexpensive.
(furuku)   Furuku narimashita.   It's become old.
(hikuku)   Hikuku narimashita.   It's become low.
(osoku)   Osoku narimashita.   It's become late.
                                                     I am late.

(tooku)   Tooku narimashita.   It's become far away.

11. Progressive Substitution

Sono pan wa sukoshi takaku narimashita ne.   That bread has become a little
                                                expensive, hasn't it.

(yasuku)   Sono pan wa sukoshi yasuku nari-   That bread has become a little
                  mashita ne.   cheaper, hasn't it.
(okashi)   Sono okashi wa sukoshi yasuku   Those cakes have become a lit-
                  narimashita ne.   tle cheaper, haven't they.
(furuku)   Sono okashi wa sukoshi furuku   Those cakes have become a lit-
                  narimashita ne.   tle old, haven't they.
(jidoosha)   Sono jidoosha wa sukoshi furuku   That car has become a little
                  narimashita ne.   old, hasn't it.
(waruku)   Sono jidoosha wa sukoshi waruku   That car has become somewhat
                  narimashita ne.   bad, hasn't it.
(uchi)   Sono uchi wa sukoshi waruku na-   That house has become somewhat
                  rimashita ne.   bad, hasn't it.
(ookiku)   Sono uchi wa sukoshi ookiku na-   That house has become a little
                  rimashita ne.   larger, hasn't it.
(toshokan)   Sono toshokan wa sukoshi ookiku   That library has become a lit-
                  narimashita ne.   tle larger, hasn't it.
(furuku)   Sono toshokan wa sukoshi furuku   That library has become a lit-
                  narimashita ne.   tle old, hasn't it.
(hon)   Sono hon wa sukoshi furuku na-   That book has become a little
                  rimashita ne.   old, hasn't it.
(takaku)   Sono hon wa sukoshi takaku na-   That book has become a little
                  rimashita ne.   expensive, hasn't it.
(pan)   Sono pan wa sukoshi takaku na-   That bread has become a little
                  rimashita ne.   expensive, hasn't it.

12. Correlation Substitution

Hon wa takaku narimashita.   Books have become expensive.

(hon o)   Hon o takaku shimashita.   They made books more expensive.
(pan wa)   Pan wa takaku narimashita.   Bread has become expensive.
(pan o)   Pan o takaku shimashita.   They made bread more expensive.
(jidoosha wa) Jidoosha wa takaku narimashita.   Cars have become expensive.
(jidoosha o)   Jidoosha o takaku shimashita.   They made cars more expensive.
(uchi wa)   Uchi wa takaku narimashita.   Houses have become expensive.
(uchi o)   Uchi o takaku shimashita.   They made their house expen-
                                                       sive. (They raised the price
                                                       of their house.)

(zasshi wa)   Zasshi wa takaku narimashita.   Magazines have become expen-
                                                       sive.
(zasshi o)   Zasshi o takaku shimashita.   They made magazines more expen-
                                                       sive.

13. Grammar and Substitution

Nagaku mo mijikaku mo arimasen.   It's neither long nor short.

(ookii,   Ookiku mo chiisaku mo arimasen.   It's neither large nor small.
  chiisai)
(tooi, chikai) Tooku mo chikaku mo arimasen.   It's neither far nor near.
(takai, yasui) Takaku mo yasuku mo arimasen.   It's neither expensive nor in-
                                                       expensive.
(atarashii,   Atarashiku mo furuku mo arimasen.   It's neither new nor old.
  furui)
(hiroi, semai) Hiroku mo semaku mo arimasen.   It's neither wide nor narrow.

14. Substitution

Ookisa wa choodo ii desu.   The size is just right.

(takasa)   Takasa wa choodo ii desu.   The height is just right.
(nagasa)   Nagasa wa choodo ii desu.   The length is just right.
(hayasa)   Hayasa wa choodo ii desu.   The speed is just right.
(hirosa)   Hirosa wa choodo ii desu.   The width is just right.

15. Grammar and Substitution

Ima made yosa ga wakarimasen deshita.   I didn't understand the value
                                                       (goodness) until now.

(ookii)   Ima made ookisa ga wakarimasen   I didn't understand the size
                  deshita.   until now.
(takai)   Ima made takasa ga wakarimasen   I didn't understand the height
                  deshita.   until now.

(nagai)	Ima made nagasa ga wakarimasen deshita.	I didn't understand the length until now.
(hiroi)	Ima made hirosa ga wakarimasen deshita.	I didn't understand the width until now.
(hayai)	Ima made hayasa ga wakarimasen deshita.	I didn't understand the speed until now.

16. Repetition

Yokatta desu.	It was good.
Warukatta desu.	It was bad.
Ookikatta desu.	It was large.
Chiisakatta desu.	It was small.
Atarashikatta desu.	It was new.
Furukatta desu.	It was old.
Takakatta desu.	It was high.
Hikukatta desu.	It was low.
Yasukatta desu.	It was cheap.
Nagakatta desu.	It was long.
Mijikakatta desu.	It was short.
Chikakatta desu.	It was near.
Hayakatta desu.	It was early.
Hirokatta desu.	It was wide.
Semakatta desu.	It was narrow.
Osokatta desu.	It was late.
Tookatta desu.	It was far away.

17. Affirmative Response

Q. Tabemono wa warukatta desu ka?   Was the food bad?
A. Ee. Tabemono wa warukatta desu ne.   Yes, the food was [really] bad!

(Yomimono wa takakatta desu ka?)   (Was the reading matter expensive?)
 Ee. Yomimono wa takakatta desu ne.   Yes, the reading matter was [really] expensive!

(Norimono wa hayakatta desu ka?)   (Was the mode of transportation fast?)
 Ee. Norimono wa hayakatta desu ne.   Yes, the mode of transportation was [really] fast!

(Tabemono wa yasukatta desu ka?)   (Was the food inexpensive?)
 Ee. Tabemono wa yasukatta desu ne.   Yes, the food was [really] inexpensive!

(Kakimono wa osokatta desu ka?)   (Were the papers late?)
 Ee. Kakimono wa osokatta desu ne.   Yes, the papers were [really] late!
(Kakemono wa furukatta desu ka?)   (Were the hangings old?)
 Ee. Kakemono wa furukatta desu ne.   Yes, the hangings were [really] old!
(Yasumi wa mijikakatta desu ka?)   (Was your vacation short?)
 Ee. Yasumi wa mijikakatta desu ne.   Yes, my vacation was [really] short!
(Hanashi wa yokatta desu ka?)   (Was the story interesting?)
 Ee. Hanashi wa yokatta desu ne.   Yes, the story was [really] interesting!
(Kaeri wa osokatta desu ka?)   (Was his return late?)
 Ee. Kaeri wa osokatta desu ne.   Yes, his return was [really] late!

(Kotae wa yokatta desu ka?)   (Was the answer good?)
Ee. Kotae wa yokatta desu ne.   Yes, the answer was [really] good!
(Odekake wa hayakatta desu ka?)   (Was his departure early?)
Ee. Odekake wa hayakatta desu ne.   Yes, his departure was [really] early!

18. Grammar (semi-formal to informal)

(Yasumi wa nishuukan desu.)   (The vacation [period] is two weeks.)
Yasumi wa nishuukan da to kikimashita. I heard that the vacation [period] is
                                      two weeks.

(Ano hanashi wa choodo ii nagasa desu.) (That story is just the right length.)
Ano hanashi wa choodo ii nagasa da to   I heard that that story is just the
  kikimashita.   right length.
(Okaeri wa goji goro desu.)   (His return is around five o'clock.)
Okaeri wa goji goro da to kikimashita. I heard that his return is around five
                                      o'clock.

(Kotae wa ashita demasu.)   (The answer will be given [out] tomor-
                                      row.)
Kotae wa ashita deru to kikimashita. I heard that the answer will be given
                                      [out] tomorrow.

(Yomimono o motto kaimasu.)   (He'll buy more reading matter.)
Yomimono o motto kau to kikimashita. I heard that he'll buy more reading mat-
                                      ter.

(Obaasan no tabemono ga chigaimasu.) (Grandmother's food is different.)
Obaasan no tabemono ga chigau to ki-   I heard that Grandmother's food is dif-
  kimashita.   ferent.
(Kakemono wa takai desu.)   (Hangings are expensive.)
Kakemono wa takai to kikimashita.   I heard that hangings are expensive.
(Yasumi wa chikai desu.)   (Vacation is near.)
Yasumi wa chikai to kikimashita.   I heard that vacation is near.
(Otoosan no kaeri wa osoi desu.)   (Father's return is late.)
Otoosan no kaeri wa osoi to kikima-   I heard that Father's return is late.
  shita.
(Hanashi wa nagakatta desu.)   (The talk was long.)
Hanashi wa nagakatta to kikimashita. I heard that the talk was long.
(Norimono wa furukatta desu.)   (The vehicles were old.)
Norimono wa furukatta to kikimashita. I heard that the vehicles were old.
(Yasumi wa mijikakatta desu.)   (Vacation was short.)
Yasumi wa mijikakatta to kikimashita. I heard that vacation was short.

CULTURAL NOTES

1. Said by a person returning to his own home, his own office, etc.

2. A welcoming phrase said by a person in the home or office of the returnee.
This phrase is sometimes in response to the previous phrase and sometimes said
first, before the returnee even says "tadaima."

EXERCISES

A. Supply the following with 1) the informal ending and 2) the semi-formal
    ending.

1. It's big.	11. It's bad.	21. It's near.
2. It was big.	12. It's small.	22. It was small.
3. It's far.	13. It was old.	23. It was bad.
4. It's early.	14. It's short.	24. It's expensive.
5. It was low.	15. It was long.	25. It was expensive.
6. It was near.	16. It's late.	26. It's long.
7. It's good.	17. It was narrow.	27. It's low.
8. It was good.	18. It's old.	28. It was short.
9. It's new.	19. It's cheap.	29. It was late.
10. It was far.	20. It was new.	30. It was wide.

B. Supply the proper form of naru or suru.

1. Nagaku _____.	Let's make it longer.
2. Nagaku _____.	It didn't become longer.
3. Mijikaku _____.	I made it shorter.
4. Mijikaku _____ ka?	Will it become shorter?
5. Yasuku _____ deshoo.	It'll probably become cheaper.
6. Yasuku _____.	He didn't make it cheaper.
7. Osoku _____.	I'm late. (I've become late.)
8. Waruku _____.	He damaged it.
9. Furuku _____.	It's become old.
10. Yoku _____.	He's recovered.
11. Chiisaku _____.	Let's make it smaller.
12. Semaku _____ deshoo.	He'll probably make it narrower.

C. Say the following.

1. Let's go early.	6. He got up late.
2. He started out late.	7. He looked at it well.
3. He spoke rapidly.	8. He'll probably buy it inexpensively.
4. I'll write it small.	9. Let's request it quickly.
5. Have you waited long?	10. He'll publish it anew.

D. Supply the missing time.

1. _____ kakarimashita.	It took one day.
2. _____ benkyoo shimashita.	I studied for one week.
3. _____ osoku narimashita.	It is three days late.
4. _____ machimashita.	I waited four weeks.
5. _____ kakaru to omoimasu.	I think it will take twenty days.
6. _____ tabemasen deshita.	I didn't eat for four days.
7. _____ osoku narimasu.	It will be seven days late.
8. _____ yasumimashita.	I rested for nine days.

9. _____ kakaru to iimashita.   He said it would take eight weeks.
10. _____ imashoo.   Let's stay six days.
11. _____ asobimashita.   I played for two days.
12. _____ ikimasu.   I'm going for five days.

E. Change the following to noun forms.

1. yomu, mono   9. kakeru, mono
2. kaeru   10. kaku, mono
3. hanasu   11. nagai
4. taberu, mono   12. noru, mono
5. ookii   13. kotaeru
6. asobu   14. hiroi
7. takai   15. ii
8. yasumu

F. Fill in the blanks.

1. Ashita kara yokka gakkoo e ikimasen.
    Ashita kara yokka no _____ desu.
2. Jidoosha no naka ni yomimono ga arimasu.
    Jidoosha no naka ni _____ ya _____ ga arimasu.
3. Densha mo hikooki mo _____ desu.
4. Tanaka-san no uchi ni pan shika arimasen.
    _____ wa sonna ni arimasen.
5. Ima uchi ni imasen.
    Ima _____ desu.
6. Kyoo wa otoosan wa goji-han ni kaeru to iimashita.
    Kyoo wa _____ ga hayai desu.
7. Yamamoto-sensee ni sono koto o kikimashita.
    Donna _____ ga demashita ka?
8. Tanaka-san wa Amerika kara kaerimashita.
    Amerika no _____ o kikimashoo.

Obaasan:	Kyooto wa ikaga deshita ka?	Grandmother:	How was Kyoto?
Otoosan:	Amari isogashiku arimasen deshita. Dakara, otera o hitotsu-futatsu mi ni iki-mashita.	Father:	I wasn't very busy. So, I went to see one or two temples.
Obaasan:	Yokatta desu ne.	Grandmother:	Wasn't that nice!
Yukio:	Kyooto kara no omiyage[1] wa nan desu ka?	Yukio:	What are your presents (souvenirs) from Kyoto?
Otoosan:	Nan deshoo ne. Kore wa obaa-sama no desu.	Father:	What could they be! This is Grandmother's.
Obaasan:	Doomo arigatoo. (Hako no naka o mimashita.) Maa, kiree na oyunomi desu ne.[3]	Grandmother:	Thank you. (She looked in the box.) My, what a pretty teacup!
Otoosan:	Saa, Yukio no wa dore datta daroo.... Aa, kore da. Hai.	Father:	Let's see. Which one was Yukio's? Oh, it's this one. Here.
Yukio:	Doomo arigatoo.	Yukio:	Thank you.

GRAMMAR

II-4.1 Verbal adjectives (negative perfectives)

The semi-formal negative perfective is the stem plus -ku arimasen deshita or the stem plus -ku nakatta desu. The informal negative perfective is -ku nakatta. The negative perfectives mean "was (were) not _____." The following shows the non-past and perfective endings of the negative form.

	Informal	Semi-formal	
Negative		
non-past	-ku nai	-ku arimasen	is (are) not _____
perfective	-ku nakatta	-ku arimasen deshita -ku nakatta desu	was (were) not _____

EXAMPLES:

Informal	Semi-formal	
Ookiku nakatta.	Ookiku arimasen deshita.	It wasn't large.
Takaku nakatta.	Takaku arimasen deshita.	It wasn't expensive.
Furuku nakatta.	Furuku arimasen deshita.	It wasn't old.
Ookiku nakatta.	Ookiku nakatta desu.	It wasn't large.

II-4.2 Adjectival nouns

(a) These are nouns which are followed by na rather than no in modifying a noun, and by ni in modifying a verb.

126

EXAMPLES:
Modifying a noun

Kiree na uchi desu.	It's a pretty house.
Shizuka na tokoro desu.	It's a quiet place.
Kiree na hito o mimashita.	I saw a pretty person.

Modifying a verb

Kiree ni narimashita.	It became pretty.
	It became clean.
Shizuka ni shimashoo.	Let's be (make it) quiet.
Kiree ni kakimashita.	He wrote it prettily.

(b) The verbal adjectives ookii and chiisai have alternate forms ooki na and chiisa na when they modify nouns. This alternate form occurs only as a noun modifier.

EXAMPLES:
Ooki na oyunomi desu ne.	It's a large teacup, isn't it!
Ooki na uchi o kaimashita.	He bought a large house.
Chiisa na eki desu.	It's a small station.

II-4.3 The copula (informal perfective)
The informal perfective of the copula is datta.

EXAMPLES:

Informal	Semi-formal	
Kuruma datta.	Kuruma deshita.	It was a car.
Kiree datta.	Kiree deshita.	It was pretty.
Kinoo datta.	Kinoo deshita.	It was yesterday.

II-4.4 The copula (informal tentative form)
The informal tentative of the copula is daroo.

EXAMPLES:

Informal	Semi-formal	
Yukio daroo.	Yukio deshoo.	It's probably Yukio.
Iku daroo.	Iku deshoo.	He'll probably go.
Isogashii daroo.	Isogashii deshoo.	He is probably busy.
Isogashikatta daroo.	Isogashikatta deshoo.	He must have been (probably was) busy.
Isogashiku nai daroo.	Isogashiku nai deshoo.	He probably isn't busy.
Isogashiku nakatta daroo.	Isogashiku nakatta deshoo.	He probably wasn't busy.

The verb or verbal adjective before daroo or deshoo is always in the informal ending in semi-formal speech.

II-4.5 The copula (negative perfective)
    The negative perfective, meaning "was (were) not" is de wa arimasen deshita
or de wa nakatta desu in the semi-formal form and de wa nakatta in the informal
form.

EXAMPLES:
    Otera de wa arimasen deshita.   It wasn't a temple.
    Tanaka-san de wa nakatta deshoo.   It wasn't Mr. Tanaka, was it?

II-4.6 Nominal form of a verb plus ni iku (kuru, etc.)
    The nominal form of a verb (II-3.4) plus ni plus a verb of motion, such as
"come" and "return," has the meaning "come to (do)," "go to (do)," etc.

EXAMPLES:
    Mi ni ikimashoo.   Let's go see [it].
    Kai ni kimashita.   He came to buy [it].
    Tabe ni kaerimashita.   He went home to eat.

II-4.7 Japanese numerals
    Numerals such as hitotsu and futatsu, which are introduced in this lesson,
are numerals of Japanese origin, as opposed to the Sino-Japanese ichi, ni, etc.,
introduced earlier. The Japanese numerals run from one through ten, and there are
a few others in addition. Hitotsu, futatsu, etc., all have two meanings respec-
tively, "one thing" or "one year of age," "two things" or "two years of age," etc.

EXAMPLES:
    Sore o / kudasai.   Please give me that one.
    Sore o hitotsu kudasai.   Please give me one of those.
    Hitotsu kudasai.   Please give me one.

    (Note that the particle o follows the actual noun and not the numeral. This
also occurs with the particles ga and wa.)

    Omiyage ga / arimasu.   There are souvenirs.
    Omiyage ga mittsu arimasu.   There are three souvenirs.
    Mittsu arimasu.   There are three.

    Mittsu wa doo desu ka?   How about three of them?
    Hatachi ni narimashita.   He became twenty years old.
    Hitotsu de kekkoo desu.   One will be fine.
    Itsutsu mo tabemashita.   He ate as many as five.

    In the last four examples, the numerals are not occurring adverbially but as
regular nouns.

                              DRILLS

1. Substitution

Kiree na tokoro desu ne.   Isn't it a pretty place!

(shizuka)   Shizuka na tokoro desu ne.   Isn't it a quiet place!
(nigiyaka)   Nigiyaka na tokoro desu ne.   Isn't it a lively place!
(ooki)   Ooki na tokoro desu ne.   Isn't it a large place!
(chiisa)   Chiisa na tokoro desu ne.   Isn't it a small place!

2. Progressive Substitution

Mae wa shizuka na machi datta to kikimashita.   I heard that it was formerly a
                                                     quiet town.

(kiree na)   Mae wa kiree na machi datta to   I heard that it was formerly a
                      kikimashita.   pretty town.
(uchi)   Mae wa kiree na uchi datta to   I heard that it was formerly a
                      kikimashita.   pretty home.
(nigiyaka na)   Mae wa nigiyaka na uchi datta   I heard that it was formerly a
                      to kikimashita.   lively home.
(omise)   Mae wa nigiyaka na omise datta   I heard that it was formerly a
                      to kikimashita.   busy store.
(chiisa na)   Mae wa chiisa na omise datta to   I heard that it was formerly a
                      kikimashita.   small store.
(yaoya)   Mae wa chiisa na yaoya datta to   I heard that it was formerly a
                      kikimashita.   small greengrocery.
(ooki na)   Mae wa ooki na yaoya datta to   I heard that it was formerly a
                      kikimashita.   large greengrocery.
(tokoro)   Mae wa ooki na tokoro datta to   I heard that it was formerly a
                      kikimashita.   large place.
(shizuka na)   Mae wa shizuka na tokoro datta   I heard that it was formerly a
                      to kikimashita   quiet place.
(machi)   Mae wa shizuka na machi datta   I heard that it was formerly a
                      to kikimashita.   quiet town.

3. Substitution

Ima yori kiree na machi datta deshoo ne.   It must have been a prettier
                                                     town than now!

(shizuka na)   Ima yori shizuka na machi datta   It must have been a quieter
                      deshoo ne.   town than now!
(nigiyaka na)   Ima yori nigiyaka na machi datta It must have been a livelier
                      deshoo ne.   town than now!
(chiisa na)   Ima yori chiisa na machi datta   It must have been a smaller
                      deshoo ne.   town than now!
(chiisai)   Ima yori chiisai machi datta   It must have been a smaller
                      deshoo ne.   town than now!
(ooki na)   Ima yori ooki na machi datta   It must have been a larger
                      deshoo ne.   town than now!
(ookii)   Ima yori ookii machi datta   It must have been a larger
                      deshoo ne.   town than now!

4. Response

(Kiree deshoo ka.)   (I wonder if it's pretty.)
 Kiree daroo to omoimasu.   I think it's probably pretty.
(Shizuka deshoo ka.)   (I wonder if it's quiet.)
 Shizuka daroo to omoimasu.   I think it's probably quiet.
(Nigiyaka deshoo ka.)   (I wonder if it's lively.)
 Nigiyaka daroo to omoimasu.   I think it's probably lively.
(Onaji deshoo ka.)   (I wonder if they're the same.)
 Onaji daroo to omoimasu.   I think they're probably the same.
(Toshokan deshoo ka.)   (I wonder if it's a library.)
 Toshokan daroo to omoimasu.   I think it's probably a library.
(Ohiru deshoo ka.)   (I wonder if it's noon.)
 Ohiru daroo to omoimasu.   I think it's probably noon.
(Nagai deshoo ka.)   (I wonder if it's long.)
 Nagai daroo to omoimasu.   I think it's probably long.
(Furui deshoo ka.)   (I wonder if it's old.)
 Furui daroo to omoimasu.   I think it's probably old.
(Omoshiroi deshoo ka.)   (I wonder if it's interesting.)
 Omoshiroi daroo to omoimasu.   I think it's probably interesting.
(Isogashii deshoo ka.)   (I wonder if he's busy.)
 Isogashii daroo to omoimasu.   I think he's probably busy.
(Kitanai deshoo ka.)   (I wonder if it's dirty.)
 Kitanai daroo to omoimasu.   I think it's probably dirty.

5. Substitution and Negative Response

Q. Michi deshita ka?   Was it a road?
A. Iie. Michi de wa arimasen deshita.   No, it wasn't a road.

(kinoo)   Kinoo deshita ka?   Was it yesterday?
             Iie. Kinoo de wa arimasen deshita.   No, it wasn't yesterday.
(otona)   Otona deshita ka?   Was it an adult?
             Iie. Otona de wa arimasen deshita.   No, it wasn't an adult.
(nigiyaka)   Nigiyaka deshita ka?   Was it lively?
             Iie. Nigiyaka de wa arimasen deshita.   No, it wasn't lively.
(shizuka)   Shizuka deshita ka?   Was it quiet?
             Iie. Shizuka de wa arimasen deshita.   No, it wasn't quiet.
(kiree)   Kiree deshita ka?   Was it pretty?
             Iie. Kiree de wa arimasen deshita.   No, it wasn't pretty.

6. Grammar and Negative Response

(omoshiroi) Q. Omoshirokatta desu ka?   Was it interesting? Was
                                             it fun?

             A. Iie. Amari omoshiroku arimasen   No, it wasn't so interest-
                 deshita.   ing.

(isogashii) Isogashikatta desu ka?   Was he busy?
             Iie. Amari isogashiku arimasen deshita.   No, he wasn't so busy.

(kitanai)	Kitanakatta desu ka?	Was it dirty?
	Iie. Amari kitanaku arimasen deshita.	No, it wasn't so dirty.
(atarashii)	Atarashikatta desu ka?	Was it new?
	Iie. Amari atarashiku arimasen deshita.	No, it wasn't so new.
(chikai)	Chikakatta desu ka?	Was it near?
	Iie. Amari chikaku arimasen deshita.	No, it wasn't so near.
(tooi)	Tookatta desu ka?	Was it far?
	Iie. Amari tooku arimasen deshita.	No, it wasn't so far.

7. Substitution

Kono otera wa ikaga desu ka?   How about this temple?

(omiyage)	Kono omiyage wa ikaga desu ka?	How about this souvenir present?
(oyunomi)	Kono oyunomi wa ikaga desu ka?	How about this teacup?
(michi)	Kono michi wa ikaga desu ka?	How about this street?
(tokee)	Kono tokee wa ikaga desu ka?	How about this clock?
(kotae)	Kono kotae wa ikaga desu ka?	How about this answer?
(hanashi)	Kono hanashi wa ikaga desu ka?	How about this story?

8. Affirmative Response

Q. Kono oyunomi wa ikaga desu ka?   How about this teacup?
A. Sono oyunomi wa kekkoo desu ne.   That teacup would be fine.

(Okashi wa ikaga desu ka?)   (How about some cakes?)
 Okashi wa kekkoo desu ne.   Cakes would be fine.
(Shizuka na tokoro wa ikaga desu ka?)   (How about a quiet place?)
 Shizuka na tokoro wa kekkoo desu ne.   A quiet place would be fine.
(Konna omiyage wa ikaga desu ka?)   (How about souvenir presents like this?)
 Konna omiyage wa kekkoo desu ne.   This kind of souvenir present is fine.
(Anna otera wa ikaga desu ka?)   (How about a temple like that?)
 Anna otera wa kekkoo desu ne.   That kind of temple is fine.
(Omoshiroi yomimono wa ikaga desu ka?)   (How about some interesting reading matter?)

 Omoshiroi yomimono wa kekkoo desu ne.   Interesting reading matter would be fine.

(Kiree na kakemono wa ikaga desu ka?)   (How about a pretty hanging?)
 Kiree na kakemono wa kekkoo desu ne.   A pretty hanging would be fine.

9. Substitution and Negative Response

(furui otera, kitanai)	Q. Ano furui otera wa ikaga deshita ka? Kitanakatta desu ka?	How was that old temple? Was it dirty?
	A. Furui otera deshita ga, sonna ni kitanaku arimasen deshita ne.	It was an old temple, but it wasn't so dirty.

(takai, kuru-   Ano takai kuruma wa ikaga deshita   How was that expensive
ma, ii)   ka? Yokatta desu ka?   car? Was it good?
                   Takai kuruma deshita ga, sonna ni   It was an expensive car,
                      yoku arimasen deshita ne.   but it wasn't so good.
(ookii machi,   Ano ookii machi wa ikaga deshita ka?   How was that large town?
omoshiroi)   Omoshirokatta desu ka?   Was it interesting?
                   Ookii machi deshita ga, sonna ni   It was a large town, but
                      omoshiroku arimasen deshita ne.   it wasn't so interest-
                                                                   ing.
(chiisa na   Ano chiisa na uchi wa ikaga deshita   How was that small house?
uchi, yasui)   ka? Yasukatta desu ka?   Was it inexpensive?
                   Chiisa na uchi deshita ga, sonna ni   It was a small house, but
                      yasuku arimasen deshita ne.   it wasn't so inexpen-
                                                                   sive.
(chotto no ya-   Ano chotto no yasumi wa ikaga deshita   How was that short vaca-
sumi, isoga-   ka? Isogashikatta desu ka?   tion? Was it busy?
shii)   Chotto no yasumi deshita ga, sonna ni   It was a short vacation,
                      isogashiku arimasen deshita ne.   but it wasn't so busy.
(nigiyaka na   Ano nigiyaka na tokoro wa ikaga   How was that busy place?
tokoro, ki-   deshita ka? Kiree deshita ka?   Was it pretty?
ree)   Nigiyaka na tokoro deshita ga, sonna   It was a busy place, but
                      ni kiree de wa arimasen deshita ne.   it wasn't so pretty.
(chiisa na to-   Ano chiisa na toshokan wa ikaga   How was that small li-
shokan, shi-   deshita ka? Shizuka deshita ka?   brary? Was it quiet?
zuka)   Chiisa na toshokan deshita ga, sonna   It was a small library,
                      ni shizuka de wa arimasen deshita ne.   but it wasn't so quiet.
(ooki na ma-   Ano ooki na machi wa ikaga deshita   How was that large town?
chi, nigi-   ka? Nigiyaka deshita ka?   Was it busy?
yaka)   Ooki na machi deshita ga, sonna ni   It was a large town, but
                      nigiyaka de wa arimasen deshita ne.   it wasn't so busy.

10. Grammar (to negatives, maintaining same level of politeness)

(Omiyage datta.)   (It was a souvenir present.)
 Omiyage de wa nakatta.   It wasn't a souvenir present.
(Oyunomi deshita.)   (It was a teacup.)
 Oyunomi de wa arimasen deshita.   It wasn't a teacup.
(Nigiyaka na michi deshita.)   (It was a lively street.)
 Nigiyaka na michi de wa arimasen   It wasn't a lively street.
   deshita.
(Kiree datta.)   (It was pretty.)
 Kiree de wa nakatta.   It wasn't pretty.
(Ookikatta.)   (It was large.)
 Ookiku nakatta.   It wasn't large.
(Isogashikatta.)   (He was busy.)
 Isogashiku nakatta.   He wasn't busy.
(Isogashikatta desu.)   (He was busy.)
 Isogashiku arimasen deshita.   He wasn't busy.
(Omoshirokatta desu.)   (It was interesting.)
 Omoshiroku arimasen deshita.   It wasn't interesting.
(Omoshiroi hon datta.)   (It was an interesting book.)
 Omoshiroi hon de wa nakatta.   It wasn't an interesting book.

(Ōoki na machi datta.)   (It was a big town.)
Ōoki na machi de wa nakatta.   It wasn't a big town.

11. Progressive Substitution

Kiree ni tabemashita.   They ate it all (clean).

(shizuka)   Shizuka ni tabemashita.   They ate quietly.
(narimashita)   Shizuka ni narimashita.   They became quiet.
(nigiyaka)   Nigiyaka ni narimashita.   They became lively.
(hanashimashita)   Nigiyaka ni hanashimashita.   They spoke in a lively [man-
                                                      ner].

(shizuka)   Shizuka ni hanashimashita.   They spoke quietly.
(shimashita)   Shizuka ni shimashita.   They were quiet.
(kiree)   Kiree ni shimashita.   They cleaned it up.
(tabemashita)   Kiree ni tabemashita.   They ate it all (clean).

12. Substitution

Omiyage o kai ni ikimashoo.   Let's go buy a souvenir pre-
                                                  sent.

(oyunomi)   Oyunomi o kai ni ikimashoo.   Let's go buy a teacup.
(tabemono)   Tabemono o kai ni ikimashoo. Let's go buy food.
(yomimono)   Yomimono o kai ni ikimashoo. Let's go buy reading matter.
(yoofuku)   Yoofuku o kai ni ikimashoo.   Let's go buy a dress.
(motto ii no)   Motto ii no o kai ni ikima-   Let's go buy a better one.
                      shoo.
(motto omoshiroi   Motto omoshiroi zasshi o kai Let's go buy a more interesting
   zasshi)   ni ikimashoo.   magazine.

13. Affirmative Response

Q. Rokuji goro ni tabe ni kaerimasen   Didn't he come home to eat around six
      deshita ka?   o'clock?
A. Ee. Tabe ni kaerimasen deshita.   No, he didn't come home to eat.

(Tanaka-san ni ai ni ikimasen deshita   (Didn't he go to meet Mr. Tanaka?)
   ka?)
   Ee. Ai ni ikimasen deshita.   No, he didn't go to meet him.
(Uchi o mi ni kimasen deshita ka?)   (Didn't they come to see the house?)
   Ee. Mi ni kimasen deshita.   No, they didn't come to see it.
(Onegai shi ni dekakemasen deshita ka?)   (Didn't they go to request it?)
   Ee. Onegai shi ni dekakemasen deshita.   No, they didn't go to request it.
(Hakone e asobi ni ikimasen deshita   (Didn't they go to Hakone to play?)
   ka?)
   Ee. Asobi ni ikimasen deshita.   No, they didn't go to play.
(Sono koto o kiki ni kimasen deshita   (Didn't they come to ask that?)
   ka?)
   Ee. Kiki ni kimasen deshita.   No, they didn't come to ask.

(Zasshi o kai ni ikimasen deshita ka?)   (Didn't they go to buy a magazine?)
Ee. Kai ni ikimasen deshita.   No, they didn't go to buy one.
(Obaasan ni ii ni ikimasen deshita ka?)   (Didn't you go tell Grandmother?)
Ee. Ii ni ikimasen deshita.   No, I didn't go tell her.

14. Grammar

(kau)	Kai ni ikimashita.	He went to buy it.
(kiku)	Kiki ni ikimashita.	He went to ask.
(yuu)	Ii ni ikimashita.	He went to tell them.
(onegai suru)	Onegai shi ni ikimashita.	He went to request it of them.
(benkyoo suru)	Benkyoo shi ni ikimashita.	He went to study.
(asobu)	Asobi ni ikimashita.	He went to play.
(ireru)	Ire ni ikimashita.	He went to deposit it (put it in).
(tomeru)	Tome ni ikimashita.	He went to stop them.
(taberu)	Tabe ni ikimashita.	He went to eat.
(miseru)	Mise ni ikimashita.	He went to show it.
(denwa o ka-keru)	Denwa o kake ni ikimashita.	He went to telephone.
(miru)	Mi ni ikimashita.	He went to see.
(au)	Ai ni ikimashita.	He went to meet him.
(hanasu)	Hanashi ni ikimashita.	He went to talk.
(dasu)	Dashi ni ikimashita.	He went to mail it.
(yasumu)	Yasumi ni ikimashita.	He went to rest.
(noru)	Nori ni ikimashita.	He went to ride it.

15. Substitution

Sore o hitotsu kudasai.   Please give me one of those.

(futatsu)	Sore o futatsu kudasai.	Please give me two of those.
(mittsu)	Sore o mittsu kudasai.	Please give me three of those.
(yottsu)	Sore o yottsu kudasai.	Please give me four of those.
(itsutsu)	Sore o itsutsu kudasai.	Please give me five of those.
(muttsu)	Sore o muttsu kudasai.	Please give me six of those.
(nanatsu)	Sore o nanatsu kudasai.	Please give me seven of those.
(yattsu)	Sore o yattsu kudasai.	Please give me eight of those.
(kokonotsu)	Sore o kokonotsu kudasai.	Please give me nine of those.
(too)	Sore o too kudasai.	Please give me ten of those.

16. Negative Response

Q. Okashi o nanatsu kaimashita ka?   Did you buy seven cakes?
A. Iie. Muttsu shika kaimasen deshita.   No, I bought only six.

(yottsu)   Okashi o yottsu kaimashita ka?   Did you buy four cakes?
              Iie. Mittsu shika kaimasen   No, I bought only three.
                deshita.

(yattsu)	Okashi o yattsu kaimashita ka?	Did you buy eight cakes?
	Iie. Nanatsu shika kaimasen deshita.	No, I bought only seven.
(futatsu)	Okashi o futatsu kaimashita ka?	Did you buy two cakes?
	Iie. Hitotsu shika kaimasen deshita.	No, I bought only one.
(mittsu)	Okashi o mittsu kaimashita ka?	Did you buy three cakes?
	Iie. Futatsu shika kaimasen deshita.	No, I bought only two.
(muttsu)	Okashi o muttsu kaimashita ka?	Did you buy six cakes?
	Iie. Itsutsu shika kaimasen deshita.	No, I bought only five.
(kokonotsu)	Okashi o kokonotsu kaimashita ka?	Did you buy nine cakes?
	Iie. Yattsu shika kaimasen deshita.	No, I bought only eight.
(itsutsu)	Okashi o itsutsu kaimashita ka?	Did you buy five cakes?
	Iie. Yottsu shika kaimasen deshita.	No, I bought only four.
(too)	Okashi o too kaimashita ka?	Did you buy ten cakes?
	Iie. Kokonotsu shika kaimasen deshita.	No, I bought only nine.

17. Substitution

	Otera o hitotsu-futatsu mi' ni ikimashita.	I went to see one or two temples.
(mittsu-yottsu)	Otera o mittsu-yottsu mi' ni ikimashita.	I went to see three or four temples.
(itsutsu-muttsu)	Otera o itsutsu-muttsu mi' ni ikimashita.	I went to see five or six temples.
(futatsu-mittsu)	Otera o futatsu-mittsu mi' ni ikimashita.	I went to see two or three temples.
(nanatsu-yattsu)	Otera o nanatsu-yattsu mi' ni ikimashita.	I went to see seven or eight temples.

18. Substitution and Negative Response

Q.	Ikutsu ni narimashita ka? Mittsu ni narimashita ka?	How old did he become? Did he turn three?
A.	Iie. Yottsu ni narimashita.	No, he became four.
(yattsu)	Ikutsu ni narimashita ka? Yattsu ni narimashita ka?	How old did he become? Did he turn eight?
	Iie. Kokonotsu ni narimashita.	No, he became nine.
(too)	Ikutsu ni narimashita ka? Too ni narimashita ka?	How old did he become? Did he turn ten?
	Iie. Juu-ichi ni narimashita.	No, he became eleven.
(nanatsu)	Ikutsu ni narimashita ka? Nanatsu ni narimashita ka?	How old did he become? Did he turn seven?
	Iie. Yattsu ni narimashita.	No, he became eight.

(itsutsu)	Ikutsu ni narimashita ka?	How old did he become? Did he
	Itsutsu ni narimashita ka?	turn five?
	Iie. Muttsu ni narimashita.	No, he became six.
(futatsu)	Ikutsu ni narimashita ka?	How old did he become? Did he
	Futatsu ni narimashita ka?	turn two?
	Iie. Mittsu ni narimashita.	No, he became three.

CULTURAL NOTES

1. There is a custom in Japan of bringing back presents to members of the family, friends, and sometimes neighbors when one has been on a trip. The actual souvenirs are inexpensive; it is the thought of sharing the pleasure of one's trip with those who remained at home.

2. The ending -sama is a politer equivalent of -san. This is an example of the use of -sama in a "kinship" form of address. The -sama ending is used more by the upper levels of society.

3. Oyunomi is a "teacup" without a handle. When one hears the term, one usually thinks of a cylindrical cup made of pottery or porcelain. Kyoto is a famous ceramic-producing area.

EXERCISES

A. Change the following to their negative forms.

1. Kiree deshita.
2. Isogashikatta desu.
3. Isogimashita.
4. Shizuka deshita.
5. Otera deshita.
6. Chikai michi deshita.
7. Chikakatta desu.
8. Nigiyaka deshita.
9. Oyunomi deshita.
10. Kitanakatta desu.
11. Mittsu deshita.
12. Omoshirokatta desu.
13. Kiree datta.
14. Takakatta.
15. Nigiyaka datta.
16. Isogashikatta.

B. Change the following to their informal equivalents.

1. Kiree deshita.
2. Kiree desu.
3. Kiree deshoo.
4. Omoshirokatta desu.
5. Omoshiroi desu.
6. Omoshiroi deshoo.
7. Kimasu.
8. Suru deshoo.
9. Shizuka deshita.
10. Kitanakatta desu.
11. Kitanai desu.
12. Shizuka deshoo.
13. Shizuka desu.
14. Isogashii deshoo.
15. Isogu deshoo.
16. Nigiyaka deshita.
17. Ii deshoo.
18. Yattsu deshita.
19. Yattsu desu.
20. Nigiyaka desu.
21. Isogashii desu.
22. Kekkoo desu.

23. Mijikakatta desu.
24. Nagai deshoo.
25. Otera deshoo.

C. Fill in the blanks, wherever possible.

1. Kiree _____ hito desu.   She's a pretty person.
2. Shizuka _____ narimashita.   It became quiet.
3. Otera _____ mi _____ ikimashita.   I went to see some temples.
4. Okashi _____ mittsu _____ arimasu. There are three cakes.
5. Mittsu _____ narimashita.   He turned three years of age.
6. Itsutsu _____ arimashita.   There were as many as five.
7. Kiree _____ tabemashita.   He ate it all.
8. Shizuka _____ tokoro desu.   It's a quiet place.
9. Kekkoo _____ mono desu.   It's a fine thing.
10. Ooki _____ mono desu.   It's a large thing.
11. Ookii _____ desu ne.   It's big, isn't it.
12. Sonna _____ ookiku arimasen.   It isn't so big.
13. Amari _____ ookikatta desu.   It was too big.
14. Shizuka _____ shimashoo.   Let's be quiet.
15. Nigiyaka _____ machi desu.   It's a lively town.

D. Say that:

1. you're returning home to eat.
2. you're going to go buy a magazine.
3. you went to see a temple.
4. he came to ask.
5. you went for a visit to Hakone.
6. he left to make the request.
7. he came to show you.
8. he went to the library to study.
9. you'll go telephone.
10. he went to stop them.

E. Listen to the following story.

    Yukio no otoosan wa Tookyoo no hito desu. Tookyoo no kaisha wa isogashii
desu. Dakara, sonna ni Kyooto ya Oosaka e wa ikimasen ga isshuukan mae ni Kyooto
e ikimashita. Kyooto ni wa kiree na otera ga arimasu. Otoosan wa sono otera o
hitotsu-futatsu mi ni ikimashita. Kiyomizu-dera e ikimashita. Sono chikaku de
obaasan e no omiyage o kaimashita. Sore wa oyunomi desu.

    Make up questions based on the above story and ask your fellow students.

Yukio:	Kyooto no juugatsu no ookii omatsuri wa nan to yuu omatsuri desu ka?	Yukio:	What's Kyoto's big October festival called?
Otoosan:	Sore wa juugatsu nijuu-ni-nichi₁ no Jidai Matsuri desu.₁ Aa. Ashita ga ni-juu-ninichi no kin'yoobi desu ne. Ashita made ita-katta n desu ga...	Father:	That's the October 22 Festival of the Ages. Oh, tomorrow is Friday the twenty-second, isn't it. I wanted to stay through tomorrow, but...
Obaasan:	Oshikatta desu ne.₂	Grandmother:	That's two bad.
Yukio:	Boku mo mitai naa.	Yukio:	I'd like to see it, too.
Otoosan:	Kyooto de ichiban ookii oma-tsuri wa Jidai Matsuri ka mo shiremasen ne. Gion Matsuri yori₃ nadakai ka mo shiremasen.	Father:	The biggest festival in Kyoto might be the Fes-tival of the Ages. It might be more famous than the Gion Festival.

GRAMMAR

II-5.1 Verbal adjectives (superlative); adjectival nouns (superlative)

Ichiban plus a verbal adjective or adjectival noun is the superlative and has the meaning "the most _____."

EXAMPLES:

Ichiban nadakai desu.	It's the most famous.
Ichiban nigiyaka desu.	It's the liveliest.
Ichiban chiisakatta desu.	It was the smallest.
Ichiban kiree ni kakimashita.	He wrote it the prettiest.
Sekai de* ichiban takai yama desu.	It's the highest mountain in the world.

*Note the use of de in designating the limitations of the superlative.

II-5.2 -tai form

The -tai form is the desiderative and has the meaning "want to _____." The ending -tai occurs after the stem of a first-conjugation verb and the ending -itai occurs after the stem of a second-conjugation verb. The -tai form is conjugated as a verbal adjective.

EXAMPLES:

First conj.	Informal	Semi-formal	
non-past	tabe-tai	tabe-tai desu	I want to eat [it]
perfective	tabe-takatta	tabe-takatta desu	I wanted to eat [it]
negative non-past	tabe-taku nai	tabe-taku arimasen (tabe-taku nai desu)	I don't want to eat [it]
negative perfective	tabe-taku nakatta	tabe-taku arimasen deshita (tabe-taku nakatta desu)	I didn't want to eat [it]

Second conj.

non-past	ik-itai	ik-itai desu	I want to go
perfective	ik-itakatta	ik-itakatta desu	I wanted to go
negative non-past	ik-itaku nai	ik-itaku arimasen (ik-itaku nai desu)	I don't want to go
negative perfective	ik-itaku nakatta	ik-itaku arimasen deshita (ik-itaku nakatta desu)	I didn't want to go

Irregular verbs

non-past	kitai	kitai desu	I want to come
non-past	shitai	shitai desu	I want to do it

(Caution: This form is not used in asking someone if he "would like to _____"
in the English way.)

II-5.3 Particle ga
     When the verb has a desiderative ending, the thing which one wants to buy,
sell, do, etc. is followed by the particle ga (or wa). The particle o also occurs
after it. The ga appears to have a more emphatic feeling and seems to occur where
there is no possibility of mistaking that noun for the subject of the sentence.
With the verbal adjective hoshii, the thing which one desires is followed by the
particle ga rather than o.

EXAMPLES:

Pan ga tabetai desu.	I want to eat bread.
Nihon no zasshi ga yomitai desu.	I want to read a Japanese magazine.
Chokoreeto ga hoshii desu.	I'd like some chocolates.
Okashi wa hoshiku arimasen.	I don't want cakes.
Sono kodomo o mitai desu ne.	My, I'd like to see those children!

II-5.4 ka mo shiremasen
     Ka mo shiremasen occurs after a verb, verbal adjective, copula or noun, and
has the meaning "may" or "it may be (that)."

EXAMPLES:

Getsuyoobi ka mo shiremasen.	It may be Monday. It may be [on] Monday.
Iku ka mo shiremasen.	He may go.
Ichiban ookii ka mo shiremasen.	It may be the biggest.

II-5.5 made ni
     Made ni occurs after a noun or a verb and indicates a time deadline, "by"
such and such a time.

EXAMPLES:

Nichiyoobi made ni kaerimasu.	I'll return by Sunday.
Tanaka-san ga kuru made ni shima-shoo.	Let's do it before (have it done by the time) Mr. Tanaka comes.

Compare the following:

Ashita made ni hanashimasu.   I'll tell them by tomorrow.
Ashita made hanashimasu.   I'll talk until tomorrow.

DRILLS

1. Repetition

(a) Tabetai.   I'd like to eat.
     Mitai.   I'd like to see it.
     Kakitai.   I'd like to write.
     Yomitai.   I'd like to read.
     Hanashitai.   I'd like to speak.
     Machitai.   I'd like to wait.
     Aitai.   I'd like to meet him.
     Wakaritai.   I'd like to understand.
     Kitai.   I'd like to come.
(b) Dekaketai.   I'd like to start out.
     Itai.   I'd like to remain.
     Kikitai.   I'd like to ask.
     Iitai.   I'd like to say it.
     Suwaritai.   I'd like to sit down.
     Shitai.   I'd like to do it.
     Asobitai.   I'd like to play.

2. Grammar

(dekakeru)   Dekaketai desu.   I'd like to start out.
(taberu)   Tabetai desu.   I'd like to eat.
(miseru)   Misetai desu.   I'd like to show it.
(deru)   Detai desu.   I'd like to attend.
(iru)   Itai desu.   I'd like to remain.
(okiru)   Okitai desu.   I'd like to get up.
(iku)   Ikitai desu.   I'd like to go.
(kaku)   Kakitai desu.   I'd like to write.
(yasumu)   Yasumitai desu.   I'd like to rest.
(dasu)   Dashitai desu.   I'd like to mail it.
(hairu)   Hairitai desu.   I'd like to enter.
(noru)   Noritai desu.   I'd like to board it.
(tomaru)   Tomaritai desu.   I'd like to stop.
(au)   Aitai desu.   I'd like to meet him.
(kuru)   Kitai desu.   I'd like to come.
(onegai suru)   Onegai shitai desu. I'd like to request it.

3. Substitution and Affirmative Response

Q. Kakemono wa ikaga desu ka?   How would you like a hanging?
A. Ee. Kakemono ga kaitai desu ne.   Yes, I'd like to buy a hanging!

(fune)   Fune wa ikaga desu ka?   How would you like a boat?
                Ee. Fune ga kaitai desu ne.   Yes, I'd like to buy a boat!
(hikooki)   Hikooki wa ikaga desu ka?   How would you like a plane?
                Ee. Hikooki ga kaitai desu ne.   Yes, I'd like to buy a plane!
(oyunomi)   Oyunomi wa ikaga desu ka?   How would you like a teacup?
                Ee. Oyunomi ga kaitai desu ne.   Yes, I'd like to buy a teacup!
(chokoreeto)   Chokoreeto wa ikaga desu ka?   How would you like some choco-
                                                   lates?

                Ee. Chokoreeto ga kaitai desu   Yes, I'd like to buy some cho-
                ne.   colates!
(anna uchi)   Anna uchi wa ikaga desu ka?   How would you like that kind of
                                                   house?

                Ee. Anna uchi ga kaitai desu   Yes, I'd like to buy that kind
                ne.   of house.

4. Substitution

Ano omatsuri wa mitakatta desu ga...   I wanted to see that festival,
                                                   but...

(shima)   Ano shima wa mitakatta desu ga...   I wanted to see that island,
                                                   but...

(yama)   Ano yama wa mitakatta desu ga...   I wanted to see that mountain,
                                                   but...

(machi)   Ano machi wa mitakatta desu ga...   I wanted to see that town,
                                                   but...

(gakkoo)   Ano gakkoo wa mitakatta desu ga...   I wanted to see that school,
                                                   but...

(shimbun) Ano shimbun wa mitakatta desu ga...   I wanted to see that newspaper,
                                                   but...

5. Substitution and Negative Response

Q. Hokkaidoo e ikimasen ka?   Won't you go to Hokkaido?
A. Ima chotto Hokkaidoo e ikitaku arimasen.   I don't want to go to Hokkaido
                                                   just now.

(Shikoku)   Shikoku e ikimasen ka?   Won't you go to Shikoku?
            Ima chotto Shikoku e ikitaku arimasen. I don't want to go to Shikoku
                                                   just now.
(Honshuu)   Honshuu e ikimasen ka?   Won't you go to Honshu?
            Ima chotto Honshuu e ikitaku arimasen. I don't want to go to Honshu
                                                   just now.
(Kyuu-   Kyuushuu e ikimasen ka?   Won't you go to Kyushu?
shuu)   Ima chotto Kyuushuu e ikitaku arima-   I don't want to go to Kyushu
            sen.   just now.

(ano ya- ma)	Ano yama e ikimasen ka? Ima chotto ano yama e ikitaku arima- sen.	Won't you go to that mountain? I don't want to go to that mountain just now.
(ano shi- ma)	Ano shima e ikimasen ka? Ima chotto ano shima e ikitaku ari- masen.	Won't you go to that island? I don't want to go to that island just now.

6. Grammar and Negative Response

(taberu)	Q. Tabetakatta desu ka? A. Tabetaku arimasen deshita.	Did you want to eat it? I didn't want to eat it.
(miseru)	Misetakatta desu ka? Misetaku arimasen deshita.	Did you want to show it? I didn't want to show it.
(kakeru)	Kaketakatta desu ka? Kaketaku arimasen deshita.	Did you want to telephone? I didn't want to telephone.
(ireru)	Iretakatta desu ka? Iretaku arimasen deshita.	Did you want to put it in? I didn't want to put it in.
(miru)	Mitakatta desu ka? Mitaku arimasen deshita.	Did you want to see it? I didn't want to see it.
(iru)	Itakatta desu ka? Itaku arimasen deshita.	Did you want to remain? I didn't want to remain.
(okiru)	Okitakatta desu ka? Okitaku arimasen deshita.	Did you want to get up? I didn't want to get up.
(au)	Aitakatta desu ka? Aitaku arimasen deshita.	Did you want to meet him? I didn't want to meet him.
(kau)	Kaitakatta desu ka? Kaitaku arimasen deshita.	Did you want to buy it? I didn't want to buy it.
(kiku)	Kikitakatta desu ka? Kikitaku arimasen deshita.	Did you want to ask? I didn't want to ask.
(dasu)	Dashitakatta desu ka? Dashitaku arimasen deshita.	Did you want to serve it? I didn't want to serve it.
(hanasu)	Hanashitakatta desu ka? Hanashitaku arimasen deshita.	Did you want to speak? I didn't want to speak.
(matsu)	Machitakatta desu ka? Machitaku arimasen deshita.	Did you want to wait? I didn't want to wait.
(suwaru)	Suwaritakatta desu ka? Suwaritaku arimasen deshita.	Did you want to sit? I didn't want to sit.
(yomu)	Yomitakatta desu ka? Yomitaku arimasen deshita.	Did you want to read it? I didn't want to read it.
(onegai suru)	Onegai shitakatta desu ka? Onegai shitaku arimasen deshita.	Did you want to request it? I didn't want to request it.
(kuru)	Kitakatta desu ka? Kitaku arimasen deshita.	Did you want to come? I didn't want to come.

7. Substitution

Nichiyoobi made ni kaeritai desu.	I'd like to return by Sunday.
(getsuyoobi) Getsuyoobi made ni kaeritai desu.	I'd like to return by Monday.
(kayoobi) Kayoobi made ni kaeritai desu.	I'd like to return by Tuesday.

(suiyoobi)	Suiyoobi made ni kaeritai desu.	I'd like to return by Wednesday.
(mokuyoobi)	Mokuyoobi made ni kaeritai desu.	I'd like to return by Thursday.
(kin'yoobi)	Kin'yoobi made ni kaeritai desu.	I'd like to return by Friday.
(doyoobi)	Doyoobi made ni kaeritai desu.	I'd like to return by Saturday.

8. Substitution

Getsuyoobi wa nannichi desu ka?   What day of the month is Monday?

(suiyoobi)	Suiyoobi wa nannichi desu ka?	What day of the month is Wednesday?
(kin'yoobi)	Kin'yoobi wa nannichi desu ka?	What day of the month is Friday?
(kayoobi)	Kayoobi wa nannichi desu ka?	What day of the month is Tuesday?
(doyoobi)	Doyoobi wa nannichi desu ka?	What day of the month is Saturday?
(mokuyoobi)	Mokuyoobi wa nannichi desu ka?	What day of the month is Thursday?
(nichiyo-obi)	Nichiyoobi wa nannichi desu ka?	What day of the month is Sunday?

9. Substitution

Tsuitachi wa nan'yoobi desu ka?   What day of the week is the first?

(futsuka)	Futsuka wa nan'yoobi desu ka?	What day of the week is the second?
(mikka)	Mikka wa nan'yoobi desu ka?	What day of the week is the third?
(yokka)	Yokka wa nan'yoobi desu ka?	What day of the week is the fourth?
(itsuka)	Itsuka wa nan'yoobi desu ka?	What day of the week is the fifth?
(muika)	Muika wa nan'yoobi desu ka?	What day of the week is the sixth?
(nanoka)	Nanoka wa nan'yoobi desu ka?	What day of the week is the seventh?
(yooka)	Yooka wa nan'yoobi desu ka?	What day of the week is the eighth?
(kokonoka)	Kokonoka wa nan'yoobi desu ka?	What day of the week is the ninth?
(tooka)	Tooka wa nan'yoobi desu ka?	What day of the week is the tenth?
(juu-ichini-chi)	Juu-ichinichi wa nan'yoobi desu ka?	What day of the week is the eleventh?
(juu-ninichi)	Juu-ninichi wa nan'yoobi desu ka?	What day of the week is the twelfth?
(juu-sannichi)	Juu-sannichi wa nan'yoobi desu ka?	What day of the week is the thirteenth?
(juu-yokka)	Juu-yokka wa nan'yoobi desu ka?	What day of the week is the fourteenth?
(juu-gonichi)	Juu-gonichi wa nan'yoobi desu ka?	What day of the week is the fifteenth?

(hatsuka)	Hatsuka wa nan'yoobi desu ka?	What day of the week is the twentieth?
(nijuu-yokka)	Nijuu-yokka wa nan'yoobi desu ka?	What day of the week is the twenty-fourth?
(sanjuunichi)	Sanjuunichi wa nan'yoobi desu ka?	What day of the week is the thirtieth?

10. Factual Response (using a calendar)

(a) Q. Getsuyoobi wa nannichi desu ka?   What day of the month is Monday?
    A. Getsuyoobi wa _____ desu.   Monday is the _____.

(b) Q. Sono tsugi no suiyoobi wa nannichi desu ka?   What day of the month is the Wednesday after that?
    A. Sono tsugi no suiyoobi wa _____ desu.   The Wednesday after that is the _____.

(c) Q. Tsuitachi wa nan'yoobi desu ka?   What day of the week is the first?
    A. Tsuitachi wa _____ desu.   The first is _____.

11. Correlation Substitution

Yokka ka itsuka no kippu ga hoshii desu ga...	I'd like a ticket for the fourth or fifth...

(muika)	Muika ka nanoka no kippu ga hoshii desu ga...	I'd like a ticket for the sixth or seventh...
(mikka)	Mikka ka yokka no kippu ga hoshii desu ga...	I'd like a ticket for the third or fourth...
(tsuitachi)	Tsuitachi ka futsuka no kippu ga hoshii desu ga...	I'd like a ticket for the first or second...
(nanoka)	Nanoka ka yooka no kippu ga hoshii desu ga...	I'd like a ticket for the seventh or eighth...
(tooka)	Tooka ka juu-ichinichi no kippu ga hoshii desu ga...	I'd like a ticket for the tenth or eleventh...
(futsuka)	Futsuka ka mikka no kippu ga hoshii desu ga...	I'd like a ticket for the second or third...
(kokonoka)	Kokonoka ka tooka no kippu ga hoshii desu ga...	I'd like a ticket for the ninth or tenth...
(juu-kunichi)	Juu-kunichi ka hatsuka no kippu ga hoshii desu ga...	I'd like a ticket for the nineteenth or twentieth...
(itsuka)	Itsuka ka muika no kippu ga hoshii desu ga...	I'd like a ticket for the fifth or sixth...
(yooka)	Yooka ka kokonoka no kippu ga hoshii desu ga...	I'd like a ticket for the eighth or ninth...
(juu-yokka)	Juu-yokka ka juu-gonichi no kippu ga hoshii desu ga...	I'd like a ticket for the fourteenth or fifteenth...

12. Substitution

Ichigatsu wa nannichi arimasu ka?   How many days are there in Jan-
                                                      uary?

(nigatsu)   Nigatsu wa nannichi arimasu ka?   How many days are there in Feb-
                                                      ruary?

(sangatsu)   Sangatsu wa nannichi arimasu   How many days are there in
                   ka?   March?

(shigatsu)   Shigatsu wa nannichi arimasu   How many days are there in
                   ka?   April?

(gogatsu)   Gogatsu wa nannichi arimasu ka?   How many days are there in May?

(rokugatsu)   Rokugatsu wa nannichi arimasu   How many days are there in
                   ka?   June?

(shichigatsu)   Shichigatsu wa nannichi arimasu   How many days are there in Ju-
                   ka?   ly?

(hachigatsu)   Hachigatsu wa nannichi arimasu   How many days are there in Au-
                   ka?   gust?

(kugatsu)   Kugatsu wa nannichi arimasu ka?   How many days are there in Sep-
                                                      tember?

(juugatsu)   Juugatsu wa nannichi arimasu   How many days are there in Oc-
                   ka?   tober?

(juu-ichigatsu)   Juu-ichigatsu wa nannichi ari-   How many days are there in No-
                   masu ka?   vember?

(juu-nigatsu)   Juu-nigatsu wa nannichi arimasu   How many days are there in De-
                   ka?   cember?

13. Progressive Substitution

Nigatsu futsuka ni umaremashita.   I was born on February second.

(sangatsu)   Sangatsu futsuka ni umarema-   I was born on March second.
                   shita.

(juu-gonichi)   Sangatsu juu-gonichi ni umare-   I was born on March fifteenth.
                   mashita.

(gogatsu)   Gogatsu juu-gonichi ni umare-   I was born on May fifteenth.
                   mashita.

(hatsuka)   Gogatsu hatsuka ni umarema-   I was born on May twentieth.
                   shita.

(kugatsu)   Kugatsu hatsuka ni umarema-   I was born on September twen-
                   shita.   tieth.

(kokonoka)   Kugatsu kokonoka ni umarema-   I was born on September ninth.
                   shita.

(shichigatsu)   Shichigatsu kokonoka ni umare-   I was born on July ninth.
                   mashita.

(yokka)   Shichigatsu yokka ni umarema-   I was born on July fourth.
                   shita.

(juu-nigatsu)   Juu-nigatsu yokka ni umarema-   I was born on December fourth.
                   shita.

(ni-juu-gonichi)   Juu-nigatsu ni-juu-gonichi ni   I was born on December twenty-
                   umaremashita.   fifth.

(nigatsu)	Nigatsu nijuu-gonichi ni umaremashita.	I was born on February twenty-fifth.
(futsuka)	Nigatsu futsuka ni umaremashita.	I was born on February second.

14. Response (asking members of the class)

Q. Nangatsu nannichi ni umaremashita ka?   On what day of what month were you born?

Q. _____-san wa nangatsu nannichi ni umaremashita ka?   On what day of what month was _____ born?

15. Substitution

Juugatsu ni wa nadakai omatsuri ga arimasu.   In October, there is a famous festival.

(kiree na)	Juugatsu ni wa kiree na omatsuri ga arimasu.	In October, there is a pretty festival.
(ooki na)	Juugatsu ni wa ooki na omatsuri ga arimasu.	In October, there is a big festival.
(omoshiroi)	Juugatsu ni wa omoshiroi omatsuri ga arimasu.	In October, there is an interesting festival.
(mitai)	Juugatsu ni wa mitai omatsuri ga arimasu.	In October, there is a festival I'd like to see.
(Kyooto no)	Juugatsu ni wa Kyooto no omatsuri ga arimasu.	In October, there is a festival in Kyoto.

16. Expansion

(omatsuri o mimashita)	Omatsuri o mimashita.	I saw a festival.
(Jidai Matsuri to yuu)	Jidai Matsuri to yuu omatsuri o mimashita.	I saw a festival called the Festival of the Ages.
(Kyooto de)	Kyooto de Jidai Matsuri to yuu omatsuri o mimashita.	I saw a festival called the Festival of the Ages in Kyoto.
(juugatsu nijuu-ninichi ni)	Juugatsu nijuu-ninichi ni Kyooto de Jidai Matsuri to yuu omatsuri o mimashita.	I saw a festival called the Festival of the Ages in Kyoto on October 22.
(mi ni ikimashita)	Mi ni ikimashita.	I went to see it.
(omatsuri o)	Omatsuri o mi ni ikimashita.	I went to see a festival.
(Aoi no Matsuri to yuu)	Aoi no Matsuri to yuu omatsuri o mi ni ikimashita.	I went to see a festival called the Hollyhock Festival.
(Kyooto e)	Kyooto e Aoi no Matsuri to yuu omatsuri o mi ni ikimashita.	I went to Kyoto to see a festival called the Hollyhock Festival.

(gogatsu juu-gonichi ni) — Gogatsu juu-gonichi ni Kyooto e Aoi no Matsuri to yuu omatsuri o mi ni ikimashita. — I went to Kyoto on May fifteenth to see a festival called the Hollyhock Festival.

(mitai desu) — Mitai desu. — I'd like to see it.

(omatsuri ga) — Omatsuri ga mitai desu. — I'd like to see a festival.

(Kyooto no) — Kyooto no omatsuri ga mitai desu. — I'd like to see a festival in Kyoto.

(Gion Matsuri to yuu) — Gion Matsuri to yuu Kyooto no omatsuri ga mitai desu. — I'd like to see a festival in Kyoto called the Gion Festival.

(nijuu-yokka made no) — Nijuu-yokka made no Gion Matsuri to yuu Kyooto no omatsuri ga mitai desu. — I'd like to see a festival in Kyoto called the Gion Festival, [which lasts] through the twenty-fourth.

(juu-rokunichi kara) — Juu-rokunichi kara nijuu-yokka made no Gion Matsuri to yuu Kyooto no omatsuri ga mitai desu. — I'd like to see a festival in Kyoto called the Gion Festival, [which lasts] from the sixteenth through the twenty-fourth.

(shichigatsu) — Shichigatsu juu-rokunichi kara nijuu-yokka made no Gion Matsuri to yuu Kyooto no omatsuri ga mitai desu. — I'd like to see a festival in Kyoto called the Gion Festival, [which lasts] from July 16 through July 24.

(mono o kaimashita) — Mono o kaimashita. — I bought something.

("Daruma" to yuu) — "Daruma" to yuu mono o kaimashita. — I bought something called a "Daruma."

(omatsuri de) — Omatsuri de "Daruma" to yuu mono o kaimashita. — I bought something called a "Daruma" at the festival.

(sangatsu muika no) — Sangatsu muika no omatsuri de "Daruma" to yuu mono o kaimashita. — I bought something called a "Daruma" at the festival on March 6.

(Tookyoo no) — Tookyoo no sangatsu muika no omatsuri de "Daruma" to yuu mono o kaimashita. — I bought something called a "Daruma" at the festival on March 6 in Tokyo.

(aitai n desu ga...) — Aitai n desu ga... — I'd like to meet him...

(hito ni) — Hito ni aitai n desu ga... — I'd like to meet a person...

(Sumisu to yuu) — Sumisu to yuu hito ni aitai n desu ga... — I'd like to meet a person named Smith...

(sono Amerika kara no) — Sono Amerika kara no Sumisu to yuu hito ni aitai n desu ga... — I'd like to meet that person named Smith from America...

(kugatsu hatsuka ni) — Kugatsu hatsuka ni sono Amerika kara no Sumisu to yuu hito ni aitai n desu ga... — I'd like to meet that person named Smith from America on September 20...

17. Substitution

Nan to yuu toshi desu ka?   What's the name of the city?
                                             (It's a city called what?)

(hito)   Nan to yuu hito desu ka?   What's the name of the person?
(omatsuri)   Nan to yuu omatsuri desu ka? What's the name of the festi-
                                             val?

(otera)   Nan to yuu otera desu ka?   What's the name of the temple?
(tokoro)   Nan to yuu tokoro desu ka?   What's the name of the place?
(shima)   Nan to yuu shima desu ka?   What's the name of the island?
(yama)   Nan to yuu yama desu ka?   What's the name of the moun-
                                             tain?

(depaato)   Nan to yuu depaato desu ka? What's the name of the depart-
                                             ment store?

18. Substitution

Nihon de ichiban ookii toshi desu.   It's the largest city in Japan.

(takai yama)   Nihon de ichiban takai yama desu.   It's the highest mountain in
                                             Japan.
(nadakai oma-   Nihon de ichiban nadakai omatsu-   It's the most famous festival
  tsuri)   ri desu.   in Japan.
(ookii shima)   Nihon de ichiban ookii shima   It's the largest island in Ja-
                  desu.   pan.
(nadakai yama) Nihon de ichiban nadakai yama   It's the most famous mountain
                  desu.   in Japan.
(nadakai to-   Nihon de ichiban nadakai toshi   It's the most famous city in
  shi)   desu.   Japan.
(kiree na oma- Nihon de ichiban kiree na oma-   It's the prettiest festival in
  tsuri)   tsuri desu.   Japan.
(nadakai hito) Nihon de ichiban nadakai hito   He's the most famous person in
                  desu.   Japan.
(kiree na to-   Nihon de ichiban kiree na toshi   It's the prettiest city in Ja-
  shi)   desu.   pan.

19. Substitution

Sekai de ichiban nagai kawa ka mo shiremasen.   It may be the longest river in
                                             the world.

(takai yama)   Sekai de ichiban takai yama ka   It may be the highest mountain
                  mo shiremasen.   in the world.
(ookii toshi)   Sekai de ichiban ookii toshi ka   It may be the largest city in
                  mo shiremasen.   the world.
(kiree na shi- Sekai de ichiban kiree na shima   It may be the prettiest island
  ma)   ka mo shiremasen.   in the world.
(hayai kisha)   Sekai de ichiban hayai kisha ka   It may be the fastest train in
                  mo shiremasen.   the world.
(nadakai yama) Sekai de ichiban nadakai yama ka   It may be the most famous moun-
                  mo shiremasen.   tain in the world.

20. Response

Q. Itsuka ni Hokkaidoo e iku deshoo   I wonder if they're going to Hokkaido on
    ka.   the fifth.
A. Itsuka ni Hokkaidoo e iku ka mo   They may go to Hokkaido on the fifth.
    shiremasen.

(Shikoku kara tooka ni kaeru deshoo   (I wonder if they'll return from Shikoku
    ka.)   on the tenth.)
 Shikoku kara tooka ni kaeru ka mo   They may return from Shikoku on the
    shiremasen.   tenth.
(Kyuushuu made mi ni kuru deshoo ka.)   (I wonder if they'll come as far as Kyushu
                                                 to see it.)
 Kyuushuu made mi ni kuru ka mo shire-   They may come as far as Kyushu to see it.
    masen.
(Kokonoka made ni Honshuu e kaeru   (I wonder if they'll return to Honshu by
    deshoo ka.)   the ninth.)
 Kokonoka made ni Honshuu e kaeru ka   They may return to Honshu by the ninth.
    mo shiremasen.
(Shikoku de ichiban ookii deshoo ka.)   (I wonder if it's the largest in Shikoku.)
 Shikoku de ichiban ookii ka mo shire-   It may be the largest in Shikoku.
    masen.
(Kyuushuu de ichiban nadakai deshoo   (I wonder if it's the most famous in Kyu-
    ka.)   shu.)
 Kyuushuu de ichiban nadakai ka mo   It may be the most famous in Kyushu.
    shiremasen.
(Kono hon ga ichiban omoshiroi deshoo   (I wonder if this book is the most inter-
    ka.)   esting.)
 Kono hon ga ichiban omoshiroi ka mo   This book may be the most interesting.
    shiremasen.
(Terebi ga ichiban hoshii deshoo ka.)   (I wonder if he wants a television [set]
                                                 the most.)
 Terebi ga ichiban hoshii ka mo shire-   He may want a television [set] the most.
    masen.
(Are ga ichiban yokatta deshoo ka.)   (I wonder if that was the best one.)
 Are ga ichiban yokatta ka mo shire-   That may have been the best one.
    masen.
(Mikka yori hayakatta deshoo ka.)   (I wonder if it was earlier than the
                                                 third.)
 Mikka yori hayakatta ka mo shirema-   It may have been earlier than the third.
    sen.

21. Substitution

Okane wa oshiku arimasen ga, anna terebi wa   I don't begrudge the money, but
   kaitaku arimasen ne.   I don't want to buy a tele-
                                                       vision [set] like that.

(kuruma)   Okane wa oshiku arimasen ga,   I don't begrudge the money, but
                anna kuruma wa kaitaku arima-   I don't want to buy a car
                sen ne.   like that.

(uchi)	Okane wa oshiku arimasen ga, anna uchi wa kaitaku arimasen ne.	I don't begrudge the money, but I don't want to buy a house like that.
(mono)	Okane wa oshiku arimasen ga, anna mono wa kaitaku arimasen ne.	I don't begrudge the money, but I don't want to buy a thing like that.
(rajio)	Okane wa oshiku arimasen ga, anna rajio wa kaitaku arimasen ne.	I don't begrudge the money, but I don't want to buy a radio like that.
(hon)	Okane wa oshiku arimasen ga, anna hon wa kaitaku arimasen ne.	I don't begrudge the money, but I don't want to buy a book like that.

CULTURAL NOTES

1. Today, it is principally a parade through the city of Kyōto, from the Imperial Palace to the Heian Shrine. The participants are dressed to represent various persons important in Japanese history.

2. Boku and naa are said by men and boys. Naa is an exclamation with a tinge of longing.

3. The Gion Festival has been celebrated with a procession through certain parts of Kyōto of decorated floats which resemble tall pavilions. The custom dates back to the ninth century when a procession marched through Kyōto to seek the protection of the gods against an epidemic of pestilence.

EXERCISES

A. On the basis of factual information, make superlative statements concerning the following.

1. Fuji-san (Mt. Fuji)
2. Eberesuto-san (Mt. Everest)
3. Makkinree-san (Mt. McKinley)
4. Mishishippi-gawa (the Mississippi River)
5. Amazon-gawa (the Amazon River)
6. Honshuu
7. Nyuuyooku (New York)
8. Nagasaki
9. Sapporo
10. Tookyoo

B. On the basis of the following statements, asnwer the questions which follow.

1. Juugatsu nijuu-ninichi ni Kyooto e ikimashita. Choodo Jidai Matsuri deshita. Dakara nigiyaka deshita.

    a.   Jidai Matsuri wa doko no omatsuri desu ka?

    b.   Sono omatsuri wa itsu desu ka?

    c.   Sono omatsuri o mi ni ikitai desu。 Doko e ikimashoo ka?

    d.   Kono hito wa Jidai Matsuri o mimashita ka?

    e.   Kiree na omatsuri deshoo ka?

2. Nihon ni wa ookii shima ga yottsu arimasu。 Sono naka de ichiban ookii no wa Honshuu desu. Sono tsugi wa Hokkaidoo ka mo shiremasen. Ookisa no ichiban chiisai no wa Shikoku desu. Kyuushuu to yuu shima mo arimasu.

    a.   Nihon ni wa ookii shima ga yattsu arimasu ka?

    b.   Dore to dore desu ka?

    c.   Sono naka de ichiban ookii no wa dore desu ka?

    d.   Hokkaidoo no ookisa wa doo desu ka?

    e.   Nan to yuu shima ga ichiban chiisai no desu ka?

3. Nichiyoobi kara doyoobi made nanoka arimasu. Nihon no gakkoo wa nichiyoobi dake oyasumi desu. Doyoobi wa yojikan gurai gakkoo e ikimasu. Getsuyoobi kara kin'yoobi made wa ichinichi gakkoo ga arimasu.

    a.   Nichiyoobi kara doyoobi made nannichi arimasu ka?

    b.   Getsuyoobi kara kin'yoobi made nannichi aru to omoimasu ka?

    c.   Nihon no seeto wa doyoobi mo benkyoo shimasu ka?

    d.   Doyoobi mo ichinichi gakkoo ni imasu ka?

    e.   Nichiyoobi wa doo desu ka? Gakkoo e ikimasu ka?

    f.   Getsuyoobi kara kin'yoobi made yojikan gurai gakkoo de benkyoo shimasu ka?

C. Answer the questions below on the basis of the following calendar.

		FEBRUARY				
S	M	T	W	Th	F	S
		1	2	3	4	5
6	7	8	9	10	11	12
13	14	15	16	17	18	19
20	21	22	23	24	25	26
27	28					

1. Nangatsu desu ka?

2. Nigatsu wa nannichi arimasu ka?

3. Tsuitachi wa nan'yoobi desu ka?

4. Sono tsugi no kayoobi wa nannichi desu ka?

5. Yokka wa nan'yoobi desu ka?

6. Nannichi to nannichi ga nichiyoobi desu ka?

7. Nannichi to nannichi ga getsuyoobi desu ka?
8. Nijuu-ninichi wa suiyoobi desu ka?
9. Nigatsu nijuu-ninichi ni wa dare ga umaremashita ka?
10. Nigatsu nijuu-ninichi ni gakkoo e ikimasu ka?
11. Nijuu-ninichi no mae no kayoobi wa nannichi deshita ka?
12. Nijuu-ninichi no tsugi no kayoobi wa nannichi desu ka?
13. Nigatsu tooka wa nan'yoobi desu ka?
14. Nigatsu juu-sannichi wa nichiyoobi desu ka?
15. Rinkaan wa nannichi ni umaremashita ka?
16. Nijuu-ninichi mo juu-ninichi mo gakkoo wa yasumi desu ka?
17. Getsuyoobi ni wa benkyoo shimasu ka?
18. Doyoobi ni mo benkyoo shimasu ka?

D. Tell (ask) your friend.

1. I don't begrudge the money, but I don't want to buy that kind of television
      [set].
2. Don't you think it's too bad?
3. Is the island called Hokkaido an interesting place?
4. A person called Tanaka wrote it.
5. I don't want to go see the place called Hiroshima.
6. This Sunday, I want to study all day.
7. I'd like to see Kyōto's Hollyhock Festival.
8. What kind of a pencil do you want?
9. I'd like to read today's newspaper.
10. What kind of thing do you want to eat?

(Nihon de wa gakkoo mo daigaku mo shigatsu kara hajimarimasu. Ima wa
juugatsu desu. Dakara, rokkagetsu
mae ni hajimarimashita. Yukio wa
ima chuugaku no nihen desu.)

(In Japan, schools as well as universi-
ties begin from April. It is now October. Therefore, [school] began six
months ago. Yukio is now in the second
year of middle school.)

Otoosan: Eego no benkyoo wa doo desu
ka?

Father: How is your study of English?

Yukio: Muzukashii desu ne. Kotoba
wa oboeyasui desu ga, ha-
nashinikui desu.

Yukio: It's difficult. The words are
easy to memorize, but it's
difficult to speak it.

Otoosan: Hachigatsu no yasumi no aida
ni daibu wasureru deshoo
ne.

Father: You probably forget quite a bit
during the August vacation.

Yukio: Ee. Narubeku benkyoo shimashita ga, daibu wasure-
mashita.

Yukio: Yes, I studied it as much as
possible, but I forgot quite
a bit.

GRAMMAR

II-6.1 -nikui, -yasui

The stem of a first-conjugation verb plus -nikui (desu) or the stem of a second-conjugation verb plus -inikui (desu) has the meaning "difficult to _____."
Similarly, the stem of a first-conjugation verb plus -yasui (desu) or the stem of
a second-conjugation verb plus -iyasui (desu) has the meaning "easy to _____."
The ending is conjugated as a verbal adjective.

EXAMPLES:

Hajimenikui desu.   It's difficult to begin.
Tabeyasui desu.   They're easy to eat.
Hanashinikui desu.*   It's difficult to speak.
Mochiyasui desu.*   It's easy to carry.
Yominikuku arimasen.   It isn't difficult to read.

*Note that the "s" stem and "t" stem are transcribed "shi" and "chi."

II-6.2 Narubeku

Narubeku modifying a verb, verbal adjective or an adjectival noun has the
meaning "as (much) as possible."

EXAMPLES:

Narubeku hayaku ikimashoo.   Let's go as quickly as possible.
Narubeku shizuka ni shimashoo.   Let's be as quiet as possible.
Narubeku tabemasu.   I'll eat as much as possible.

II-6.3 Counters

Examples of counters have occurred in various lessons already. En (the Japanese unit of currency), and ji (for "o'clock") are examples of counters. There

153

are many others in addition to these in Japanese. Some counters occur in combination with Japanese numerals and some in combination with Sino-Japanese numerals.

Counters exist in English also. One says "a head" of lettuce, "a loaf" of bread, "a bar" of candy, etc. In these examples, the counters vary depending on the noun in question. In Japanese, the counters are for certain categories of nouns, and the categories are classified by shape or kind. There is a counter for large animals, one for small animals, one for flat, rectangular objects, one for long, cylindrical objects, etc.

Contractions may occur between the number and the counter. Any or all of the numbers 1, 3, 6, 8, and 10 form contractions, depending on the initial consonant of the counter.

EXAMPLES:

"h" counter (cupfuls)	"k" counter (months duration)	"s" counter (volumes)
ippai	ikkagetsu	issatsu
nihai	nikagetsu	nisatsu
sambai	sankagetsu	sansatsu
yonhai	yonkagetsu	yonsatsu
gohai	gokagetsu	gosatsu
roppai	rokkagetsu	rokusatsu
nanahai	nanakagetsu	nanasatsu
happai, hachihai	hakkagetsu	hassatsu
kyuuhai	kyuukagetsu	kyuusatsu
jippai, juppai	jikkagetsu, jukkagetsu	jissatsu, jussatsu

"t" counter (art objects)	"ch" counter (Western-style clothing)
itten	itchaku
niten	nichaku
santen	sanchaku
yonten	yonchaku
goten	gochaku
rokuten	rokuchaku
nanaten	nanachaku
hatten	hatchaku
kyuuten	kyuuchaku
jitten, jutten	jitchaku, jutchaku

DRILLS

1. Substitution

Ikkagetsu mae ni hajimarimashita.   It began one month ago.

(nikagetsu)	Nikagetsu mae ni hajimarimashita.	It began two months ago.
(sankagetsu)	Sankagetsu mae ni hajimarimashita.	It began three months ago.
(yonkagetsu)	Yonkagetsu mae ni hajimarimashita.	It began four months ago.
(gokagetsu)	Gokagetsu mae ni hajimarimashita.	It began five months ago.
(rokkagetsu)	Rokkagetsu mae ni hajimarimashita.	It began six months ago.
(nanakagetsu)	Nanakagetsu mae ni hajimarimashita.	It began seven months ago.

(hakkagetsu)	Hakkagetsu mae ni hajimarimashita.	It began eight months ago.
(kyuukagetsu)	Kyuukagetsu mae ni hajimarimashita.	It began nine months ago.
(jikkagetsu)	Jikkagetsu mae ni hajimarimashita.	It began ten months ago.
(juu-ikka-getsu)	Juu-ikkagetsu mae ni hajimarimashita.	It began eleven months ago.

2. Substitution and Response

Q. Nikagetsu kakarimasu ka?		Will it take two months?
A. Sankagetsu kakaru ka mo shiremasen.		It may take three months.

(nanakagetsu)	Nanakagetsu kakarimasu ka?	Will it take seven months?
	Hakkagetsu kakaru ka mo shiremasen.	It may take eight months.
(gokagetsu)	Gokagetsu kakarimasu ka?	Will it take five months?
	Rokkagetsu kakaru ka mo shiremasen.	It may take six months.
(ikkagetsu)	Ikkagetsu kakarimasu ka?	Will it take one month?
	Nikagetsu kakaru ka mo shiremasen.	It may take two months.
(sankagetsu)	Sankagetsu kakarimasu ka?	Will it take three months?
	Yonkagetsu kakaru ka mo shiremasen.	It may take four months.
(rokkagetsu)	Rokkagetsu kakarimasu ka?	Will it take six months?
	Nanakagetsu kakaru ka mo shiremasen.	It may take seven months.
(kyuukagetsu)	Kyuukagetsu kakarimasu ka?	Will it take nine months?
	Jikkagetsu kakaru ka mo shiremasen.	It may take ten months.

3. Substitution

Eego no benkyoo wa ichinen shimashita.		I studied English for one year.

(ninen)	Eego no benkyoo wa ninen shimashita.	I studied English for two years.
(sannen)	Eego no benkyoo wa sannen shimashita.	I studied English for three years.
(yonen)	Eego no benkyoo wa yonen shimashita.	I studied English for four years.
(gonen)	Eego no benkyoo wa gonen shimashita.	I studied English for five years.
(rokunen)	Eego no benkyoo wa rokunen shimashita.	I studied English for six years.
(shichinen)	Eego no benkyoo wa shichinen shima-shita.	I studied English for seven years.
(hachinen)	Eego no benkyoo wa hachinen shima-shita.	I studied English for eight years.
(kyuunen)	Eego no benkyoo wa kyuunen shimashita.	I studied English for nine years.
(juunen)	Eego no benkyoo wa juunen shimashita.	I studied English for ten years.

4. Progressive Substitution

Ichinen to gokagetsu tsuzukemashita.   I continued it one year
                                                      and five months.

(ninen)   Ninen to gokagetsu tsuzukemashita.   I continued it two years
                                                      and five months.

(sankagetsu)   Ninen to sankagetsu tsuzukemashita. I continued it two years
                                                      and three months.

(gonen)   Gonen to sankagetsu tsuzukemashita. I continued it five years
                                                      and three months.

(nikagetsu)   Gonen to nikagetsu tsuzukemashita.   I continued it five years
                                                      and two months.

(sannen)   Sannen to nikagetsu tsuzukemashita. I continued it three years
                                                      and two months.

(yonkagetsu)   Sannen to yonkagetsu tsuzukemashita. I continued it three years
                                                      and four months.

(ichinen)   Ichinen to yonkagetsu tsuzukemashita. I continued it one year
                                                      and four months.

(gokagetsu)   Ichinen to gokagetsu tsuzukemashita. I continued it one year
                                                      and five months.

5. Expansion

(rokunen made   Rokunen made arimasu.   It goes up through the
  arimasu)   sixth year.
(ichinen kara)   Ichinen kara rokunen made arimasu.   It goes from the first
                                                      year through the sixth
                                                      year.

(shoogakkoo   Shoogakkoo wa ichinen kara rokunen   Elementary school goes
  wa)   made arimasu.   from the first year
                                                      through the sixth year.
(Nihon no)   Nihon no shoogakkoo wa ichinen kara Elementary school in Japan
                   rokunen made arimasu.   goes from the first year
                                                      through the sixth year.

(sannen made   Sannen made arimasu.   It goes up through the
  arimasu)   third year.
(ichinen kara)   Ichinen kara sannen made arimasu.   It goes from the first
                                                      year through the third
                                                      year.

(chuugakkoo   Chuugakkoo wa ichinen kara sannen   Middle school goes from
  wa)   made arimasu.   the first year through
                                                      the third year.
(Nihon no)   Nihon no chuugakkoo wa ichinen kara Middle school in Japan
                   sannen made arimasu.   goes from the first year
                                                      through the third year.

(sannen made   Sannen made arimasu.   It goes up through the
  arimasu)   third year.

(ichinen kara)	Ichinen kara sannen made arimasu.	It goes from the first year through the third year.
(kootoo-gakkoo mo)	Kootoo-gakkoo mo ichinen kara sannen made arimasu.	High school also goes from the first year through the third year.
(Nihon no)	Nihon no kootoo-gakkoo mo ichinen kara sannen made arimasu.	High school in Japan also goes from the first year through the third year.

6. Substitution

	Daigaku no benkyoo wa muzukashii desu ka?	Are studies at the university difficult?
(shoogakkoo)	Shoogakkoo no benkyoo wa muzukashii desu ka?	Are studies in elementary school difficult?
(chuugakkoo)	Chuugakkoo no benkyoo wa muzukashii desu ka?	Are studies in middle school difficult?
(chuugaku)	Chuugaku no benkyoo wa muzukashii desu ka?	Are studies in middle school difficult?
(kootoo-gakkoo)	Kootoo-gakkoo no benkyoo wa muzukashii desu ka?	Are studies in high school difficult?
(eego)	Eego no benkyoo wa muzukashii desu ka?	Is the study of English difficult?
(nihongo)	Nihongo no benkyoo wa muzukashii desu ka?	Is the study of Japanese difficult?
(shiken)	Shiken no benkyoo wa muzukashii desu ka?	Is studying for exams difficult?
(rekishi)	Rekishi no benkyoo wa muzukashii desu ka?	Is the study of history difficult?
(chiri)	Chiri no benkyoo wa muzukashii desu ka?	Is the study of geography difficult?

7. Substitution and Affirmative Response

Q.	Chuugakkoo wa shoogakkoo yori muzukashii desu ka?	Is middle school more difficult than elementary school?
A.	Ee. Chuugakkoo wa shoogakkoo yori daibu muzukashii desu ne.	Yes, middle school is quite a bit more difficult than elementary school.
(kootoo-gakkoo, chuugaku)	Kootoo-gakkoo wa chuugaku yori muzukashii desu ka?	Is high school more difficult than middle school?
	Ee. Kootoo-gakkoo wa chuugaku yori daibu muzukashii desu ne.	Yes, high school is quite a bit more difficult than middle school.

(daigaku, koo-
too-gakkoo)
	Daigaku wa kootoo-gakkoo yori
	   muzukashii desu ka?
	Ee. Daigaku wa kootoo-gakkoo
	   yori daibu muzukashii desu ne.
		Is the university more diffi-
		cult than high school?
		Yes, the university is quite a
		bit more difficult than high
		school.

(eego, nihon-
go)
	Eego wa nihongo yori muzukashii
	   desu ka?
	Ee. Eego wa nihongo yori daibu
	   muzukashii desu ne.
		Is English more difficult than
		Japanese?
		Yes, English is quite a bit
		more difficult than Japanese.

(rekishi,
chiri)
	Rekishi wa chiri yori muzukashii
	   desu ka?
	Ee. Rekishi wa chiri yori daibu
	   muzukashii desu ne.
		Is history more difficult than
		geography?
		Yes, history is quite a bit
		more difficult than geogra-
		phy.

(kono shiken,
mae no shi-
ken)
	Kono shiken wa mae no shiken yo-
	   ri muzukashii desu ka?
	Ee. Kono shiken wa mae no shi-
	   ken yori daibu muzukashii desu
	   ne.
		Is this exam more difficult
		than the previous exam?
		Yes, this exam is quite a bit
		more difficult than the pre-
		vious exam.

8. Substitution

Nihongo wa eego hodo muzukashiku arimasen.		Japanese is not as difficult as English.
(chiri, reki- shi)	Chiri wa rekishi hodo muzuka- shiku arimasen.	Geography is not as difficult as history.
(kootoo-gak- koo, dai- gaku)	Kootoo-gakkoo wa daigaku hodo muzukashiku arimasen.	High schools are not as diffi- cult as universities.
(shoogakkoo, chuugaku)	Shoogakkoo wa chuugaku hodo muzukashiku arimasen.	Elementary schools are not as difficult as middle schools.
(kono shiken, mae no shi- ken)	Kono shiken wa mae no shiken hodo muzukashiku arimasen.	This exam is not as difficult as the previous exam.

(chuugaku
ichinen,
chuugaku
ninen)
	Chuugaku ichinen wa chuugaku
	   ninen hodo muzukashiku ari-
	   masen.
		The first year of middle school
		is not as difficult as the
		second year of middle school.

9. Grammar

(Nihongo wa eego hodo muzukashiku arimasen.)	(Japanese is not as difficult as English.)
Nihongo no hoo ga yasashii desu.	Japanese is easier.

(Kono tekisuto wa sono tekisuto hodo
   muzukashiku arimasen.)
	(This text is not as difficult as that
	   text.)

Kono tekisuto no hoo ga yasashii desu.	This text is easier.

(Kootoo-gakkoo wa daigaku hodo muzu-
   kashiku arimasen.)
	(High schools are not as difficult as uni-
	   versities.)

Kootoo-gakkoo no hoo ga yasashii desu.	High schools are easier.

(Rekishi wa chiri hodo muzukashiku
  arimasen.)
Rekishi no hoo ga yasashii desu.
(Chiri wa rekishi hodo muzukashiku
  arimasen.)
Chiri no hoo ga yasashii desu.
(Shoogakkoo wa chuugakkoo hodo muzu-
  kashiku arimasen.)
Shoogakkoo no hoo ga yasashii desu.
(Sono shiken wa kono shiken hodo
  muzukashiku arimasen.)
Sono shiken no hoo ga yasashii desu.

(History is not as difficult as geogra-
  phy.)
History is easier.
(Geography is not as difficult as his-
  tory.)
Geography is easier.
(Elementary school is not as difficult as
  middle school.)
Elementary school is easier.
(That exam is not as difficult as this
  exam.)
That exam is easier.

10. Substitution and Opposite Response

Q. Eego no shiken wa muzukashikatta desu ka?
A. Iie. Eego no shiken wa yasashikatta desu.

Was the English exam difficult?
No, the English exam was easy.

(rekishi)   Rekishi no shiken wa muzukashi-
                    katta desu ka?
                  Iie. Rekishi no shiken wa ya-
                    sashikatta desu.

Was the history exam difficult?

No, the history exam was easy.

(chuugaku   Chuugaku nihen no shiken wa mu-
  nihen)   zukashikatta desu ka?

                  Iie. Chuugaku nihen no shiken
                    wa yasashikatta desu.

Were the exams in the second
  year of middle school difficult?

No, the exams in the second
  year of middle school were
  easy.

(kugatsu)   Kugatsu no shiken wa muzukashi-
                    katta desu ka?
                  Iie. Kugatsu no shiken wa ya-
                    sashikatta desu.

Was the September exam difficult?
No, the September exam was
  easy.

(nihongo)   Nihongo no shiken wa muzukashi-
                    katta desu ka?
                  Iie. Nihongo no shiken wa ya-
                    sashikatta desu.

Was the Japanese exam difficult?
No, the Japanese exam was easy.

(chiri)   Chiri no shiken wa muzukashi-
                    katta desu ka?
                  Iie. Chiri no shiken wa yasa-
                    shikatta desu.

Was the geography exam difficult?
No, the geography exam was
  easy.

11. Substitution

Rekishi to chiri no benkyoo o hajimemashita ga,
  yasashiku arimasen.

I began the study of history
  and geography, but it isn't
  easy.

(nihongo,   Nihongo to furansugo no benkyoo
  furansugo)   o hajimemashita ga, yasashiku
                    arimasen.

I began the study of Japanese
  and French, but it isn't
  easy.

(eego, furansugo)	Eego to furansugo no benkyoo o hajimemashita ga, yasashiku arimasen.	I began the study of English and French, but it isn't easy.
(nihongo, supeingo)	Nihongo to supeingo no benkyoo o hajimemashita ga, yasashiku arimasen.	I began the study of Japanese and Spanish, but it isn't easy.
(Amerika no rekishi, chiri)	Amerika no rekishi to chiri no benkyoo o hajimemashita ga, yasashiku arimasen.	I began the study of American history and geography, but it isn't easy.
(Nihon no rekishi, chiri)	Nihon no rekishi to chiri no benkyoo o hajimemashita ga, yasashiku arimasen.	I began the study of Japanese history and geography, but it isn't easy.

12. Progressive Substitution

Wakarinikui koto o iimasu.		He says things which are difficult to understand.
(iinikui)	Iinikui koto o iimasu.	He says things which are difficult to say.
(onegai shimasu)	Iinikui koto o onegai shimasu.	He makes a request that's difficult to say.
(shinikui)	Shinikui koto o onegai shimasu.	He requests things which are difficult to do.
(shimasu)	Shinikui koto o shimasu.	He does things which are difficult to do.
(wakarinikui)	Wakarinikui koto o shimasu.	He does things which are difficult to understand.
(iimasu)	Wakarinikui koto o iimasu.	He says things which are difficult to understand.

13. Opposite Response

Q.	Mochiyasui desu ka?	Is it easy to carry?
A.	Iie. Mochinikui desu.	No, it's difficult to carry.
(Wasureyasui desu ka?)		(Is it easy to forget?)
Iie. Wasurenikui desu.		No, it's difficult to forget.
(Hanashiyasui desu ka?)		(Is it easy to speak?)
Iie. Hanashinikui desu.		No, it's difficult to speak.
(Dashiyasui desu ka?)		(Is it easy to get it out?)
Iie. Dashinikui desu.		No, it's difficult to get it out.
(Deyasui desu ka?)		(Is it easy to get out?)
Iie. Denikui desu.		No, it's difficult to get out.
(Tomeyasui desu ka?)		(Is it easy to stop them?)
Iie. Tomenikui desu.		No, it's difficult to stop them.
(Tomariyasui desu ka?)		(Is it easy to stop?)
Iie. Tomarinikui desu.		No, it's difficult to stop.
(Ireyasui desu ka?)		(Is it easy to put in?)
Iie. Irenikui desu.		No, it's difficult to put in.

(Hairiyasui desu ka?)   (Is it easy to get in?)
  Iie. Hairinikui desu.   No, it's difficult to get in.
(Kaiyasui desu ka?)   (Is it easy to buy?)
  Iie. Kainikui desu.   No, it's difficult to buy.
(Yomiyasui desu ka?)   (Is it easy to read?)
  Iie. Yominikui desu.   No, it's difficult to read.
(Shiyasui desu ka?)   (Is it easy to do?)
  Iie. Shinikui desu.   No, it's difficult to do.
(Kiyasui desu ka?)   (Is it easy to come?)
  Iie. Kinikui desu.   No, it's difficult to come.

14. Response

Q. Eego to nihongo to dotchi no hoo   Between English and Japanese, which is
      ga hanashiyasui desu ka?   easier to speak?
A. Watakushi wa eego no hoo ga hana-   For me, it's easier to speak English.
      shiyasui desu.

(Eego to furansugo to dotchi no hoo   (Between English and French, which is
    ga yomiyasui desu ka?)   easier to read?)
  Watakushi wa eego no hoo ga yomiyasui   For me, it's easier to read English.
    desu.
(Ii to atarashii to dotchi no hoo ga   (Between "atarashii" and "ii," which is
    iiyasui desu ka?)   easier to say?)
  Watakushi wa ii no hoo ga iiyasui   For me, it's easier to say "ii."
    desu.
(Chiisai hako to ookii hako to dotchi   (Between large boxes and small boxes,
    no hoo ga mochiyasui desu ka?)   which are easier to carry?)
  Watakushi wa chiisai hako no hoo ga   For me, it's easier to carry small boxes.
    mochiyasui desu.
(Supeingo no kotoba to eego no kotoba   (Between English words and Spanish words,
    tc dotchi no hoo ga wasureyasui   which are easier to forget?)
    desu ka?)
  Watakushi wa supeingo no kotoba no   For me, it's easier to forget Spanish
    hoo ga wasureyasui desu.   words.
(Tabemono to kakemono to dotchi no   (Between food and hangings, which is
    hoo ga kaiyasui desu ka?)   easier to buy?)
  Watakushi wa tabemono no hoo ga kai-   For me, it's easier to buy food.
    yasui desu.
(Shizuka na tokoro to nigiyaka na to-   (Between a lively place and a quiet place,
    koro to dotchi no hoo ga benkyoo   which is easier to study in?)
    shiyasui desu ka?)
  Watakushi wa shizuka na tokoro no hoo   For me, it's easier to study in a quiet
    ga benkyoo shiyasui desu.   place.

15. Substitution

Ikkagetsu gurai wa tsuzukeyasui to   I think it's easy to continue it for
omoimasu. Narubeku ikkagetsu tsu-   about a month. I'll do my best to con-
zukemashoo.   tinue it for one month.

(nikagetsu)	Nikagetsu gurai wa tsuzukeyasui to omoimasu. Narubeku nika-getsu tsuzukemashoo.	I think it's easy to continue it for about two months.. I'll do my best to continue it for two months.
(yojikan)	Yojikan gurai wa tsuzukeyasui to omoimasu. Narubeku yojikan tsuzukemashoo.	I think it's easy to continue it for about four hours. I'll do my best to continue it for four hours.
(yonshuukan)	Yonshuukan gurai wa tsuzukeyasui to omoimasu. Narubeku yonshuu-kan tsuzukemashoo.	I think it's easy to continue it for about four weeks. I'll do my best to continue it for four weeks.
(rokushuukan)	Rokushuukan gurai wa tsuzukeya-sui to omoimasu. Narubeku rokushuukan tsuzukemashoo.	I think it's easy to continue it for about six weeks. I'll do my best to continue it for six weeks.
(ichinen)	Ichinen gurai wa tsuzukeyasui to omoimasu. Narubeku ichinen tsuzukemashoo.	I think it's easy to continue it for about a year. I'll do my best to continue it for one year.

16. Progressive Substitution

	Iiyasuku narimashita.	It's become easier to say.
(wasurenikuku)	Wasurenikuku narimashita.	It's become more difficult to forget.
(shimashoo)	Wasurenikuku shimashoo.	Let's make it more difficult to forget.
(noriyasuku)	Noriyasuku shimashoo.	Let's make it easier to get on.
(narimashita)	Noriyasuku narimashita.	It's become easier to get on.
(mochinikuku)	Mochinikuku narimashita.	It's become more difficult to carry.
(arimasen)	Mochinikuku arimasen.	It isn't difficult to carry.
(hajimenikuku)	Hajimenikuku arimasen.	It isn't difficult to begin it.
(narimasu)	Hajimenikuku narimasu.	It'll become difficult to be-gin it.
(tsuzukeni-kuku)	Tsuzukenikuku narimasu.	It'll become difficult to con-tinue.
(arimasen)	Tsuzukenikuku arimasen.	It isn't difficult to continue.
(iiyasuku)	Iiyasuku arimasen.	It isn't easy to say.
(narimashita)	Iiyasuku narimashita.	It's become easier to say.

17. Opposite Response

Q.	Ano shoogakkoo wa hairiyasukatta deshoo ka ne.	I wonder if it was easy to get into that elementary school.
A.	Ano shoogakkoo wa hairinikukatta daroo to omoimasu.	I think it must have been difficult to get into that elementary school.

(Chikatetsu de ikiyasukatta deshoo ka ne.)

Chikatetsu de ikinikukatta daroo to omoimasu.

(Sensee ni onegai shiyasukatta deshoo ka ne.)

Sensee ni onegai shinikukatta daroo to omoimasu.

(Ushiro kara miyasukatta deshoo ka ne.)

Ushiro kara minikukatta daroo to omoimasu.

(Suiyoobi ni wa denikukatta deshoo ka ne.)

Suiyoobi ni wa deyasukatta daroo to omoimasu.

(Tanaka-san no uchi ni wa yorinikukatta deshoo ka ne.)

Tanaka-san no uchi ni wa yoriyasukatta daroo to omoimasu.

(I wonder if it was easy to go by subway.)

I think it must have been difficult to go by subway.

(I wonder if it was easy to request it of the teacher.)

I think it must have been difficult to request it of the teacher.

(I wonder if it was easy to see from the rear.)

I think it must have been difficult to see from the rear.

(I wonder if it was difficult to attend on Wednesday.)

I think it must have been easy to attend on Wednesday.

(I wonder if it was difficult to drop by at Mr. Tanaka's house.)

I think it must have been easy to drop by at Mr. Tanaka's house.

EXERCISES

A. Supply the following forms.

	-yasui	inf. perf.	inf. neg.	semi-formal neg.
Example:				
taberu	tabeyasui	tabeyasukatta	tabeyasuku nai	tabeyasuku arimasen

1. motsu
2. yomu
3. au
4. dasu
5. naru
6. kiku
7. wasureru
8. miru
9. suru
10. kuru

	-nikui	inf. perf.	inf. neg.	semi-formal neg.

11. matsu
12. yasumu
13. yuu
14. hanasu
15. suwaru
16. iku
17. kotaeru
18. okiru

19. onegai suru
20. isogu

B. Answer the following questions.

1. Nihon no gakkoo wa nangatsu ni hajimarimasu ka?
2. Yasumi wa shichigatsu hatsuka goro kara kugatsu made desu. Dono gurai no
       oyasumi desu ka?
3. Shigatsu kara oyasumi made dono gurai arimasu ka?
4. Kugatsu kara yonkagetsu benkyoo shimasu. Suru to nangatsu ni narimasu ka?
5. Shoogakkoo no ue no gakkoo wa nan to iimasu ka?
6. Shoogakkoo wa nannen made arimasu ka?
7. Amerika mo onaji desu ka? Nannen arimasu ka?
8. Chuugaku wa nannen arimasu ka?
9. Chuugaku de no benkyoo wa shoogakkoo yori muzukashii to omoimasu ka?
10. Kootoo-gakkoo wa shoogakkoo no sugu ue desu ka?
11. Kootoo-gakkoo wa nannen arimasu ka?
12. Kootoo-gakkoo de wa nani o benkyoo shimasu ka?
13. Anata wa daigaku ni hairitai desu ka?
14. Dono daigaku ni hairitai n desu ka?

C. Tell (ask) your friend.

1. I continued the study of English for as many as five years.
2. I am in the third year of middle school.
3. I was in America for one year and seven months.
4. I entered the university six months ago.
5. Nine months ago is quite some time ago.
6. It began (from) about three months ago.
7. The history exam in September was difficult.
8. You made the exam as easy as possible.
9. Those words are difficult to forget.
10. I think that English is easier than French.

Yukio:	Raishuu no getsuyoo wa chiri no shiken desu.	Yukio:	There's an exam in geography on Monday of next week.
Otoosan:	Kondo no sensee wa yoku shiken o suru ne. Isshuukan-oki da ne.	Father:	The teacher [you have] this year gives exams often, doesn't he. It's every other week, isn't it.
Yukio:	Ee. Chotto oosugite, komarimasu. Keredomo, sonna ni muzukashii shiken de wa arimasen. Sengetsu wa san-do arimashita. Dakara, ni-shuukan-goto deshita.	Yukio:	Yes. It's a little too often and I have a hard time. However, they aren't such difficult exams. There were three last month. So, it was every two weeks.
Otoosan:	Chiri no benkyoo wa omoshi-roi?	Father:	Is the study of geography interesting?
Yukio:	Ee. Kore kara Ura-Nihon to Omote-Nihon o kuraberu' n desu. Ura-Nihon ni wa ooki na toshi ga sukunai desu ne.	Yukio:	Yes. We're going to compare the Japan Sea side (back Japan) and the Pacific Ocean side (front Japan). Large cities are scarce on the Japan Sea side, aren't they.

(tsuzuku)

(to be continued)

GRAMMAR

II-7.1 Verbal adjectives (gerund form)

(a) The stem of the verbal adjective plus -kute is the gerund form. The construction "A" wa ookikute, komarimasu means "A being big, I am in difficulty."

EXAMPLES:

Chiisakute, yominikui desu.	It's small and difficult to read. (Being small, it's difficult to read.)
Shiken wa muzukashikute, komari-masu.	I have a difficult time because the exams are difficult. (The exams being diffi-cult, I have a difficult time.)
Kakinikukute, komarimashita.	It was difficult to write and I had a hard time.

(b) The gerund of the negative nai is nakute.

EXAMPLES:

Takaku nakute, yokatta desu ne.	Isn't it good that it wasn't expensive.
Yasuku nakute, warui desu ne.	It's too bad it isn't inexpensive.

II-7.2 Sugiru

(a) The stem of a verbal adjective plus sugiru forms a compound with the idea of "too _____." The newly formed compound is conjugated as a first-conjuga-tion verb.

EXAMPLES:
    Kore wa chiisasugimasu.   This is too small.
    Chotto takasugimasen ka?   Isn't it a little too expensive?

    (b) Sugiru also forms a compound with the adjectival noun.

EXAMPLES:
    Nigiyaka-sugite, komarimasu.   I have difficulty because it's too live-
                                        ly.

    Kyoo wa chotto shizuka-sugimasen   Isn't it a little too quiet today?
      ka?

    (c) Sugiru forms a compound with the stem of a first-conjugation verb and
-isugiru with the stem of a second-conjugation verb.

EXAMPLES:
    Tabesugimashita.   I ate too much.
    Ano hito wa hanashisugimasu.   That person talks too much.
    Sore wa mochisugi desu.   That's carrying too much.

II-7.3 -oki (ni)

    The suffix -oki occurs after a numeral or a numeral-counter combination. It
is the nominal form of the verb oku; in this use it means "leaving" so much time
(or space) between occurrences.

EXAMPLES:
    Ichinichi-oki ni demasu.   It leaves every other day.
    Nijikan-oki ni nomimasu.   I drink it every three hours.
    Nijippun-oki ni toorimasu.*   It passes by every twenty minutes.

*Note that in the higher numbers, oki has more of a meaning of "every" rather than
"leaving" so much interval in between.

II-7.4 -goto (ni)

    (a) The suffix -goto (ni) occurs after a numeral or a numeral-counter combi-
nation with the meaning "every" so often or at regular "intervals."

EXAMPLES:
    Ano shimbun wa nishuukan-goto ni   That newspaper comes out once every two
      demasu.   weeks.
    Ichijikan-goto ni toorimasu.   It passes every hour.

    (b) The suffix also occurs after regular time nouns.

EXAMPLES:
    Hi-goto ni yoku narimasu.   He improves every day (day by day).
    Nichiyoobi-goto ni asobi ni de-   He goes out every Sunday.
      kakemasu.

DRILLS

1. Substitution

Senshuu kita no hoo e ikimashita.   He went north last week.

(higashi)   Senshuu higashi no hoo e ikima-   He went east last week.
                     shita.
(nishi)   Senshuu nishi no hoo e ikimashi-   He went west last week.
                     ta.
(minami)   Senshuu minami no hoo e ikima-   He went south last week.
                     shita.
(Kyuushuu)   Senshuu Kyuushuu no hoo e iki-   He went to Kyushu last week.
                     mashita.
(Ura-Nihon)   Senshuu Ura-Nihon no hoo e iki-   He went to the Japan Sea side
                     mashita.   of Japan last week.
(Omote-Nihon)   Senshuu Omote-Nihon no hoo e   He went to the Pacific Ocean
                     ikimashita.   side of Japan last week.

2. Substitution

Sengetsu wa yuki no hi ga ookatta desu.   Last month there were many
                                                        snowy days.

(ame no hi)   Sengetsu wa ame no hi ga ookatta   Last month there were many
                     desu.   rainy days.
(shiken)   Sengetsu wa shiken ga ookatta   Last month there were many
                     desu.   exams.
(benkyoo)   Sengetsu wa benkyoo ga ookatta   Last month there was a lot of
                     desu.   studying to do.
(isogashii hi)   Sengetsu wa isogashii hi ga oo-   Last month there were many busy
                     katta desu.   days.
(yasumi)   Sengetsu wa yasumi ga ookatta   Last month there were many hol-
                     desu.   idays.
(omatsuri)   Sengetsu wa omatsuri ga ookatta   Last month there were many fes-
                     desu.   tivals.

3. Substitution

Senjitsu wa ame deshita.   It was rainy the other day.

(yuki)   Senjitsu wa yuki deshita.   It was snowy the other day.
(omoshiroi   Senjitsu wa omoshiroi hanashi   It was an interesting talk the
  hanashi)   deshita.   other day.
(yasashii   Senjitsu wa yasashii shiken   It was an easy exam the other
  shiken)   deshita.   day.
(isogashii hi)   Senjitsu wa isogashii hi deshita.   It was a busy day the other
                                                        day.
(nigiyaka)   Senjitsu wa nigiyaka deshita.   It was lively the other day.

4. Affirmative Response

Q. Rainen ikimasu ka?   Will you go next year?
A. Ee. Rainen ikitai to omoimasu   Yes, I would like to go next year...
       ga...

(Rainen mo tsuzukemasu ka?)   (Will you continue it next year, also?)
Ee. Rainen mo tsuzuketai to omoimasu   Yes, I would like to continue it next
   ga...   year, also...
(Raigetsu made machimasu ka?)   (Will you wait until next month?)
Ee. Raigetsu made machitai to omoi-   Yes, I would like to wait until next
   masu ga...   month...
(Raigetsu shimasu ka?)   (Will you do it next month?)
Ee. Raigetsu shitai to omoimasu ga...   Yes, I would like to do it next month...
(Raishuu kaerimasu ka?)   (Will you return next week?)
Ee. Raishuu kaeritai to omoimasu   Yes, I would like to return next week...
   ga...
(Ashita kakemasu ka?)   (Will you telephone tomorrow?)
Ee. Ashita kaketai to omoimasu ga...   Yes, I would like to telephone tomor-
                                             row...
(Rainen kakimasu ka?)   (Will you write it next year?)
Ee. Rainen kakitai to omoimasu ga...   Yes, I would like to write it next
                                             year...
(Rainen hairimasu ka?)   (Will you enter next year?)
Ee. Rainen hairitai to omoimasu   Yes, I would like to enter next year...
   ga...
(Raigetsu demasu ka?)   (Will you attend next month?)
Ee. Raigetsu detai to omoimasu ga...   Yes, I would like to attend next month...
(Raishuu kaimasu ka?)   (Will you buy it next week?)
Ee. Raishuu kaitai to omoimasu ga...   Yes, I would like to buy it next week...

5. Progressive Substitution

Kongetsu wa yasumi desu.   This month is vacation [for
                                             me].

(konshuu)   Konshuu wa yasumi desu.   This week is vacation.
(shizuka desu) Konshuu wa shizuka desu.   This week is quiet.
(komban)   Komban wa shizuka desu.   This evening is quiet.
(nigiyaka   Komban wa nigiyaka deshoo.   This evening will probably be
   deshoo)   lively.
(raishuu)   Raishuu wa nigiyaka deshoo. Next week will probably be
                                              lively.
(omatsuri   Raishuu wa omatsuri desu.   Next week is the festival.
   desu)
(raigetsu)   Raigetsu wa omatsuri desu.   Next month is the festival.
(kiree deshoo) Raigetsu wa kiree deshoo.   Next month will probably be
                                              pretty.
(rainen)   Rainen wa kiree deshoo.   Next year will probably be
                                              pretty.
(isogashii   Rainen wa isogashii desu.   Next year will be busy.
   desu)

(kongetsu)   Kongetsu wa isogashii desu.   This month is busy.
(yasumi)   Kongetsu wa yasumi desu.   This month is vacation.

6. Affirmative Response

Q. Kondo no nichiyoo wa ikaga desu ka?   How would this Sunday be?
A. Kondo no nichiyoo wa kekkoo desu.   This Sunday would be fine.

(kayoo)   Kondo no kayoo wa ikaga desu ka?   How would this Tuesday be?
               Kondo no kayoo wa kekkoo desu.   This Tuesday would be fine.
(kin'yoo)   Kondo no kin'yoo wa ikaga desu   How would this Friday be?
                   ka?
               Kondo no kin'yoo wa kekkoo desu.   This Friday would be fine.
(oyasumi no   Kondo no oyasumi no hi wa ikaga   How would this next holiday
  hi)   desu ka?   be?
               Kondo no oyasumi no hi wa kekkoo   This next holiday would be
                   desu.   fine.
(gakkoo)   Kondo no gakkoo wa ikaga desu ka?   How is the new school?
               Kondo no gakkoo wa kekkoo desu.   The new school is fine.
(uchi)   Kondo no uchi wa ikaga desu ka?   How is the new house?
               Kondo no uchi wa kekkoo desu.   The new house is fine.

7. Grammar and Substitution

(omoshiroi)   Kondo mo omoshirokatta desu.   It was interesting this time
                                                      also.

(muzukashii)   Kondo mo muzukashikatta desu.   It was difficult this time
                                                      also.

(takai)   Kondo mo takakatta desu.   It was expensive this time
                                                      also.

(ii)   Kondo mo yokatta desu.   It was good this time also.
(warui)   Kondo mo warukatta desu.   It was bad this time also.
(omoshiroku   Kondo mo omoshiroku arimasen   It was uninteresting this time
  nai)   deshita.   also.
(yoku nai)   Kondo mo yoku arimasen deshita.   It was not good this time
                                                      either.
(nigiyaka da) Kondo mo nigiyaka deshita.   It was lively this time also.
(kiree da)   Kondo mo kiree deshita.   It was pretty this time also.
(kiree de wa   Kondo mo kiree de wa arimasen   It was not pretty this time
  nai)   deshita.   either.
(yasuku nai)   Kondo mo yasuku arimasen deshita.   It was not inexpensive this
                                                      time either.
(yasui)   Kondo mo yasukatta desu.   It was inexpensive this time
                                                      also.
(isogashii)   Kondo mo isogashikatta desu.   It was busy this time also.
(nagaku nai)   Kondo mo nagaku arimasen deshita.   It didn't take long this time
                                                      either.

8. Substitution

Nido ka sando kurabemashita.   I compared it two or three times.

(sando, yodo)   Sando ka yodo kurabemashita.   I compared it three or four times.
(ichido, nido)   Ichido ka nido kurabema-   I compared it once or twice.
                   shita.
(godo, rokudo)   Godo ka rokudo kurabema-   I compared it five or six times.
                   shita.
(rokudo, nana-   Rokudo ka nanado kurabema-   I compared it six or seven times.
  do)   shita.
(shichido,   Shichido ka hachido kurabe-   I compared it seven or eight times.
  hachido)   mashita.

9. Substitution

Nido to kikitaku arimasen.   I don't want to hear it ever again.

(kurabetaku   Nido to kurabetaku arimasen.   I don't want to compare it ever
  arimasen)   again.
(denwa o kake-   Nido to denwa o kaketaku   I don't want to telephone ever
  taku arima-   arimasen.   again.
  sen)
(hajimetaku   Nido to hajimetaku arimasen.   I don't want to begin it ever again.
  arimasen)
(yoritaku   Nido to yoritaku arimasen.   I don't want to drop by ever again.
  arimasen)
(noritaku   Nido to noritaku arimasen.   I don't want to ride it ever again.
  arimasen)
(tabetaku   Nido to tabetaku arimasen.   I don't want to eat it ever again.
  arimasen)

10. Substitution and Affirmative Response

Q. Chotto muzukashisugimasen ka?   Isn't it a little too difficult?
A. Chotto muzukashisugiru ka mo shiremasen. It may be a little too difficult.

(yasashisugi-   Chotto yasashisugimasen ka?   Isn't it a little too easy?
  masen)   Chotto yasashisugiru ka mo   It may be a little too easy.
                   shiremasen.
(yosugimasen)   Chotto yosugimasen ka?   Isn't it a little too good?
                 Chotto yosugiru ka mo shi-   It may be a little too good.
                   remasen.
(ookisugima-   Chotto ookisugimasen ka?   Isn't it a little too big?
  sen)   Chotto ookisugiru ka mo   It may be a little too big.
                   shiremasen.
(takasugima-   Chotto takasugimasen ka?   Isn't it a little too expensive?
  sen)   Chotto takasugiru ka mo   It may be a little too expensive.
                   shiremasen.

(hayasugima-sen)	Chotto hayasugimasen ka?	Isn't it a little too early?
	Chotto hayasugiru ka mo shiremasen.	It may be a little too early.
(kitanasugi-masen)	Chotto kitanasugimasen ka?	Isn't it a little too dirty?
	Chotto kitanasugiru ka mo shiremasen.	It may be a little too dirty.
(semasugima-sen)	Chotto semasugimasen ka?	Isn't it a little too narrow?
	Chotto semasugiru ka mo shiremasen.	It may be a little too narrow.
(nadakasugi-masen)	Chotto nadakasugimasen ka?	Isn't it a little too famous?
	Chotto nadakasugiru ka mo shiremasen.	It may be a little too famous.
(sukunasugi-masen)	Chotto sukunasugimasen ka?	Isn't it a little too few?
	Chotto sukunasugiru ka mo shiremasen.	It may be a little too few.
(mijikasugi-masen)	Chotto mijikasugimasen ka?	Isn't it a little too short?
	Chotto mijikasugiru ka mo shiremasen.	It may be a little too short.
(toosugimasen)	Chotto toosugimasen ka?	Isn't it a little too far?
	Chotto toosugiru ka mo shiremasen.	It may be a little too far.
(hirosugima-sen)	Chotto hirosugimasen ka?	Isn't it a little too wide?
	Chotto hirosugiru ka mo shiremasen.	It may be a little too wide.
(furusugima-sen)	Chotto furusugimasen ka?	Isn't it a little too old?
	Chotto furusugiru ka mo shiremasen.	It may be a little too old.
(hikusugima-sen)	Chotto hikusugimasen ka?	Isn't it a little too low?
	Chotto hikusugiru ka mo shiremasen.	It may be a little too low.

11. Grammar

(sukunai)	Sukunasugimasu.	It's too few.
(nagai)	Nagasugimasu.	It's too long.
(kitanai)	Kitanasugimasu.	It's too dirty.
(chiisai)	Chiisasugimasu.	It's too small.
(chikai)	Chikasugimasu.	It's too near.
(ii)	Yosugimasu.	It's too good.
(ookii)	Ookisugimasu.	It's too big.
(atarashii)	Atarashisugimasu.	It's too new.
(ooi)	Oosugimasu.	It's too many.
(osoi)	Ososugimasu.	It's too late.
(hiroi)	Hirosugimasu.	It's too wide.
(tooi)	Toosugimasu.	It's too far.
(yasui)	Yasusugimasu.	It's too cheap.
(warui)	Warusugimasu.	It's too bad.
(hikui)	Hikusugimasu.	It's too low.
(furui)	Furusugimasu.	It's too old.

12. Grammar and Affirmative Response

Q. Sukoshi tabesugimashita ka?   Did you eat a little too much?
A. Ee. Sukoshi tabesugimashita.   Yes, I ate a little too much.

(yomisugiru)   Sukoshi yomisugimashita ka?   Did you read a little too much?
(kaisugiru)   Sukoshi kaisugimashita ka?   Did you buy a little too much?
(yasumisugiru)   Sukoshi yasumisugimashita   Did you take too many holidays?
                   ka?
(ikisugiru)   Sukoshi ikisugimashita ka?   Did you go a little beyond?
(arisugiru)   Sukoshi arisugimashita ka?   Was there a little too much?
(asobisugiru)   Sukoshi asobisugimashita ka?   Did you play a little too much?
(nagaku kaka-   Sukoshi nagaku kakarisugima-   Did it take a little too long?
  risugiru)   shita ka?
(isogisugiru)   Sukoshi isogisugimashita ka?   Did you hurry a little too much?
(iresugiru)   Sukoshi iresugimashita ka?   Did you put in a little too much?
(oosugiru)   Sukoshi oosugimashita ka?   Was it a few too many?
(sukunasugiru)   Sukoshi sukunasugimashita   Was it a little too few?
                   ka?
(isogashisugi-   Sukoshi isogashisugimashita   Was it a little too busy?
  ru)   ka?
(nigiyaka-   Sukoshi nigiyaka-sugimashita   Was it a little too lively?
  sugiru)   ka?
(kiree-sugiru)   Sukoshi kiree-sugimashita   Was it a little too pretty?
                   ka?
(shizuka-   Sukoshi shizuka-sugimashita   Was it a little too quiet?
  sugiru)   ka?

13. Grammar

(motsu)   Mochisugimashita.   He carried too much.
(matsu)   Machisugimashita.   He waited too long.
(yuu)   Iisugimashita.   He said too much.
(kau)   Kaisugimashita.   He bought too much.
(tomaru)   Tomarisugimashita.   He stopped too often.
(noru)   Norisugimashita.   He rode too much.
(hanasu)   Hanashisugimashita.   He spoke too much.
(dasu)   Dashisugimashita.   He served too much.
(iku)   Ikisugimashita.   He went too far.
(kaku)   Kakisugimashita.   He wrote too much.
(yomu)   Yomisugimashita.   He read too much.
(yasumu)   Yasumisugimashita.   He rested too much.
(kuru)   Kisugimashita.   He came too often.
(benkyoo suru) Benkyoo shisugimashita.   He studied too much.
(taberu)   Tabesugimashita.   He ate too much.
(tsuzukeru)   Tsuzukesugimashita.   He continued it for too long.
(miru)   Misugimashita.   He looked too long.

14. Substitution

Jippun-goto ni demasu.   It leaves every ten minutes.

(juu-gofun-goto ni)   Juu-gofun-goto ni demasu.   It leaves every fifteen min-
                                                      utes.
(nijippun-goto ni)   Nijippun-goto ni demasu.   It leaves every twenty minutes.
(ichijikan-goto ni)   Ichijikan-goto ni demasu.   It leaves every hour.
(sanjikan-goto ni)   Sanjikan-goto ni demasu.   It leaves every three hours.
(mikka-goto ni)   Mikka-goto ni demasu.   It leaves every third day.
(yokka-goto ni)   Yokka-goto ni demasu.   It leaves every fourth day.
(isshuukan-goto ni)   Isshuukan-goto ni demasu.   It leaves every week.
(nishuukan-goto ni)   Nishuukan-goto ni demasu.   It leaves every two weeks.
(sankagetsu-goto   Sankagetsu-goto ni demasu.   It leaves every three months.
  ni)
(rokkagetsu-goto   Rokkagetsu-goto ni demasu.   It leaves every six months.
  ni)
(ninen-goto ni)   Ninen-goto ni demasu.   It leaves every two years.

15. Progressive Substitution

Futsuka-oki ni shimasu.   I do it every three days.

(ichinichi)   Ichinichi-oki ni shimasu.   I do it every two days.
(kurabemasu)   Ichinichi-oki ni kurabemasu.   I compare them every other day.
(ikkagetsu)   Ikkagetsu-oki ni kurabemasu.   I compare them every other
                                                     month.
(ikimasu)   Ikkagetsu-oki ni ikimasu.   I go every other month.
(nikagetsu)   Nikagetsu-oki ni ikimasu.   I go every three months.
(demasu)   Nikagetsu-oki ni demasu.   It leaves every three months.
(ichijikan)   Ichijikan-oki ni demasu.   It leaves every other hour.
(yasumimasu)   Ichijikan-oki ni yasumimasu.   I rest every other hour.
(ichinen)   Ichinen-oki ni yasumimasu.   I rest every other year.
(yorimasu)   Ichinen-oki ni yorimasu.   It stops (drops in) every other
                                                     year.
(futsuka)   Futsuka-oki ni yorimasu.   I drop by every three days.
(shimasu)   Futsuka-oki ni shimasu.   I do it every three days.

16. Affirmative Response (goto to oki)

Q. Mikka-goto ni demasu ka?   Does it leave every three days?
A. Ee. Futsuka-oki ni demasu.   Yes, it leaves every three days.

(Futsuka-goto ni ikimasu ka?)   (Do you go there every two days?)
Ee. Ichinichi-oki ni ikimasu.   Yes, I go there every other day.
(Nikagetsu-goto ni aimasu ka?)   (Do you see him every two months?)
Ee. Ikkagetsu-oki ni aimasu.   Yes, I see him every other month.
(Nishuukan-goto ni kaimasu ka?)   (Do you buy it every two weeks?)
Ee. Isshuukan-oki ni kaimasu.   Yes, I buy it every other week.
(Sannen-goto ni demasu ka?)   (Do you attend once in three years?)
Ee. Ninen-oki ni demasu.   Yes, I attend once in three years.

(Yojikan-goto ni tabemasu ka?)   (Do you eat every four hours?)
Ee. Sanjikan-oki ni tabemasu.   Yes, I eat every four hours.

17. Grammar

(muzukashii)   Muzukashikute, komarimasu.   It's difficult and I have a diffi-
                                                    cult time.

(kakinikui)   Kakinikukute, komarimasu.   It's difficult to write and I have
                                                    a difficult time.

(mochinikui)   Mochinikukute, komarimasu.   It's difficult to hold and I have
                                                    a difficult time.

(isogashii)   Isogashikute, komarimasu.   I'm busy and have a difficult time.

(kitanai)   Kitanakute, komarimasu.   It's dirty and I have a difficult
                                                    time.

(hoshii)   Hoshikute, komarimasu.   I want it and I have a difficult
                                                    time.

(nadakai)   Nadakakute, komarimasu.   He's famous and I have a difficult
                                                    time.

(ooi)   Ookute, komarimasu.   There are many and I have a diffi-
                                                    cult time.

(sukunai)   Sukunakute, komarimasu.   They are few and I have a difficult
                                                    time.

(takai)   Takakute, komarimasu.   It's expensive and I have a diffi-
                                                    cult time.

(chiisai)   Chiisakute, komarimasu.   It's small and I have a difficult
                                                    time.

18. Grammar (forming one sentence from two)

(Hi ga nagai desu.) (Ii desu.)   (The days are long.) (They are nice.)
 Hi ga nagakute, ii desu.   The days are long and nice.
(Heya ga semai desu.) (Ooi desu.)   (The rooms are narrow.) (There are many.)
 Heya ga semakute, ooi desu.   The rooms are narrow and many.
(Uchi ga sukunai desu.) (Takai desu.)   (Houses are few.) (They are expensive.)
 Uchi ga sukunakute, takai desu.   Houses are few and expensive.
(Ano kisha wa kitanai desu.) (Osoi   (That train is dirty.) (It is slow.)
  desu.)
 Ano kisha wa kitanakute, osoi desu.   That train is dirty and slow.
(Ano hito wa nadakai desu.) (Isoga-   (That person is famous.) (He is busy.)
 shii desu.)
 Ano hito wa nadakakute, isogashii   That person is famous and busy.
  desu.
(Kono zasshi wa omoshiroi desu.)   (This magazine is interesting.) (It is
  (Yasui desu.)   inexpensive.)
 Kono zasshi wa omoshirokute, yasui   This magazine is interesting and inex-
  desu.   pensive.
(Ano uchi wa furui desu.) (Ookii   (That house is old.) (It is large.)
  desu.)
 Ano uchi wa furukute, ookii desu.   That house is old and large.

(Ano yama wa yuki ga ooi desu.)   (There is a lot of snow on that mountain.)
  (Kiree desu.)   (It is pretty.)
Ano yama wa yuki ga ookute, kiree   There is a lot of snow on that mountain
  desu.   and it is pretty.

19.   Expansion

(daibu chigai-masu)	Daibu chigaimasu.	They differ quite a bit.
(Ura-Nihon to)	Ura-Nihon to daibu chigai-masu.	It differs quite a bit from the Japan Sea side (back Japan).
(Omote-Nihon to)	Omote-Nihon to Ura-Nihon to daibu chigaimasu.	The Pacific Ocean side (front Japan) and the Japan Sea side differ quite a bit.
(yuki ga suku-nai desu)	Yuki ga sukunai desu.	There is little snow.
(Omote-Nihon wa)	Omote-Nihon wa yuki ga suku-nai desu.	Front-Japan has little snow.
(Ura-Nihon wa yuki ga oo-kute)	Ura-Nihon wa yuki ga ookute, Omote-Nihon wa yuki ga sukunai desu.	Back-Japan has a lot of snow and Front-Japan has little snow.
(sonna ni oo-kiku arima-sen)	Sonna ni ookiku arimasen.	They aren't so large.
(Ura-Nihon no toshi wa)	Ura-Nihon no toshi wa sonna ni ookiku arimasen.	Cities on the Japan Sea side are not so large.
(Omote-Nihon no toshi wa ookii kere-domo)	Omote-Nihon no toshi wa oo-kii keredomo, Ura-Nihon no toshi wa sonna ni ookiku arimasen.	Cities on the Pacific side of Japan are large, but the cities on the Japan Sea side are not so large.
(takai yama ga arimasu)	Takai yama ga arimasu.	There are high mountains.
(aida ni)	Aida ni takai yama ga ari-masu.	There are high mountains in between.
(Omote-Nihon to Ura-Nihon no)	Omote-Nihon to Ura-Nihon no aida ni takai yama ga ari-masu.	There are high mountains between Front and Back-Japan.
(raigetsu no zasshi ni demasu)	Raigetsu no zasshi ni de-masu.	It will appear in next month's issue.
(tsuzuki wa)	Tsuzuki wa raigetsu no zasshi ni demasu.	The continuation will appear in next month's issue.
(kono hana-shi no)	Kono hanashi no tsuzuki wa raigetsu no zasshi ni de-masu.	The continuation of this story will appear in next month's issue.

(Hokkaidoo desu)	Hokkaidoo desu.	It's Hokkaidō.
(ichiban kita no shima wa)	Ichiban kita no shima wa Hokkaidoo desu.	The northernmost island is Hokkaidō.
(shima no naka de)	Shima no naka de ichiban kita no shima wa Hokkaidoo desu.	Of the islands, the northernmost is Hokkaidō.
(Nihon no yottsu no ooki na)	Nihon no yottsu no ooki na shima no naka de ichiban kita no shima wa Hokkaidoo desu.	Of Japan's four big islands, the northernmost is Hokkaidō.
(ichiban minami desu)	Ichiban minami desu.	It's the southernmost.
(Kyuushuu to yuu shima ga)	Kyuushuu to yuu shima ga ichiban minami desu.	The island called Kyūshū is the southernmost.
(sono yottsu no ooki na shima no naka de)	Sono yottsu no ooki na shima no naka de Kyuushuu to yuu shima ga ichiban minami desu.	Of those four large islands, the one called Kyūshū is the southernmost.
(daibu arimasu)	Daibu arimasu.	There is quite a bit.
(higashi kara nishi e mo)	Higashi kara nishi e mo daibu arimasu.	There is quite a bit from east to west also.
(kita kara minami e nagai desu ga)	Kita kara minami e nagai desu ga, higashi kara nishi e mo daibu arimasu.	It's long from north to south, but there is quite a bit from east to west also.
(Honshuu wa)	Honshuu wa kita kara minami e nagai desu ga, higashi kara nishi e mo daibu arimasu.	Honshū is long from north to south, but there is quite a bit from east to west also.

EXERCISES

A. Supply the missing word which would complete the sentence and make it a true
     statement.

1. Nihon wa ooki na shima ga _____ arimasu.
2. Sono naka de ichiban _____ no shima wa Hokkaidoo desu.
3. Hokkaidoo wa _____ no kita ni arimasu.
4. Honshuu wa kita kara _____ e nagai desu.
5. Honshuu wa _____ kara nishi e mo daibu arimasu.
6. _____ wa Kyuushuu yori chiisai desu.
7. Omote-Nihon wa _____ yori ooki na toshi ga ooi desu.
8. Ura-Nihon wa _____ ga ooi desu.
9. Shichigatsu wa _____ ga nagai desu.
10. Juunigatsu wa hi ga _____ desu.
11. Kongetsu wa sangatsu desu. _____ wa shigatsu desu.
12. _____ mo konshuu mo isogashikatta desu.

B.   Make single sentences of the following sets of sentences.

1.   Nihon wa yama ga ooi desu.   Komarimasu.
2.   Ano hon wa wakarinikukatta desu.   Komarimashita.
3.   Kore wa takai desu.   Yosugimasu.
4.   Sono gakkoo no hoo ga chikai desu.   Ii to omoimasu.
5.   Heya ga chiisai desu.   Konna ookii mono wa hairimasen.
6.   Ano machi wa furui desu.   Omoshiroi tokoro desu.
7.   Yasumi ga nagai desu.   Ii desu ne.
8.   Kore wa chiisai desu.   Takasugimasu.
9.   Ano hon yori atarashii desu.   Ii desu.
10. Kono michi wa hiroi desu.   Atarashii desu.

C.   Supply the missing items.

1.   _____-oki ni asobi ni kimasu.   He comes for a visit every other year.
2.   _____-goto ni asobi ni ki-   He comes for a visit once every two
     masu.   years.
3.   _____-goto ni muzukashiku   It becomes more difficult by the day.
     narimasu.
4.   _____-oki ni nori ni kitai   I'd like to come ride every three days.
     desu.
5.   _____-goto wa oosugimasen ka?   Isn't every two days too frequent?
6.   _____-oki ni shiken ga ari-   There is an exam every other week.
     masu.
7.   _____-goto ni dekakemasu.   He goes out once every three weeks.
8.   _____-goto ni kimasu.   It comes every ten minutes.
9.   _____-oki ni demasu.   One leaves every four days.
10. _____-oki wa ikaga desu ka?   How about every other month?

D.   Read (or listen to) the following passage, then answer the questions which
     follow.

     Yukio-san wa raishuu kara Ura-Nihon no koto o benkyoo shimasu. Keredomo,
sonna ni Ura-Nihon no koto o shirimasen. Dakara, kyoo toshokan e chiri ya rekishi
no hon o yomi ni ikimashita. Ura-Nihon no toshi no koto ya, omatsuri ya, yama ya,
kotoba no chigai no koto kara benkyoo o hajimemashita. Nihon no hito wa Ura-Nihon
to iimasu ga, sono Ura-Nihon no kita to minami wa daibu chigau to Yukio wa wakarimashita. Yukio wa kono hon mo ano hon mo yomitai n desu. Hon ga ookute komarimasu. Ashita mo toshokan de sono benkyoo o tsuzukeru to omoimasu.

1.   Yukio-san wa raishuu kara nani o hajimemasu ka?
2.   Yukio-san wa Ura-Nihon no koto o sonna ni shirimasen ka?
3.   Dakara, kyoo wa doko e ikimashita ka?
4.   Dooshite soko e ikimashita ka?
5.   Donna hon o yomi ni ikimashita ka?
6.   Benkyoo wa nani kara hajimemashita ka?
7.   Ura-Nihon ni yama ga ooi to omoimasu ka?   Dooshite desu ka?
8.   Ura-Nihon wa kita mo minami mo onaji desu ka?
9.   Yukio wa donna koto ga wakarimashita ka?
10. Yomitai hon wa sukunai desu ka?

11. Ashita mo toshokan e iku deshoo ka?
12. Ashita wa nani o suru deshoo ka?

E. Tell your friend:

1. that you ate too much.
2. that you bought too much. Therefore, you have no money.
3. that there was not an exam last week. Therefore, there may be one this week.
4. that the exam the other day was difficult.
5. that you heard there is more snow this year.
6. that you never want to eat it again.
7. that you saw (met) him two or three times.
8. that rainy days were too few last month.

Yukio:	Sono hoka ni doo chigaimasu ka?	Yukio:	Besides that, how do they differ?
Otoosan:	Soo desu ne. Omote-Nihon to Ura-Nihon no aida ni takai yama ga aru deshoo. Sono yama no nishi wa samukute yuki ga ooi n desu.	Father:	Let's see. There are some high mountains between Pacific and Japan-Sea Honshū, aren't there. It's cold west of those mountains and there is lots of snow.
Yukio:	Fuji-san mo yuki de shiroi desu ne. Fuji-san mo sono yama no hitotsu desu ka?	Yukio:	Mt. Fuji is also white with snow, isn't it. Is Mt. Fuji also among those mountains?
Obaasan:	Yukio, sore wa chigaimasu yo. Fuji-san wa hoka no yama no hitotsu desu. Honshuu o higashi to nishi ni wakeru takai yama ga aru n desu. Sono hitotsu desu.	Grandmother:	No, that's wrong, Yukio. Mt. Fuji belongs to another mountain [range]. There are high mountains which divide Honshū into east and west. It belongs to that.
Yukio:	Aa, soo desu ka. Motto kiki-tai koto ga takusan arimasu ga...	Yukio:	Oh, I see. There's lots more I want to ask...
Otoosan:	Yukio wa chiri no benkyoo ga suki desu ne.	Father:	You like the study of geography, don't you.

GRAMMAR

II-8.1 Modifiers

In Units I and II, modifiers of nouns have been introduced. They have been "noun plus no," "adjectival noun plus na," and informal forms of verbal adjectives.

EXAMPLES:

Ame no hi wa ooi desu.   Rainy days are numerous.
  (Ame no modifying hi)
Kiree na uchi desu ne.   It's a pretty house, isn't it.
  (Kiree na modifying uchi)
Ookii, ii uchi desu.   It's a large, nice house.
  (Ookii, ii modifying uchi)
Takaku nai jidoosha ga kaitai   I want to buy a car that's not expensive.
  desu.
  (Takaku nai modifying jidoosha)
Muzukashikatta shiken wa itsu no   The exam that was difficult was which
  deshita ka?   (when's) exam?
  (Muzukashikatta modifying shiken)

Similarly, the informal forms of verbs also modify nouns. (Only the non-past

179

forms of verbs have been introduced in the informal form. Other informal forms
will be introduced in Unit III.)

EXAMPLES:
    Yomu hon ga arimasen.   I don't have a book to read.
    Yomu no ga suki desu.   I like to read (reading).
    Miru tokoro wa takusan arimasu.   There are many places to see.

The subject of the modifier is followed by no. (It also occurs with ga.)

EXAMPLES:
    Yukio no tabetai okashi wa dore   Which is the cake that you want to eat,
      desu ka?   Yukio?
    Yukio-san no taberu no wa hayai Yukio eats fast. (Yukio's eating is
      desu.   fast.)
Compare with:
    Yukio-san wa taberu no ga hayai Yukio is fast in eating. (As for Yukio,
      desu.   his eating is fast.)

II-8.2 Noun no
    The noun no is modified by a noun, an adjectival noun plus na, an informal
form of the verbal adjective, or an informal form of the verb. The non-past verb
modifying no has a gerundial meaning (for example, reading, writing, etc.) in
English.

EXAMPLES:
    Benkyoo suru no wa omoshiroi desu. Studying is fun.
    Taberu no ga suki desu.   He likes to eat (eating).

II-8.3 Noun form of colors
    Colors such as akai and shiroi are verbal adjectives. The noun form for such
colors is the -ku form, without the final -ku ending.

EXAMPLES:
    Kiiro wa kiree na iro desu ne.   Yellow is a pretty color, isn't it.
    Aka desu.   It's red (also said of a red traffic
                             light).
    Ao ni narimashita.   It's become green.

(Aoi describes green as well as blue, particularly in reference to colors of na-
ture such as the color of the water, leaves, and grass.)

DRILLS

1. Substitution

Aoi yoofuku ga suki desu.   I like blue dresses.

(shiroi)   Shiroi yoofuku ga suki desu.   I like white dresses.
(kuroi)   Kuroi yoofuku ga suki desu.   I like black dresses.
(akai)   Akai yoofuku ga suki desu.   I like red dresses.

(kiiroi)	Kiiroi yoofuku ga suki desu.	I like yellow dresses.
(chairo no)	Chairo no yoofuku ga suki desu.	I like brown dresses.
(midori no)	Midori no yoofuku ga suki desu.	I like green dresses.

2. Affirmative Response (using objects)

Q. Kiiroi desu ka?   Is it yellow?
A. Ee. Kiiroi desu.   Yes, it's yellow.

(akai)	Akai desu ka?	Is it red?
(kuroi)	Kuroi desu ka?	Is it black?
(shiroi)	Shiroi desu ka?	Is it white?
(aoi)	Aoi desu ka?	Is it blue?
(midori)	Midori desu ka?	Is it green?
(chairo)	Chairo desu ka?	Is it brown?

3. Substitution and Negative Response

Q. Akaku narimashita ka?   Did he blush (become red)?
A. Iie. Akaku arimasen yo.   No, he isn't red!

(aoku)	Aoku narimashita ka?	Did he turn pale?
	Iie. Aoku arimasen yo.	No, he isn't pale!
(shiroku)	Shiroku narimashita ka?	Has it become white?
	Iie. Shiroku arimasen yo.	No, it isn't white!
(kuroku)	Kuroku narimashita ka?	Has it turned dark?
	Iie. Kuroku arimasen yo.	No, it isn't dark!
(kiiroku)	Kiiroku narimashita ka?	Has it turned yellow?
	Iie. Kiiroku arimasen yo.	No, it isn't yellow!
(chairo ni)	Chairo ni narimashita ka?	Has it become brown?
	Iie. Chairo de wa arimasen yo.	No, it isn't brown!
(midori ni)	Midori ni narimashita ka?	Has it become green?
	Iie. Midori de wa arimasen yo.	No, it isn't green!

4. Substitution and Negative Response

Q. Ichiban suki na iro wa ao desu ka?   Is blue your favorite color?
A. Iie. Ichiban suki na iro wa ao de wa ari-   No, blue isn't my favorite
    masen.   color.

(chairo)	Ichiban suki na iro wa chairo desu ka?	Is brown your favorite color?
	Iie. Ichiban suki na iro wa chairo de wa arimasen.	No, brown isn't my favorite color.
(aka)	Ichiban suki na iro wa aka desu ka?	Is red your favorite color?
	Iie. Ichiban suki na iro wa aka de wa arimasen.	No, red isn't my favorite color.

(midori)	Ichiban suki na iro wa midori desu ka?	Is green your favorite color?
	Iie. Ichiban suki na iro wa midori de wa arimasen.	No, green isn't my favorite color.
(kuro)	Ichiban suki na iro wa kuro desu ka?	Is black your favorite color?
	Iie. Ichiban suki na iro wa kuro de wa arimasen.	No, black isn't my favorite color.
(shiro)	Ichiban suki na iro wa shiro desu ka?	Is white your favorite color?
	Iie. Ichiban suki na iro wa shiro de wa arimasen.	No, white isn't my favorite color.
(kiiro)	Ichiban suki na iro wa kiiro desu ka?	Is yellow your favorite color?
	Iie. Ichiban suki na iro wa kiiro de wa arimasen.	No, yellow isn't my favorite color.

5. Response (using objects)

Q. Kono _____ wa nani iro desu ka?   What color is this _____ ?
A. Sore wa _____ desu.   That's _____ .

6. Substitution

Joozu ni narimashita.   He's become skillful.

(heta)	Heta ni narimashita.	He's become unskillful.
(suki)	Suki ni narimashita.	He's gotten to like it.
(kirai)	Kirai ni narimashita.	He's gotten to dislike it.
(shizuka)	Shizuka ni narimashita.	He's become quiet.

7. Substitution

Sore ga kirai na n desu.   That's what he dislikes.

(suki)	Sore ga suki na n desu.	That's what he likes.
(joozu)	Sore ga joozu na n desu.	That's what he's good at.
(heta)	Sore ga heta na n desu.	That's what he's poor at.

8. Progressive Substitution

Ryokoo suru no wa suki de wa arimasen ga...   I don't [particularly] like
                                                     traveling, but...

(onegai suru)	Onegai suru no wa suki de wa arimasen ga...	I don't [particularly] like making requests, but...
(kirai)	Onegai suru no wa kirai de wa arimasen ga...	I don't [particularly] dislike making requests, but...

(hanasu)	Hanasu no wa kirai de wa arimasen ga...	I don't [particularly] dislike speaking, but...
(heta)	Hanasu no wa heta de wa arimasen ga...	I'm not [particularly] poor at speaking, but...
(kaku)	Kaku no wa heta de wa arimasen ga...	I'm not [particularly] poor at writing, but...
(joozu)	Kaku no wa joozu de wa arimasen ga...	I'm not [particularly] skillful at writing, but...
(miru)	Miru no wa joozu de wa arimasen ga...	I'm not [particularly] skillful at judging (looking), but...
(kirai)	Miru no wa kirai de wa arimasen ga...	I don't [particularly] dislike seeing it, but...
(ryokoo suru)	Ryokoo suru no wa kirai de wa arimasen ga...	I don't [particularly] dislike traveling, but...
(suki)	Ryokoo suru no wa suki de wa arimasen ga...	I don't [particularly] like traveling, but...

9. Affirmative Response

Q. Shigatsu goro wa attakai desu ka?   Is it warm around April?
A. Ee. Shigatsu goro wa attakai desu.   Yes, it's warm around April.

(Kugatsu goro wa atatakai desu ka?)   (Is it warm around September?)
(Shichigatsu goro wa atsui desu ka?)   (Is it hot around July?)
(Juugatsu goro wa suzushii desu ka?)   (Is it cool around October?)
(Nigatsu goro wa samui desu ka?)   (Is it cold around February?)
(Kita no hoo wa samui desu ka?)   (Is the North cold?)
(Minami no hoo wa atsui desu ka?)   (Is the South hot?)
(Nishi no hoo wa suzushii desu ka?)   (Is the West cool?)

10. Substitution and Negative Response

Q. Chotto atsuku arimasen ka?   Isn't it a little hot?
A. Iie. Atsuku wa arimasen.   No, it isn't hot.

(samuku)	Chotto samuku arimasen ka?	Isn't it a little cold?
	Iie. Samuku wa arimasen.	No, it isn't cold.
(attakaku)	Chotto attakaku arimasen ka?	Isn't it a little warm?
	Iie. Attakaku wa arimasen.	No, it isn't warm.
(atatakaku)	Chotto atatakaku arimasen ka?	Isn't it a little warm?
	Iie. Atatakaku wa arimasen.	No, it isn't warm.
(suzushiku)	Chotto suzushiku arimasen ka?	Isn't it a little cool?
	Iie. Suzushiku wa arimasen.	No, it isn't cool.

11. Grammar (combining two sentences into one)

(Hokkaidoo wa samui desu.)   (Hokkaido is cold.)
(Yuki ga ooi desu.)   (There is a lot of snow.)
 Hokkaidoo wa samukute, yuki ga ooi   Hokkaido is cold and there is a lot of
   desu.   snow.

(Kyooto wa hachigatsu atsui desu.)   (Kyoto is hot in August.)
(Suki de wa arimasen.)   (I don't like it.)
Kyooto wa hachigatsu atsukute suki   Kyoto is hot in August and I don't like
   de wa arimasen.   it.

(Yokohama wa Tookyoo yori chotto suzu-   (Yokohama is a little cooler than Tokyo.)
   shii desu.)
(Ii to omoimasu.)   (I think it's nice.)
Yokohama wa Tookyoo yori chotto suzu-   Yokohama is a little cooler than Tokyo
   shikute ii to omoimasu.   and I think it's nice.

(Nagasaki wa attakai desu.)   (Nagasaki is warm.)
(Yuki no hi wa sukunai desu.)   (Snowy days are few in number.)
Nagasaki wa attakakute, yuki no hi wa   Nagasaki is warm, and snowy days are
   sukunai desu.   few in number.

(Omote-Nihon wa Ura-Nihon hodo samuku   (The Pacific Ocean side of Honshu is not
   nai desu.)   as cold as the Japan Sea side.)
(Ookii toshi ga arimasu.)   (There are large cities.)
Omote-Nihon wa Ura-Nihon hodo samuku   The Pacific Ocean side of Honshu is not
   nakute, ookii toshi ga arimasu.   as cold as the Japan Sea side, and
                                                there are large cities.

12. Progressive Substitution

Tsumetai ocha wa ikaga desu ka?   How about some iced tea?

(atsui)   Atsui ocha wa ikaga desu ka?   How about some hot tea?
(mono)   Atsui mono wa ikaga desu ka?   How about something hot?
(atatakai)   Atatakai mono wa ikaga desu ka?   How about something warm?
(pan)   Atatakai pan wa ikaga desu ka?   How about some warm bread?
(yasui)   Yasui pan wa ikaga desu ka?   How about some cheap bread?
(oyunomi)   Yasui oyunomi wa ikaga desu ka?   How about a cheap teacup?
(akai)   Akai oyunomi wa ikaga desu ka?   How about a red teacup?
(yoofuku)   Akai yoofuku wa ikaga desu ka?   How about a red dress?
(attakai)   Attakai yoofuku wa ikaga desu ka?   How about some warm clothes?
(tabemono)   Attakai tabemono wa ikaga desu   How about some warm food?
                 ka?
(tsumetai)   Tsumetai tabemono wa ikaga desu   How about some cold food?
                 ka?
(ocha)   Tsumetai ocha wa ikaga desu ka?   How about some iced tea?

13. Progressive Substitution

Tsumetai mizu ga nomitai desu.   I would like to drink some
                                                         cold water.

(mono)   Tsumetai mono ga nomitai desu.   I would like to drink some-
                                                         thing cold.
(atsui)   Atsui mono ga nomitai desu.   I would like to drink some-
                                                         thing hot.

(ocha)	Atsui ocha ga nomitai desu.	I would like to drink some hot tea.
(ii)	Ii ocha ga nomitai desu.	I would like to drink some good tea.
(mono)	Ii mono ga nomitai desu.	I would like to drink something good.
(tsumetai)	Tsumetai mono ga nomitai desu.	I would like to drink something cold.
(mizu)	Tsumetai mizu ga nomitai desu.	I would like to drink some cold water.

14. Progressive Substitution

Okiru no ga osoi desu.   He's late in rising.

(hajimeru)	Hajimeru no ga osoi desu.	He's slow in beginning it.
(joozu)	Hajimeru no ga joozu desu.	He's good at beginning it.
(hanasu)	Hanasu no ga joozu desu.	He's good at speaking.
(heta)	Hanasu no ga heta desu.	He's poor at speaking.
(wakeru)	Wakeru no ga heta desu.	He's unskillful in dividing it.
(omoshiroi)	Wakeru no ga omoshiroi desu.	It's fun to divide it.
(ryokoo suru)	Ryokoo suru no ga omoshiroi desu.	It's fun to travel.
(suki)	Ryokoo suru no ga suki desu.	He likes to travel.
(nomu)	Nomu no ga suki desu.	He likes to drink it.
(hayai)	Nomu no ga hayai desu.	He's fast at drinking it.
(okiru)	Okiru no ga hayai desu.	He's early in rising.
(osoi)	Okiru no ga osoi desu.	He's late in rising.

15. Substitution

Ryokoo suru no wa itsu desu ka?   When will you be taking your trip?

(kaeru)	Kaeru no wa itsu desu ka?	When will you be returning?
(umareru)	Umareru no wa itsu desu ka?	When will it be born?
(tsuzukeru)	Tsuzukeru no wa itsu desu ka?	When will you continue it?
(wakaru)	Wakaru no wa itsu desu ka?	When will you know?
(kuraberu)	Kuraberu no wa itsu desu ka?	When will you compare them?
(hajimeru)	Hajimeru no wa itsu desu ka?	When will you begin it?
(yoru)	Yoru no wa itsu desu ka?	When will you drop by?

16. Substitution and Appropriate Response

Q. Yomitai no wa nan desu ka?   What is it that you would like to read?

A. _____ desu.

| (kurabetai) | Kurabetai no wa nan desu ka? | What is it that you would like to compare? |

(kaitai)   Kaitai no wa nan desu ka?   What is it that you would like
                                                      to buy?

(naritai)   Naritai no wa nan desu ka?   What is it that you would like
                                                      to become?

(tabetai)   Tabetai no wa nan desu ka?   What is it that you would like
                                                      to eat?

(benkyoo shi-   Benkyoo shitai no wa nan desu ka? What is it that you would like
 tai)   to study?

(waketai)   Waketai no wa nan desu ka?   What is it that you would like
                                                      to divide?

17. Expansion

Rainen Nihon o ryokoo suru no wa dare desu ka?   Who is it that's going to trav-
                                                      el in Japan next year?

(dare desu ka) Dare desu ka?   Who is it?

(ryokoo suru   Ryokoo suru no wa dare desu ka?   Who is it that's going to trav-
 no wa)   el?

(Nihon o)   Nihon o ryokoo suru no wa dare   Who is it that's going to trav-
                   desu ka?   el in Japan?

(rainen)   Rainen Nihon o ryokoo suru no wa   Who is it that's going to trav-
                   dare desu ka?   el in Japan next year?

Kiiroi yoofuku ga suki na no wa dare deshita ka?   Who was it that liked yellow
                                                      dresses?

(dare deshita   Dare deshita ka?   Who was it?
 ka)

(suki na no   Suki na no wa dare deshita ka?   Who was it that liked it?
 wa)

(kiiroi yoo-   Kiiroi yoofuku ga suki na no wa   Who was it that liked yellow
 fuku ga)   dare deshita ka?   dresses?

Atsui ocha o onegai shitai no wa dare desu ka?   Who is it that wants to request
                                                      hot tea?

(dare desu ka) Dare desu ka?   Who is it?

(onegai shitai Onegai shitai no wa dare desu ka? Who is it that wants to request
 no wa)   it?

(atsui ocha o) Atsui ocha o onegai shitai no wa   Who is it that wants to request
                   dare desu ka?   hot tea?

Hoka no nomimono no hoo ga ii to omou no wa dare   Who are the ones who think some
   to dare desu ka?   other beverage would be bet-
                                                      ter?

(dare to dare   Dare to dare desu ka?   Who are they?
 desu ka)

(ii to omou   Ii to omou no wa dare to dare   Who are the ones who think it's
 no wa)   desu ka?   good?

(nomimono
  no hoo ga)
	Nomimono no hoo ga ii to omou
	  no wa dare to dare desu ka?
		Who are the ones who think that
		  a beverage would be better?

(hoka no)	Hoka no nomimono no hoo ga ii to
	  omou no wa dare to dare desu ka?
		Who are the ones who think some
		  other beverage would be bet-
		  ter?

	Ichiban gakkoo o yasumu no wa dare desu ka?	Who is it that misses school the most?
(dare desu ka)	Dare desu ka?	Who is it?
(yasumu no wa)	Yasumu no wa dare desu ka?	Who is it that takes holidays?
(gakkoo o)	Gakkoo o yasumu no wa dare desu ka?	Who is it that misses school?

(ichiban)	Ichiban gakkoo o yasumu no wa
	  dare desu ka?
		Who is it that misses school
		  the most?

18. Substitution

Miru tokoro wa sukunaku arimasen.		Places to see are not few [in number].
(asobu)	Asobu tokoro wa sukunaku arima- sen.	Places to play are not few.
(yasumu)	Yasumu tokoro wa sukunaku arima- sen.	Places to rest are not few.
(tomaru)	Tomaru tokoro wa sukunaku arima- sen.	Places to stay are not few.
(yoru)	Yoru tokoro wa sukunaku arimasen.	Places to drop by are not few.

(mi ni ikitai)	Mi ni ikitai tokoro wa sukunaku
	  arimasen.
		Places I'd like to go see are
		  not few.

(tabe ni iki-
  tai)
	Tabe ni ikitai tokoro wa suku-
	  naku arimasen.
		Places I'd like to go eat are
		  not few.

19. Substitution

Tanaka-san no asa okiru jikan wa nanji desu ka?		What time does Mr. Tanaka arise in the morning?

(ban yasumu)	Tanaka-san no ban yasumu jikan
	  wa nanji desu ka?
		What time does Mr. Tanaka re-
		  tire at night?

(ohiru taberu)	Tanaka-san no ohiru taberu jikan
	  wa nanji desu ka?
		What time does Mr. Tanaka eat
		  at noon?

(gogo kaeru)	Tanaka-san no gogo kaeru jikan
	  wa nanji desu ka?
		What time does Mr. Tanaka re-
		  turn in the afternoon?

(asa dekakeru)	Tanaka-san no asa dekakeru jikan
	  wa nanji desu ka?
		What time does Mr. Tanaka start
		  out in the morning?

20. Grammar

(Tanaka-san wa asa goji-han ni oki-   (Mrs. Tanaka gets up at five-thirty in
  masu.)   the morning.)
 Tanaka-san no asa okiru no wa goji-   [The time when] Mrs. Tanaka gets up in
  han desu.   the morning is five-thirty.
(Sensee wa asa shichiji-han ni kimasu.)   (The teacher comes at seven-thirty in
                                                  the morning.)
 Sensee no asa kuru no wa shichiji-han   [The time when] the teacher comes in the
  desu.   morning is seven-thirty.
(Jiroo wa ban ocha o nomimasu.)   (Jiro drinks tea in the evening.)
 Jiroo no ban nomu no wa ocha desu.   [What] Jiro drinks in the evening is
                                                  tea.
(Ano seeto wa okashi ga tabetai desu.)   (That pupil wants to eat cakes.)
 Ano seeto no tabetai no wa okashi   [What] that pupil wants to eat is cakes.
  desu.
(Yamada-san wa eego ga benkyoo shitai   (Mr. Yamada wants to study English.)
  n desu.)
 Yamada-san no benkyoo shitai no wa   [What] Mr. Yamada wants to study is
  eego desu.   English.
(Yamamoto-san wa ao ga suki desu.)   (Mrs. Yamamoto likes blue.)
 Yamamoto-san no suki na no wa ao desu.   [The color which] Mrs. Yamamoto likes
                                                  is blue.

EXERCISES

A. Supply the missing colors.

  1. Yama wa yuki de _____ desu.
  2. Sensee ga Yukio-san ni, "Joozu ni kotaemashita ne," to iimashita. Suru to
        Yukio-san wa _____ narimashita.
  3. _____ yoofuku wa ban tooku kara miyasui desu.
  4. Tooku kara ichiban minikui yoofuku no iro wa _____ deshoo.
  5. Chokoreeto wa _____ desu.
  6. Kyoo wa ii hi desu. Mizu no iro wa kiree na _____ desu.
  7. Amerika de wa _____ kokuban no hoo ga ooi desu.
  8. Ame no ooi tokoro wa _____ desu.
  9. Ao ni kiiro o iremashita. _____ ni narimashita.

B. Complete the following and make them true statements, using "warm," "hot,"
      "cold," etc.

  1. Nihon de wa ichigatsu wa _____ desu.
  2. Shigatsu wa gogatsu hodo _____ arimasen.
  3. Juuichigatsu wa juunigatsu hodo _____ arimasen.
  4. Shichigatsu to hachigatsu wa _____ desu.
  5. Dakara, sonna ni _____ nai tokoro e ikimasu.
  6. Hokkaidoo wa shichigatsu ya hachigatsu wa _____, ichigatsu ya nigatsu
        wa _____ desu.
  7. Kyooto wa hachigatsu wa _____, ichigatsu wa _____ desu.

8. Juunigatsu ya ichigatsu wa Nihon no uchi wa _____ arimasen.
9. Hachigatsu wa _____ ocha o nomimasu ga, juunigatsu wa _____ no o nomimasu.
10. Hachigatsu wa _____ tokoro e ikitai desu.

C. Answer the following questions on the basis of factual information you know concerning Japan.

1. Honshuu ni wa takai yama ga arimasu ka?
2. Sono yama wa Honshuu o futatsu ni wakemasu ka?
3. Amerika ni chikai hoo wa nan to iimasu ka?
4. Amerika kara tooi hoo wa nan to iimasu ka?
5. Fuji-san mo sono yama no hitotsu desu ka?
6. Sono yama mo Honshuu o futatsu ni wakemasu ka?
7. Doo wakemasu ka?
8. Sono higashi ni aru toshi no ookii no wa dore desu ka?
9. Kyooto ya Oosaka wa sono nishi ni aru toshi desu ka?
10. Sono nishi Nihon to higashi Nihon no aida ni aru yama wa takai desu ka?
11. De wa, shichi-hachigatsu wa suzushikute, ichi-nigatsu wa samui deshoo ne.
12. Fuji-san no ue wa nani iro desu ka?
13. Omote-Nihon to Ura-Nihon to samusa wa doo chigaimasu ka?
14. Omote-Nihon to Ura-Nihon to dotchi no hoo ga ookii toshi ga ooi deshoo ka?
15. Sukii (ski) no suki na hito wa dotchi e sukii o shi ni iku deshoo ka?

D. Fill in the blanks with one of the following, koto, mono, hito or tokoro.

1. Kikitai _____ ga takusan arimasu.   There's a lot I'd like to ask.
2. Tabetai _____ ga arimasu ka?   Is there something you would like to eat?
3. Atsuku nai _____ e ikimashoo.   Let's go where it isn't hot.
4. Samui _____ wa kirai desu.   I don't like places that are cold.
5. Omoshiroi _____ ni aimashita.   I met an interesting person.
6. Miru _____ ga takusan arimasu.   There are a lot of places to see.
7. Rokuji ni okiru _____ wa dare to dare desu ka?   Who are the ones who arise at six o'clock?
8. Tanaka-san no _____ ga shimbun ni demashita.   That matter concerning Mr. Tanaka appeared in the newspapers.
9. Ashita kuru _____ ni onegai shimashoo.   Let's request it of the people who will be coming tomorrow.
10. Motto ireru _____ o kudasai.   Please give me more things to put in.

E. Complete the following statements, using doko, itsu, nan or dare.

1. Ashita hajimaru no wa _____ desu ka?   What time does it begin tomorrow? (What time is it that it's beginning tomorrow?)
2. Yoku wasureru no wa _____ desu ka?   Who is it that often forgets?

3. Ashita benkyoo suru no wa _____   What is it that we're studying tomorrow?
   desu ka?

4. Raishuu iku no wa _____ desu   Where is it that we're going next week?
   ka?

5. Kyoo hanasu no wa _____ desu   Who is it that's going to speak today?
   ka?

F. Say the following in Japanese, using no.

1. What Yukio likes is this.
2. Where is it that Mr. Yamada wants to travel?
3. Is this what your mother doesn't like?
4. What is the time that your father arises?
5. Which is the one the teacher wants to read?
6. What is it that Yukio wants to become?
7. Around what time is it that Yukio retires?
8. I understand well what Yukio is saying (says).
9. The one who's unskillful is Taro.
10. He's skillful at writing it, but he's slow.

REVIEW

A. Respond to the following questions.

1. Kyoo wa nan'yoobi desu ka?
2. Kyoo wa nannichi desu ka?
3. Nigatsu wa nannichi arimasu ka?
4. Shichigatsu wa nannichi arimasu ka?
5. Nangatsu nannichi ni umaremashita ka?
6. Hachigatsu wa gakkoo ga yasumi desu ka?
7. Ikkagetsu no yasumi desu ka?
8. Doyoobi mo nichiyoobi mo gakkoo ga arimasu ka?
9. Isshuukan wa nannichi arimasu ka?
10. Isshuukan ni nannichi yasumi ga arimasu ka?

B. Answer the following questions on the basis of the calendar below.

November						
Sun	Mon	Tue	Wed	Thu	Fri	Sat
	1	2	3	4	5	6
7	8	9	10	11	12	13
14	15	16	17	18	19	20
21	22	23	24	25	26	27
28	29	30				

1. Nangatsu desu ka?
2. Kongetsu wa samuku narimasu ka?
3. Sengetsu wa nangatsu deshita ka?
4. Raigetsu wa nangatsu desu ka?
5. Kongetsu wa rokushuukan arimasu ka?
6. Kyoo wa nan'yoobi desu ka?
7. Kyoo wa nannichi desu ka?
8. Ashita wa nan'yoobi desu ka?
9. Ashita wa nannichi desu ka?
10. Tsuitachi wa nan'yoobi desu ka?
11. Futsuka no tsugi no kayoobi wa nannichi desu ka?
12. Sono mae no hi wa nannichi desu ka?
13. Nanoka wa nan'yoobi desu ka?
14. Sono hi ni gakkoo e ikimasu ka?
15. Juu-ichigatsu mikka wa yasumi no hi deshoo ka? (Sensee ni kikimashoo.)
16. Juu-sannichi no tsugi no doyoobi wa nannichi desu ka?

191

17. Juu-ichigatsu ni wa oyasumi ga futsuka arimasu ka? (Sensee ni kikimashoo.)
18. Juu-ichigatsu juu-gonichi wa nan'yoobi desu ka? (Sono hi, nanatsu to itsutsu
  . to mittsu no kodomo wa nani o suru deshoo ka? Sensee ni kikimashoo.)
19. Raigetsu no tsuitachi wa nan'yoobi desu ka?
20. Juu-ichigatsu to juu-nigatsu to kurabemashoo. Dotchi no hoo ga samui
    deshoo ka?

C. Answer the questions below on the basis of the following 1965 train schedule.

	Train (Hikari-goo)	Train (Sakura-goo)	(Hikari) 2nd Class	(Sakura) 2nd Class
Tookyoo Lv.	9:00	16:35		
Yokohama	----	17:01		
Nagoya Lv.	11:29	21:21	1920 yen	
Kyooto Lv.	12:34	23:13	2420 yen	
Oosaka Arr.	13:00	23:50	2480 yen	
Koobe		0:16		
Hiroshima		4:43		
Nagasaki		12:28		3230 yen (without sleeper)

1. Tookyoo kara Oosaka made ikitai n desu ga, dono kisha ga ichiban hayai desu
      ka?
2. Sono kisha wa nanji ni Tookyoo o demasu ka?
3. Gozen kuji deshoo ka, gogo deshoo ka?
4. Yokohama ni tomarimasu ka?
5. Doko to doko ni tomarimasu ka?
6. Sono kisha wa doko made ikimasu ka?
7. Koobe e mo ikimasu ka?
8. Tookyoo kara Oosaka made Hikari-goo de nanjikan gurai kakarimasu ka?
9. Tookyoo kara Nagoya made nanjikan gurai kakarimasu ka?
10. Nagoya kara Kyooto made nanjikan gurai kakarimasu ka?
11. Ima no kisha wa sanjikan de Tookyoo kara Oosaka made ikimasu. Kuji no kisha
      wa nanji ni Oosaka-eki ni hairimasu ka?
12. Ima no kisha no hoo ga hayai desu ne. Dono gurai hayai desu ka?
13. Tookyoo kara Oosaka made iku n desu ga, Kyooto made yori motto takai desu ka?
14. Dono gurai takai desu ka?
15. Nagasaki made ikitai n desu ga, dono kisha de ikimashoo ka?
16. Sono kisha wa Yokohama ni tomarimasu ka?
17. Tookyoo kara Yokohama made nampun gurai kakarimasu ka?
18. Sakura-goo wa Hikari-goo yori hayai desu ka?
19. Hikari-goo wa Sakura-goo yori hayai desu ka?
20. Tookyoo kara Nagasaki made nanjikan gurai kakarimasu ka?
21. Nagasaki wa Tookyoo ni chikai desu ka?
22. Yokohama wa Tookyoo kara tooi desu ka?
23. Hiroshima wa Tookyoo yori Nagasaki ni chikai desu ka?

D. Complete the following by telling what (etc.) it is you would (or would not)
    like to do. (Watch the particles.)

Example: Yomitai desu.
          Shimbun ga yomitai desu.

 1. Kaitai desu.
 2. Ryokoo shitai desu.
 3. Hoshii desu.
 4. Kaeritai desu.
 5. Waketai desu.
 6. Hajimetai desu.
 7. Wasuretai desu.
 8. Nomitaku arimasen.
 9. Kurabetaku arimasen.
10. Tsuzuketaku arimasen.

E. Answer the following questions on the basis of the facts provided in the les-
    sons of Unit II.

 1. Yukio-san no uchi wa doko desu ka?
 2. Yukio-san no uchi wa chiisai uchi desu ka?
 3. Tonari no uchi ni iru hito wa dare desu ka?
 4. Yukio-san no uchi to tonari no uchi to dotchi no hoo ga ookii desu ka?
 5. Yukio-san no uchi wa atarashii desu ka?
 6. Senjitsu Yukio-san no otoosan wa doko kara kaerimashita ka?
 7. Kyooto kara Tookyoo made Shinkansen de dono gurai kakarimasu ka?
 8. Yukio-san no otoosan wa "tadaima" to iimashita. Suru to obaasan wa nan to
     iimashita ka?
 9. Otoosan no okaeri wa hayakatta desu ka?
10. Nannichi hayakatta desu ka?
11. Kaisha kara wa itsu kaeru to kikimashita ka?
12. Obaasan e no omiyage wa nan deshita ka?
13. Donna oyunomi deshita ka?
14. Obaasan no omiyage wa hako no naka ni arimashita ka?
15. Obaasan wa nan to iimashita ka?
16. Otoosan wa sono oyunomi o doko de kaimashita ka?
17. Omiyage no suki na hito wa dare desu ka?
18. Otoosan wa kondo Kyooto no otera o mi ni ikimashita ka?
19. Kyooto wa miru tokoro ga ooi desu ka?
20. Otoosan wa nannichi ni Kyooto kara kaerimashita ka?
21. Kyooto de wa isogashikatta desu ka?
22. Donna tokoro e ikimashita ka?
23. Ashita Kyooto de wa nani ga arimasu ka?
24. Sono omatsuri wa itsu desu ka?
25. Otoosan wa nani ga mitakatta desu ka?
26. Dare ga "Oshikatta desu ne" to iimashita ka?
27. Yukio-san wa oyasumi no aida ni narubeku nani o shimashita ka?
28. Keredomo sono eego o daibu wasuremashita ka?
29. Sono oyasumi wa itsu deshita ka?
30. Eego wa hanashinikui desu ka?

31. Kotoba mo oboenikui desu ka?
32. Yukio-san wa ima chuugaku ichinen desu ka?
33. Itsu kara ninen ni narimashita ka?
34. Nihon no gakkoo wa nangatsu ni hajimarimasu ka?
35. Yukio-san no suki na benkyoo wa nan deshoo ka?
36. Raishuu aru shiken wa nan no shiken desu ka?
37. Sono sensee wa yoku shiken o shimasu ka?
38. Isshuukan-oki wa nanshuukan-goto desu ka?
39. Sengetsu wa nando shiken ga arimashita ka?
40. Yukio-san wa shiken ga oosugiru to omoimasu ka?

F. Listen to the following passage. Then answer the questions which follow.

      Yukio-san wa raishuu chuugaku no chi̅ri no jikan ni Omote-Nihon to Ura-Nihon
no kot̅o o benkyoo shima̅su. Ichiban suki̅ na no wa chi̅ri no benkyoo desu.
      Honshuu no kit̅a kara minami ni taka̅i yama̅ ga arimasu. O̅oku no hit̅o wa sono
yama̅ de Nihon o futatsu̅ ni wakemasu. Sono futatsu̅ o Omote-Nihon to Ura-Nihon to
iimasu. Amerika ni chika̅i hoo ga Omote-Nihon desu. Omote-Nihon to Ura-Nihon wa
daibu chigaima̅su. Omote-Nihon wa a̅me ga o̅okute, Ura-Nihon wa yuk̅i ga o̅oi desu.
Da̅kara, Ura-Nihon no hoo ga samu̅i koto ga wakarima̅su. Ura-Nihon no mizu mo Omote-
Nihon no yori tsumeta̅i desu. O̅oki̅i to̅shi wa Omote-Nihon no hoo ga takusan ari-
ma̅su.
      Yo̅ku Honshuu o higashi̅ to nishi ni̅ mo wakema̅su. Fuji̅-san no chika̅ku ga aida
ni narima̅su. Fuji̅-san wa Nihon de ichiban ta̅kakute, nadaka̅i yama̅ desu. Honshuu
no higashi no ho̅o no ichiban ooki̅i to̅shi wa Tookyoo desu. Sono Tookyoo wa Nihon
de ichiban ooki̅i to̅shi desu. Kyo̅oto ya Oosaka ga Nihon no nishi no ho̅o no ooki̅i
to̅shi desu.

1. Chiri no benkyoo no suki na no wa dare desu ka?
2. Omote-Nihon to Ura-Nihon o benkyoo suru no wa itsu desu ka?
3. Chuugaku no seeto wa dare desu ka?
4. Honshuu o Omote-Nihon to Ura-Nihon ni wakeru no wa nan desu ka?
5. Honshuu no kita kara minami ni aru takai mono wa nan desu ka?
6. Amerika ni chikai hoo wa dotchi desu ka?
7. Daibu chigau no wa doko to doko desu ka?
8. Ame no ooi no wa dotchi desu ka?
9. Yuki no ooi no wa dotchi desu ka?
10. De wa soko wa juu-nigatsu wa shirokute kiree deshoo ne.
11. Samui hoo wa dotchi desu ka?
12. Ookii toshi no takusan aru no wa Ura-Nihon desu ka?
13. Honshuu o higashi to nishi ni wakeru no mo yama desu ka?
14. Nihon de ichiban takai yama wa dore desu ka?
15. Nihon no ichiban nadakai yama wa dore desu ka?
16. Fuji-san yori motto takakute nadakai yama ga Nihon ni arimasu ka?
17. Fuji-san no takasa no koto ga hanashi ni demashita ka?
18. Sekai ni Fuji-san yori takai yama ga arimasu ka?
19. Nihon no ichiban ookii toshi wa Oosaka desu ka?
20. Kyooto ya Oosaka wa nishi no hoo ni aru ookii toshi desu ka?
21. Nihon no ichiban ookii shima wa dore deshoo ka?
22. Sono shima no minami ni aru shima wa nan to iimasu ka?

G. Change the verbs in the parentheses to their proper forms.

1. Nichiyoobi wa gakkoo wa (yasumu)   Sunday is a holiday.
        desu.
2. Omoshiroi (hanasu) o kikimashita.   I heard an interesting story.
3. (Tsuzuku) wa doko desu ka?   Where is the continuation?
4. Furansugo no (benkyoo suru) wa   The study of French is interesting.
        omoshiroi desu.
5. Hokkaidoo no (ryokoo suru) wa   I will do my traveling in Hokkaidō next
        rainen shimasu.   year.
6. Omoshiroi (kotaeru) ga demashita.   Some interesting answers were presented.

H. Tell the following story in your own words in Japanese.

    Yesterday, at Mr. Tanaka's home, I met Mr. Smith. He's a man who comes to
Japan often. This Mr. Smith likes Japanese cars. About two weeks ago he bought
a blue Japanese car. Mr. Smith said it's better than the bigger American cars.
He said that Japanese cars are inexpensive and good. That's why he bought this
car this time. I also like Japanese cars, but I think that big American cars are
prettier. On the way home, I went home in Mr. Smith's car. Blue is pretty, but
red cars are prettier, I think.

Vocabulary Index by Lesson

Lesson 5

chokoreeto
ikura
okane
okashi
shimbun
ten'in
zasshi
doozo
kono, etc.
-en
dashimasu
deshita
kaimasu
onegai shimasu
kudasai

Lesson 6

koko, etc.
teeryuujo
toshokan
yuubinkyoku
sugi
sugu
gogo
gozen
gurai
-byoo
-fun, -pun
asobimasu
benkyoo shimasu
hanashimasu
kakarimasu
kakimasu
machimasu
mimasu
yomimasu

Lesson 7

aida
anata
hito
kodomo
otona
seeto
sensee
tomodachi
watakushi
chigau
iru

isogu
suru
wakaru

Lesson 8

denwa
ima
koto
rajio
doo
soo
doomo
osaki ni
suru to
au
deru
hairu
ireru
kakeru
kiku
kotaeru
miseru
noru
omou
tomaru
tomeru
suwaru
yuu

Unit II
Lesson 1

heya
dotchi
hoo
kore, etc.
atarashii
chiisai
chikai
furui
hayai
hikui
hiroi
ii
mijikai
nagai
ookii
osoi
semai
takai
warui
yasui

shiru

Lesson 2

mono
otoosan
terebi
tokoro
Shinkansen
onaji
konna, etc.
Hakone
Hiroshima
Koobe
Kyooto
Nagasaki
Nagoya
Oosaka
Sapporo
Tookyoo
Yokohama

Lesson 3

hanashi
kaeri
kakemono
kakimono
kotae
nomimono
norimono
obaasan
odekake
tabemono
yasumu
yomimono
yoofuku
motto
sukoshi
choodo
-nichi
-ka
naru

Lesson 4

hitotsu, etc.
kekkoo
kiree
michi
nigiyaka
(o)miyage
shizuka

(o)tera
(o)yunomi
amari
chotto
dakara
ikaga
isogashii
kitanai
omoshiroi

Lesson 5

boku
kippu
(o)matsuri
sekai
shima
toshi
yama
Hokkaidoo
Honshuu
Kyuushuu
Shikoku
tsugi
getsuyoobi, etc.
-yoobi
hoshii
nadakai
oshii
umareru

Lesson 6

chiri
chuugakkoo
chuugaku
daigaku
eego
kootoo-gakkoo
kotoba
rekishi
shiken
shoogakkoo
daibu
narubeku
-go
-kagetsu
-nen
-nikui
-yasui
muzukashii
yasashii
hajimaru

hajimeru

motsu

tsuzukeru

wasureru

suzushii

tsumetai

nomu

ryokoo suru

wakeru

Lesson 7

ame

hi

higashi

kita

kotoshi

minami

nishi

omote

ura

yuki

keredomo

-do

-getsu

-jitsu

kon-

rai-

sen-

-goto

-oki

-sugiru

ooi

sukunai

komaru

kuraberu

Lesson 8

chairo

heta

hoka

iro

joozu

kirai

midori

mizu

ocha

suki

takusan

akai

aoi

atsui

atatakai, attakai

kiiroi

kuroi

samui

shiroi

Alphabetical Vocabulary Index

Numbers refer to Units and Lessons.
With the exception of countries, proper nouns are not included.

doyoo II-7
doyoobi II-5

ee I-1
eego II-6
eki I-4
-en I-5
empitsu I-1

-fun I-6
fune I-3
furansugo II-6
furui II-1
futatsu II-4

gakkoo I-3
-gatsu II-5
-getsu II-7
getsuyoo II-7
getsuyoobi II-5
go (five) I-1
-go (language) II-6
gochisoo-sama I-2
gogo I-6
goro I-2
-goto II-7
gozen I-6
gurai (time) I-6

hachi (eight) I-1
hai I-5
hairu I-8
hajimaru II-6
hajimeru II-6
hako I-4
-han I-2
hanashi II-3
hanasu I-7, hanashimasu I-6
hatachi II-4
hatsuka II-5
hayai II-1
hayasa II-3
heta II-8
heya II-1
hi II-7
higashi II-7
hikooki I-3
hikui II-1
hiroi II-1
hirosa II-3
hiru I-2
hito I-7

hitotsu II-4
hodo II-2
hoka II-8
hon I-1
hon'ya I-4
hoo II-1
hoshii II-5

ichi I-1
ichiban II-5
ii II-1
iie I-1
ikaga II-4
iku I-7, ikimasu I-3
ikura I-5
ikutsu II-4
ima I-8
irasshaimase I-5
ireru I-8
iro II-8
iru (be) I-7
isogashii II-4
isogu I-7
isu I-4
itadakimasu I-1
itsu I-6
itsutsu II-4
itte irasshai I-2
itte mairimasu I-2

jettoki I-3
-ji I-1
jidoosha I-3
-jikan II-2
joozu II-8
juu (ten) I-1

-ka (days) II-3
kaeri II-3
kaeru I-7, kaerimasu I-2
-kagetsu II-6
kaisha I-3
kakaru I-7, kakarimasu I-6
kakemono II-3
kakeru I-8
kakimono II-3
kaku I-7, kakimasu I-6
kara II-2
kasu I-7
kau I-7, kaimasu I-5
kawa II-5
kayoo II-7

omoshiroi II-4
omote II-7
omou I-8
onaji II-2
onegai suru I-7, onegai shimasu I-5
ooi II-7
ookii II-1
ookisa II-3
osaki ni I-8
oshii II-5
osoi II-1
otera II-4
otona I-7
otoosan II-2
oyunomi II-4

pan I-4
pan'ya I-4
-pun I-6

rai- II-7
rajio I-8
rekishi II-6
roku (six) I-1
ryokoo suru II-8

saa II-4
samui II-8
-san I-1
san I-1
seeto I-7
sekai II-5
semai II-1
sen- II-7
senjitsu II-7
sensee I-7
shichi I-1
shika I-8
shiken II-6
shima II-5
shimbun I-5
shiro II-8
shiroi II-8
shiru II-1
shita I-4
shizuka II-4
shoogakkoo II-6
-shuukan II-3
soba I-4
soko I-6
sonna (sonna ni) II-2
sono I-5
soo I-8

sore II-1
sotchi II-1
sugi I-6
-sugiru II-7
sugu I-6
suiyoo II-7
suiyoobi II-5
suki II-8
sukoshi II-3
sukunai II-7
suru I-7
suru to I-8
suwaru I-8
suzushii II-8

taberu I-7, tabemasu I-2
tabemono II-3
tadaima II-3
takai II-1
takasa II-3
takusan II-8
takushii I-3
teeryuujo I-6
tekisuto I-1
ten'in I-5
terebi II-5
tokee I-1
tokoro II-2
tomaru I-8
tomeru I-8
tomodachi I-7
tonari I-4
too II-4
tooi II-1
tooku II-3
tooru I-8
tororii basu I-3
toshi (city) II-5
toshokan I-6
tsugi II-5
tsuitachi II-5
tsukue I-4
tsumetai II-8
tsuzukeru II-6
tsuzuki II-7
tsuzuku II-7

uchi I-3
ue I-4
umareru II-5
ura II-7
ushiro I-4

Grammar Index

Adjectival noun II-4.2
Adjectives, see Verbal adjectives
aru (arimasu) I-4.2

Colors II-8.3
Comparative (positive) II-1.3
Copula, desu I-1.1, deshita I-5.1,
  negative (semi-formal) I-7.3,
  tentative (semi-formal) I-7.4, da
  II-3.5, perfective (informal) II-4.4,
  tentative (informal) II-4.4, negative
  perfective II-4.5
Counters II-6.3

dake I-8.4
de (by) I-3.4
de (at) I-6.3
deshita I-5.1
Desiderative II-5.2
desu I-1.1

e I-3.3

ga (particle) I-4.3, II-5.3
ga (conjunction) I-6.2
Gerunds, see Verb, Verbal adjective,
  Copula
goro I-2.4
-goto II-7.4
gurai I-6.4

hodo II-2.2,

iru I-7.2

ka (interrogative) I-1.4
-ka -ka I-1.5
ka (or) II-1.5

ka mo shiremasen II-5.4
kara II-2.3
koko I-6.5
kono series II-2.5
konna series II-2.5

made II-2.4
made ni II-5.5
-masen form I-3.1
-masen deshita I-6.1
-mashita I-4.1
-mashoo I-3.2
-masu form I-2.1
mo I-7.5
mo...mo I-7.6
mo (after counter) II-2.6
Modifiers II-8.1

n desu II-1.8
narubeku II-6.2
ne II-1.6
Negatives, -masen I-3.1, -masen deshita
  I-6.1, copula (semi-formal negative)
  I-7.3, verbal adjectives II-2.1,
  verbal adjectives (negative perfective) II-4.1
Negative question I-3.5
ni (after time) I-2.3, to I-4.5
-nikui II-6.1
no I-4.4
no (noun) II-8.2
Nominal form of verbs II-3.4, plus iku
  (etc) II-4.6
Nouns I-1.2, also Introduction, Adjectival nouns II-4.2
Noun form of colors II-8.3
Numerals (Japanese) II-4.7

195j